THE GROWING EDGE

Vermont Villages, 1840-1880

by

T. D. Seymour Bassett

Vermont Historical Society
Montpelier
Vermont

© 1992 by T. D. Seymour Bassett

All rights reserved. No part of this book may be reproduced in any form or by any electronic or mechanical means including information storage and retrieval without permission in writing from the publisher, except by a reviewer who may quote brief passages.

Library of Congress Cataloging-in-Publication Data

Bassett, T. D. (Thomas D. Seymour)
    The growing edge: Vermont villages, 1840-1880 / by T. D. Seymour Bassett.
        p. cm.
    Includes bibliographical references and index.
    ISBN 0-934720-36-3
    1. Villages—Vermont—History—19th century. 2. Vermont—History.
I. Title.
F53.B38 1992
974.3'03—dc20

92-14661
CIP

EDITOR: Susan Bartlett Weber
INDEXER: Reidun Dahle Nuquist
TYPESETTING & DESIGN: Kristin Peterson-Ishaq and the Center for Research on Vermont
COVER DESIGN: The Laughing Bear Associates

To My Family

My grandfathers moved off farms to cities. My mother found an urban market for her singing and my father, while preferring to read his Homer under the Philosopher's Oak on the edge of a meadow in full sight of the Green Mountains, was at home where many congregated. My brother, a newspaperman and teacher in five cities, took a fatherly and shaping interest in my growth. My sister, Catharine Bassett Hagar, has been a valuable presence and reminder of our diverse paths to the present. Patricia Reynolds Bassett, an excellent teacher, patiently heard my rehearsals. Mary Jane Gray showed concentration in the midst of family hubbub and could edit foolishness out of a text. Gifts from Alice Cook Bassett are more than tongue can tell. Our children and our children's children tell me how many more things there are in the world than forty years of Vermont villages.

Contents

Foreword — vii

Preface — ix

1. Rural Life in 1840 — 1
2. Burlington in 1840: An Inland Port — 15
3. The End of a World and the Dawn of Industrialism — 31
4. Village Industry — 49
5. Village Business and Social Conditions — 71
6. Urban Culture: Arts, Schools, Churches, Families — 87
7. The Press and Politics — 103
8. Villages Go to War for Freedom and Unity — 129
9. Postwar Village Industry — 155
10. Village Society Reshaped — 175
11. Burlington: A Vermont City, 1865-80 — 197

Index — 221

Illustrations

1. *Burlington Harbor, ca. 1848* — 14
2. *Burlington in 1841* — 19
3. *Vermont Post Roads, 1837-1841* — 28
4. *Vermont Railroads, Quarries, Mines, and Large Towns, 1848-1880* — 48
5. *Sheldons & Slason's Marble Quarry* — 63
6. *Underclyffe, St. Johnsbury* — 66
7. *Camp Holbrook, Brattleboro, 1862-1865* — 135
8. *Brattleboro Military Hospital, 1863-1865* — 135
9. *St. Francis Xavier's Church and Rectory, 1876* — 179
10. *City of Burlington, 1873* — 209

Foreword

Tom Bassett's *The Growing Edge* began life in March 1952 as "The Urban Penetration of Rural Vermont," weighing eight pounds, two ounces, and measuring eight hundred pages. A Harvard Ph.D. dissertation under the direction of Arthur Schlesinger, Sr., a celebrated pioneer of American urban history, it had all the Schlesinger, Sr., earmarks. It was encyclopedic, a bit short on explicit theory, and definitive in its scope. Its contribution to Vermont history was instantly apparent and in most larger states it would have been published in an abridged version by an academic or commercial press long ago.

With the University of Vermont then lacking an academic press affiliation and other presses deterred by the limited marketing opportunities Vermont provided, the dissertation was instead photocopied and relegated to the bowels of selected libraries. Purists may note that photocopying added almost a pound and a half, the weight of an average book, to its size. Yet despite all encumbrances, "The Urban Penetration of Rural Vermont" prospered as did few other works of its genre. Its quality and importance overcame its limited marketability in the sense that over the past twenty or so years it has been cited in virtually every study of nineteenth-century Vermont, and it has become one of the most sought-after dissertations in the University of Vermont's special collections.

When the Vermont Historical Society decided to make this work available to an even wider audience, I was proud for the society and pleased for Tom Bassett. Familiar with an earlier unsuccessful society effort to publish "Urban Penetration," however, and knowing that shortening was an economic necessity, I was apprehensive over how revising to shorten it would affect the quality and usefulness of the text. Upon reading this new version, weighing one pound, five ounces, I confess my fears were unfounded. *The Growing Edge* is an even stronger effort than its original. As Professor Bassett notes in his own preface, he found that "sap boiled down is sweeter."

Revision has also provided an opportunity to incorporate more recent scholarship and identify unarticulated assumptions. The concept of urbanization, Bassett's main theme, has undergone particular readjustment. The demarcation between urban and rural is less clear in 1992 than it seemed in 1952. During the 1950s it was accepted as a self-evident truth that the good life could or should be best lived in cities. There was virtual unanimity among historians and sociologists (our grandest universities are usually located in urban centers) that urban was urbane, rural was hayseed. Indeed, the growth of civilization was the growth of cities.

Years have tempered these earlier certainties, and that is one of the reasons the publication of *The Growing Edge* is so timely. The realization that industry and technology no longer require huge population aggregates casts a different perspective on the Vermont experience. Historians who grappled with the reasons why Vermont remained "hitched to the post" while other states galloped toward the future may now redefine their task to explain how Vermont positioned itself to adapt to the era of cellular phones and personal computers.

There are, of course, other models perhaps more appropriate for the Vermont experience, and Bassett might well reject the two I have posited above. All, however, will draw upon his exhaustive research and balanced judgments, which will now be available to inform old friends and a much wider range of new readers.

Vermonters are prone to boast that Vergennes is the smallest (or second smallest) city in the United States. It is sometimes noted that Burlington is the smallest biggest city in the United States. No state in the entire United States can boast a largest city as small as Burlington. Both Vergennes and Burlington serve to distinguish Vermont from most of its sister states, and this should be of interest to anyone attracted by the nineteenth century, the development of the American economy, or the manifold problems and questions posed by the history of urban centers in the United States.

SAMUEL B. HAND
University of Vermont

Preface

I am a city boy exposed since my youth to the myth that all virtues belong to the country. I believe in the truth it contains—that space and sky and leaves and dirt in temperate combination are essential to well-being. As the son of a professor who believed in the contemporary value of the history of Greek cities, from Homeric to Hellenic, I assumed that accumulations of artifacts, archives, knowledge, books, and ideas, and the peaceful differing among people preferring to use different parts of those accumulations, are essential to human vitality. I belong to the growing number who think the country is a nice place to visit but I wouldn't want to live there. After I graduated from college, I sampled various metropolitan, rural, and minimally urban settings like the Burlington I started from and I chose to return to Burlington. That may be why I chose to write about a subject that gives prominence to Burlington. In my childhood it was a village where the newspaper editor thought the first robin was news.

Not only my life, but also my education pointed me toward urban history. Ralph Henry Gabriel demonstrated to me at Yale that a historian could write about a locality (his subject was Long Island) as a serious scholarly subject. I chose for my senior paper under his direction the ideas of Lewis Mumford. His *Technics and Civilization* (1934) had just come out, and his *The Culture of Cities* (1938) showed him a crusader to make cities livable. I looked for a thesis subject within the framework of urban-industrialism and the Civil War. I wondered what happened to the losers but did not find a way to get at the sources in the South. I went home and looked for reasons why the Republican Party, born on the eve of the war, had controlled the state for a century. When I showed my first chapters to Frederick Merk, he saw that I was interested in the social background more than the political story, and sent me to Arthur Meier Schlesinger.

I chose the Civil War period because I wondered why, in a country that had all the machinery the pacifist says will prevent war, the machinery failed. The sections had a common legislature and a supreme court to mediate differences, a literate population capable of using the information distributed by the press to decide issues democratically, virtual disarmament, and so on. Yet the war came. In college, Sherman Kent had persuaded me that penetrating a plethora of recent sources is worthy historical work. Only Walter Crockett, Arthur Stone, Harold Wilson, and Winston Flint had looked seriously at the history of Vermont in the century after 1850, and their focus was either political or rural. I did not relish revising the eighteenth-century myths Vermonters long lived by and thought it was time to move on.

Harvard awarded me a Ph.D. in 1952 and Professor Schlesinger said the eight-hundred-page pile of information, entitled "The Urban Penetration of Rural Vermont," should be published in full. The next summer Arthur Wallace Peach, director of the Vermont Historical Society, said that he would raise the money to publish it, but "Pop" was an enthusiast who could complete less than he hoped. At the University of Vermont from 1958, I kept studying Vermont history. When in 1990 the Vermont Historical Society offered to publish a shortened version, I revised and found that sap boiled down is sweeter. If I were starting today I would deal more with women, children, and family life and learn how to quantify. I leave those subjects and methods for others.

I focus on towns between 2,500 people, the census definition of "urban" until the end of the nineteenth century, and 8,000, its later minimum, a hazy "urban frontier" zone from which Rutland and Burlington emerged after the Civil War. I call them railroad towns, centers, central places, large towns, county seats or shire towns, and villages. Although small towns by national standards, they were the dozen or so largest places in rural Vermont. Unquestionably rural in 1840, Vermont entered a period when urban influence kept increasing. Its villages were the focal points of politics, trade, transportation, industry, education, and religion. Except for the family, found in all locales, every social and cultural activity not in a setting of fields, woods, and mountains centered in the village.

Town historians write chiefly about the villages within their town, but rarely index "village" or record when the town's villages were incorporated, because the legal village is merely formal, not functional. Andrew and Edith Nuquist's study, *Vermont State Government and Administration* (1966), concluded for the sixty-three or more villages in the 1960s, "the form of the system is less important than the personnel" (544-545), which overlapped with town officers. Middlebury (1832), Springfield (1833) and Woodstock (1836) led a short parade of incorporated villages, which by 1880 had lengthened to almost a score, including Rutland and Castleton (1847), Bennington (1849), St. Johnsbury (1852), Brattleboro (1854), and St. Albans (1859). Vergennes, incorporated as a city in 1788, behaved like a village. Burlington, never incorporated as a village either, behaved like a village until the legislature chartered part of the town as a city in 1864. Boosters led movements to incorporate villages or cities in order to tax themselves for more urban services than the farming part of town wanted: fire and police protection, water supply, sewers, streets, sidewalks, parks, trees, slaughterhouses, restraint of animals from running at large. In three cases—Burlington, Windsor, and Montpelier—the towns were partitioned to solve the problem. (The later carving of Rutland was for Redfield Proctor's reasons.) In Lyndon those who live in "the Center"—that is, the former center—speak of "the Ville," the current center, yet there was a center before either, the unincorporated Lyndon Corner. Walter Hard in *A Matter of Fifty Houses* (1952) was thinking of the average Vermont village in a town of fifteen hundred, which had not grown since 1840, whose "population center" was the cemetery. Another kind of village was on the boundary where urban and rural met and the urban prevailed.

For half a century I have bombarded historians, librarians, and archivists all over the country with questions. To all these professionals, but especially over the long years to the members of the Department of History at the University of Vermont and the staff of the Vermont Historical Society, thank you. David J. Blow, who knows most about the history of Burlington, has been my honest critic, unfailingly generous in making his unpublished research available to me. Thanks also to my editor, Susan Bartlett Weber, for insisting on clarity and consistency, and to Kristin Peterson-Ishaq, coordinator of the Center for Research on Vermont at the University of Vermont, for producing the final result.

1. Rural Life in 1840

A century and a half ago, Vermont had a unique character that has not entirely vanished. The stiff-necked independence of its people and their opposition to federal encroachments are symbolic traditions rooted in its earliest history as an independent republic. The twig was bent by the Green Mountain Boys' successful resistance to New York, Canada, and the Continental Congress. When their interests seemed to conflict with federal policy, Vermonters readily invoked the states' rights doctrine. When they said "foreign" or "abroad" they frequently meant "out-of-state." The Vermont individuality was also shaped partly by reactions common to all provinces against cultural centers and partly by the state-federal balance then: people depended on Washington for little.

In topography, climate, and population Vermont differed in minor ways from neighboring states. The Connecticut River, New England's best source of waterpower and a trade route from New Hampshire and Vermont to Connecticut through the early nineteenth century, marked its eastern boundary. Lake Champlain, the best inland waterway available to New England, flanked Vermont on the west, and with its outlet, the Richelieu River, oriented western Vermont trade toward Canada. When the Northern Canal cut through the low watershed between the lake and the Hudson River in 1823 the flow was reversed, toward New York.[1] Differences between eastern and western Vermont were sharpened because the Green Mountains divided the state longitudinally. Their extension southward straddled state boundaries while in New Hampshire and Maine the mountains did not divide the settled areas. The Green Mountains were narrow enough to leave a larger proportion of good farmland than Maine and New Hampshire enjoyed. Hence Vermont remained agrarian longer. Vermont alone in the Northeast was an inland state with no large commercial centers. Its climate was predominantly Canadian and continental. Narrow Lake Champlain could not temper the northwesters as Lake Ontario did for New York, nor did the coastal storms often reach so far inland in their full force.

---

[1] Chilton Williamson, *Vermont in Quandary, 1763-1825* (Montpelier: Vermont Historical Society, 1949), discusses politics and diplomacy as conditioned by Vermont's Canadian trade.

The characteristics of the people, fixed soon after the War of 1812, were like those of the rest of New England.[2] But its French Canadian and Irish immigration, first a seepage and then in waves, did not affect the state in the same way it did other parts of New England. The influx by 1840 consisted of transient "hired men," choppers, itinerant craftsmen, or settlers on the poorer "abandoned farms" of the lower Champlain Valley. The Canadians among them were within walking distance of their former homes. An island of Welsh developed in the 1850s around the slate quarries. The flow from Central Europe scarcely touched Vermont except in transit.

Its political and social history had its own individuality. No state but Vermont voted for William Wirt, the Anti-Masonic candidate for president in 1832. No state was so consistently Republican as Vermont for a century after 1854. The conflict between orthodox Protestants and the religious radicals, which resulted in Connecticut conservatism and the ferment of upstate New York, was almost a draw in Vermont. Its tolerance of the whole range of religious views from zealous commitment to indifference has been notable in all periods.[3]

In 1840, four out of five Vermonters were farmers, as most of their ancestors had been in 1640. Vermont farmers lived an outdoor life, gathering forest products, tilling the soil and tending livestock. Spread out evenly over the uneven land, they dwelt in separate homesteads on their own or hired acres. Their fathers or grandfathers had cut, burned off, and farmed the land, although a good many families had several times moved short distances from their original Vermont homes.

Their first labor had been the removal of the forest. After a cleared area was planted in the spring, all hands fell to chopping down the adjacent woods. The first dry spell in August was the time for the "burn." Whatever was left was dragged off and the charred stumps fired again, removed with oxen or horses, or left to rot. Where the rivers had enough water to move logs and the timber was good for masts, spars, planking, and boards, wasteful burning had been superseded by logging out the good timber first, then burning the brush and small growth. While this process of clearing was going on, as it still was in the mountains and in the north, the people lived in houses of logs or rough boards over hewn timber frames. They had one big all-purpose room and a loft, with the

---

[2]T. D. Seymour Bassett, "Migration to Vermont, 1761-1836," *Vermont Geographer* (1975), 7-20, suggests how early Vermont character and institutions were shaped by the character of the migrants.

[3]Randolph A. Roth draws a profile of early Vermont religion and society in *The Democratic Dilemma: Religion, Reform, and the Social Order in the Connecticut River Valley of Vermont, 1791-1850* (New York: Cambridge University Press, 1987).

stock close by. Recent clearing and minimal housing accounted for the slovenly look of the landscape.

Farmers aimed to move into frame and clapboard, one-and-a-half or two-story dwellings. Most houses were "wood-colored" (unpainted) or only infrequently painted, especially in the years after 1837 when money was unusually scarce. The prosperous minority who had inherited a valley farm and had worked it well, or had developed a cash specialty, like Martin Flint's exceptional clover seed business in Randolph,[4] or had multiplied their merino flocks and added farm to farm for pasture had large, comfortable, and expensive houses. The stone or brick had been quarried or baked in the neighborhood; the timbers and flooring cut from the woods on the farm.[5] If the owner preferred wooden construction, as he usually did, he could afford to add the stylish classical revival ornamentation and to paint with the standard mixture of white lead and linseed oil. His barns, especially if he were a wool grower, were new, and some were bigger than his house. These received coats of native red ochre (hematite) mixed with oil or, earlier, with skim milk.

Farming by families on homesteads was an unending struggle against odds. Less than half of Vermont was fit for cultivation or even grazing, once the forest humus had been burned, leached, or cropped off. Probably less than a sixth of the state had what is classified today as first-class soil. The Champlain Valley, a wedge with its point in western Rutland County and including the western halves of the lake counties, contained the highest percentage of this good land.[6] Its soil consisted of the prehistoric sedimentary deposits of an enlarged Lake Champlain, glacial scrapings and decomposed limestone rocks similar to those of southeastern Pennsylvania and the Shenandoah Valley. It was comparatively level, calcareous, and deep. The long bowl of Orleans County, the basins of the upper Winooski and White rivers and the narrower valleys of the other streams, with a few stone-free terraces and old glacial pond beds, comprised the rest of the good land. Otherwise,

---

[4]Abby Maria Hemenway, ed. *Vermont Historical Gazetteer: A Local History of All the Towns in the State, Civil, Educational, Biographical, Religious and Military*. (Burlington, Vt.: A. M. Hemenway, 1867-91; 5 vols.), 2:1059.

[5]Herbert Wheaton Congdon, *Old Vermont Houses*, 2d ed. (New York: A. A. Knopf, 1946), 7, 33, 57-58, 92, and *passim*.

[6]See the soil map prepared by the Vermont Agricultural Experiment Station and attached to W. J. Latimer and others, "Soil Survey (Reconnaissance) of Vermont," U. S. Department of Agriculture, Bureau of Chemistry and Soils *Bulletin* No. 43, ser. 1930 (Washington: Government Printing Office, 1933), and the "General Soil Map" prepared by the University of Vermont Department of Geography for the State Central Planning Office, July 1963.

the farmer had to contend with shallow, rough, acid, stony, or sandy soils. Where the forest humus had not yet been exhausted he could make a living on inferior locations, but not for long. One could not permanently farm the Green Mountains nor raise crops on other large areas fit only for grass and trees.

Not only was much of the land of poor quality, the uncertain weather could spoil crops and damage herds on the best farms. "The year without any summer," 1816, was the worst, but irregular frosts nipped the newly sprouted crops and blossoming apples in the late spring and cut off the corn and potatoes before they had fully matured. The average growing season varied from almost 160 days near the lake to less than a hundred days in the southern mountains and northeastern Essex County.

Flood damage increased as settlers built in the floodplain and removed the forest cover. The ice shoves of spring and the freshets of the warm months proved a constant threat to buildings and bridges near the rivers, and deposits of gravel kept spoiling the intervales. Two-thirds of the average annual precipitation, ranging from under thirty-four inches near the lake to over fifty in the mountains, fell during the growing months. It was always a gamble, however, whether the rain would be spaced to make the crops flourish or to interfere with planting, haying, and harvesting. Snowfall averaged just over six feet in the eastern and western valleys and from seven to ten and more in the mountains. A sudden cold wave, not warned by any weather bureau, or a sudden snowstorm burying stock under a caved-in roof, brought losses in spite of emergency measures.[7]

The farmer's prosperity related to his location: the farther from the village, the more travel time spent on errands; the farther from markets, the less received for produce. The heavy clays of some parts of the Champlain Valley were not only hard to drain and plow, but turned to mire in wet weather. Grand Isle County, a group of three main islands and a peninsula jutting down from Canada, had some of the best farmland in the state and a long growing season, but its ferries were subject to the hazards of sudden storms and the somewhat irregular services of the operators. The sandbar connecting South Hero with the delta land north of the mouth of the Lamoille River in

---

[7] See weather tables compiled by Charles E. Allen, *Burlington, Vermont: Statistics 1763 to 1893* (Burlington: Free Press Association, 1893), 17-25; Robert S. Ingram and Samuel C. Wiggans, *Climate of Burlington, Vermont* (Burlington: Agricultural Experiment Station, University of Vermont, 1968); and the maps of mean temperatures, annual precipitation and snowfall, and mean growing season in Harold A. Meeks, *The Geographic Regions of Vermont: A Study in Maps* (Hanover: Dartmouth College, Department of Geography, 1975), 26-30; and for one extreme, T. D. Seymour Bassett, "The Cold Summer of 1816--Fact and Folklore," *New England Galaxy* 15 (Summer 1973): 15-19.

Milton had not yet been improved to provide uninterrupted communication. An open winter kept sledges and sleighs in the barn and deprived the farmer of his quickest means of transportation. Too many winter thaws prevented his teaming across lakes, although while "the broad lake" near Burlington remained open, boats could continue freighting and ferrying to and from New York ports. Usually Lake Champlain was closed in February and March, and there were one or two months of good sleighing on the land. After a heavy snow, all hands turned out to clear or pack roads for the stage and their own vehicles. Good roads were essential to prosperous farming, and yet without them, farms were insulated from distant competition and urban attractions.

Prosperity blessed the farmers whose fathers had paid for their land and who had good luck with weather and prices, good soil, good stock, tight buildings, and sharpened tools, and who got their work done at the right times. Even then, their non-agricultural skills and resources contributed much to their prosperity. Following the Vermont practice of husbandry around the seasons will give a closer picture of the way the farmer's products were prepared for market. It will help to explain whether he adorned the natural landscape with a comfortable farmhouse, convenient barns, and careful cultivation, or only a shack, shelters, and weedy fields.

As the old corn snow began to disappear in March and the roads became impassable with mud and ruts, the careful farmer had finished his preparations for the agricultural new year.[8] He had repaired his buildings and fences. He had taken his tools to the blacksmith or fixed them himself. He had bought or cleaned his seed, pruned his orchard, hauled his logs and cordwood, returned from his last trip to the gristmill or otherwise disposed of last year's harvest, and engaged extra hands for the season. Since December he had gotten along, in most cases, with the labor of his family. He had just enough hay and other provender to carry his lean stock until the new grass came. If he could, he withheld his stock from wet or new pastures until the grass afforded a full bite, or the ground was dry enough not to be damaged by trampling. If he had been fortunate enough to have a surplus of feed, he had either sold it at the best prices in the late winter or, if near

---

[8] Local almanacs such as *Walton's Vermont Register and Farmer's Almanac*, published ever since 1818 with varying imprints, show the work of each season in the farmer's calendar. They contain space for the owners' memoranda, and many of the almanacs with these notes have been preserved. See also the more extended journals of Henry Stevens, John Whittemore, and Seth Shaler Arnold in Vermont Historical Society *Proceedings* 2 (September 1931): 115-128, 6 (December 1938): 317-351, 8 (June 1940): 107-193. Although a few widows and daughters operated farms for brief periods, the jobs I am describing were almost always run and done by men.

a highway, had used it to feed transient droves headed for market downcountry. If short, he had sold or butchered what he could not feed.

The snow was still deep enough in the woods for the oxen to pull the big wooden tank on runners when the sap started running in the sugarbush early in March. The farmer had nothing but chores (feeding and milking the animals) to interfere with tapping his maple grove with axe or augur and boiling the sap down to syrup in the sugarhouse. If it alternately thawed by day and froze by night, he would have a good yield. Light "sugar snows" kept the traction easy for the team. "Sugaring off" was a social occasion celebrating the end of the sugaring season.

The spring began with special attention to lambing, calving, and other increases of stock, then preparing the land as it dried out, followed by sowing, and ending with sheep shearing about the middle of June. The well-drained slopes were the first plowed, harrowed, and planted with frost-resistant seed. Local foundries provided most of the cast-iron plows, the harrows were toothed drags rather than discs, and most seed was broadcast by hand, not drilled. The main supply of fertilizer was barnyard manure, drawn whenever the snow was right for sledding. Some added clay to the sandiest fields. Advertisements for plaster of paris (made from gypsum) and lime suggest some use on acid soils. A few farmers still cleared woods for wheat, which they rotated with rye, clover, and grass. Gradually the meadows and bottomlands dried, until by the end of May or early June the crops were in. Then came hoeing and hilling potatoes and corn (horse cultivators appeared in the next decade), weeding row crops, and perhaps a short breather while everything grew and the hired man did the chores. All hands always had a day off for June training (militia inspection). Women had charge of the dairy and the vegetable garden. When it rained "outside," the almanac said, the husband gardened—meaning he could work in a light drizzle and duck into the kitchen to avoid a downpour, but would not want to be caught in a field far from the house during a deluge. Peas, beans, turnips, and other roots, regularly grown for family use, were often cultivated on a larger scale as winter fodder for cattle and sheep. Farmers were beginning to understand that legumes captured nitrogen for the soil. Since it was still the practice to wash the wool on the backs of the sheep, shearing waited until the brooks had warmed. Work was speeded by exchange between neighbors.

The principal work from June to Thanksgiving in early December was gathering into barns, but there were innumerable odd jobs. The wool was either taken to the mill, held for a better price, or disposed of to traveling buyers. A bull, ram, or stallion might be hired for servicing or a colt altered. Ground had to be prepared for rye and wheat in August, planted in September. Fall plowing was advisable for land that would not drain early enough the following spring.

When the grass was tall enough to cut—that is, just before it went to seed—scythes were sharpened and extra day labor hired for July and August. Over a third of the total man days of farm work was needed in those two months. The farmer in 1840 was able to hire hands at seventy-five cents a day. He paid more than the industrialist for labor during the next fifty years. Put another way, what he produced paid for less and less farm labor. From the point of view of the farmhand, the purchasing power of his wages steadily increased.[9] Until recently, rum had been a regular part of the haymakers' perquisites, but the temperance movement had virtually killed the custom. The hay had to be cut by hand, tedded (turned) by hand or with horse rake, forked onto wagons, and hurried into the barn as soon as it was dry, lest thunderstorms spoil it. The working day lasted as long as the daylight. Vermont farmers used very little machinery on their rough fields.

The harvesting continued through late summer and fall. Wheat, rye, and oats ripened in August; corn in September. Sometimes they cut a second crop of hay, or "rowen." The adept used scythes with cradles; many still bent over with sickles. The harvesters hand-tied the sheaves of grain and simply leaned Indian corn together in shocks. Cornhusking and apple picking continued to Halloween. The windfalls and culls from the orchard were pressed at the cider mill or at home or fed to the pigs. The better grades of apple were sold, dried, or made into sauce. Parties of a dozen or so young men and women would peel, quarter, and string apples for drying in the shed chamber and end the evening with cake, pie, and dancing. When the farmer knew how much feed he would have for the winter he decided what animals to fatten and butcher after the cold weather set in. He might drive stock to the slaughterhouse and take the hides to the tannery. The women made tallow candles and sometimes glue from horns and hoofs. For home consumption quarters were hung to freeze outside or the meat was pickled in brine. In October, before the ground froze hard, the potatoes, rutabagas, and other roots were dug and dumped in root cellars or buried in well-drained pits under straw and earth. What time off the farmer allowed himself during the busy season was either for the Fourth of July celebration, which not even haying interfered with, a little fishing and berrying, or the parties that were a way of thanking neighbor volunteers after a piece of cooperative work. Business, politics, and pleasure were usually combined. In the late fall he enjoyed hunting for some of his winter food.

---

[9]Thurston M. Adams, *Prices Paid by Farmers for Goods and Services and Received by Them for Farm Products, 1790-1871; Wages of Farm Labor, 1780-1837.* Vermont Agricultural Experiment Station Bulletin 507 (Burlington: Agricultural Experiment Station, University of Vermont, 1944), 43-54. My discussion of farm economy is based chiefly on this monograph.

When all was safely gathered in, the governor proclaimed a day of Thanksgiving, usually the first Thursday in December. The better-attended winter term of district school now opened. The farmer who threshed his grain and shelled his corn early in the winter and kept his apples picked over cheated the rats and rot. Hay was often salted for the cattle and late corn chopped for fodder in the strawcutter. The saying went that good shelter and plenty of straw saved feed, but the practice fell below this standard. Clean dairies required frequent whitewashings. Christmas was celebrated less than New Year's, but winter was the season for visits, singing school, spelling bees, sleigh rides, and balls. Even the exhausting work of combating a fire was a welcome break in the winter routine. A good farmer did not make much money in cold weather, unless he went into the woods; but he did the things necessary to bring a good harvest the next year, and he enjoyed himself.

Farmers knew nature best, but they also knew intimately the relatively few persons nearby with whom they dealt. Most of their trips were no farther than the adjacent towns or the county seat. The nature of farming tied them to their land.

Their communication was as simple and limited as their travel. Farmers were rarely illiterate, for they had had at least a few terms of district school. Less than two in one thousand white adult Vermonters in 1840 could neither read nor write. Perhaps a third subscribed to the local weekly newspaper with ten pounds of butter, one or two bushels of rye, or other produce. A few took religious or agricultural periodicals. These papers recounted the news of the world outside Vermont, and the fires, floods, elections, and annual meetings around the state. For the most part, gossip was the main source of local news. Farmers did not take much time to read and were suspicious of secondhand book learning. Their writing was equally limited, in the main, to keeping track of their distant relatives and making a rough record of their obligations and advances to others.

Their social activities were face to face visiting among families or at the meetinghouse, the public house, the schoolhouse, or the county courthouse—if the town boasted separate buildings for these functions. In warm weather there were camp meetings, barn dances and bees, rallies, and fairs. Going to meeting on Sunday offered a chance to dress up, meet friends, and collect mail. The taverns, strung at short distances along the highways, provided supper and lodging if overnight journeys could not be broken at the homes of friends, relatives, or business associates. A trip to the next town to fetch a harness, shoe a horse, or settle a note could conveniently be combined with a meal and storytelling at the inn. The town hall, church, or academy building were the natural places for singing school concerts, lyceums, and meetings of local organizations. Twice a year, the meetinghouse—often called "town house" or "town room"—was put to the official purpose for which it was built: to hold town meeting in March and to hold the state election in September. Those who attended these meetings to discuss local affairs or elect officers had some personal concern—the bounty on foxes, the repair of their own roads, revision of school districts, or other parochial business, perhaps a temperance or antislavery petition. At some time in their lives most country people became involved in a case at the courthouse or had need to consult the records of the county clerk or probate judge. Political parties held their conventions at the county seat. June training, the Independence Day speechmaking and banquet in the grove (or in the tavern if the weather was "inclement"), revival meetings or work bees were social activities relieving the isolation of farm life. Sometimes people quite forgot the serious purposes for which these meetings were called. Daniel Webster's address to ten thousand at Stratton during the Whig campaign of 1840, for example, was a great picnic and a chance to hear the "godlike Daniel."

Vermont's most valuable export was people to the West and to the cities that soon produced cheaper farm produce and industrial goods than Vermonters could. A slight gain in Vermont's population since 1820 reflected the stimulation of the Hudson-Champlain-Richelieu trade route, which brought cheaper western wheat, flour, and fat cattle. What new product could Vermont farmers raise and sell to advantage? They thought it was wool, especially if Webster's Whig Party could win them a higher wool tariff.[10]

The fame of Vermont merinos, which western and foreign breeders kept buying years after the Civil War, has tended to obscure the fact that most Vermonters were general farmers, even at the height of the sheep boom of 1830-45. Wool growing as a highly developed and profitable specialty was limited for the most part to large-scale operators in Addison, Rutland, Windsor, and Orange counties. The sheep population was densest in the Champlain shore towns from Benson to St. Albans and the towns along the Connecticut River from Westminster to Thetford. The ordinary farmer, to be sure, had a flock of "grade" sheep (unimproved breeds), but even in 1840 the total value of wool sales at average prices was only sixty-four percent of the value of the butter and cheese made on the farm.[11]

---

[10]Lewis Stilwell, "Migration from Vermont, 1776-1860," Vermont Historical Society *Proceedings* 5 (June 1937): 63-246, details the people drain. Harold F. Wilson, *The Hill Country of Northern New England; Its Social and Economic History, 1790-1930* (1936; reprint, New York: AMS Press, 1967), 75-94, summarizes the conditions that made Vermont a leader in sheep raising for over a decade.

[11]T. M. Adams, *Prices and Wages*, 22.

It is easy to see why, in the absence of any kind of accounting among farmers except the most sketchy recording of purchases, sales, and debts, the wool growers and the general public believed that wool was *the* Vermont staple. Wool "*was* the most important *single* source of Vermont income" in the decade before 1840, rocketing to prominence since 1824, apparently because of the higher tariff.[12] Protection was a major article of Whig faith, ritually repeated, and the tariff directly affected wool prices. Ever led on by the hope of greater protection for a commodity that in its peak years averaged less than a quarter of their income, the farmers chased the tariff will-o'-the-wisp for decades. Tariff historians, however, have not ascribed the major influence on wool prices to the tariff on wool.[13]

People focused on wool for two other reasons. The violently fluctuating and speculative market, with prices up to 1845 relatively higher than for important staples in general, kept farmers' thoughts on the rosy uncertainty of a high price and a heavy clip. Besides, the prosperity of large-scale breeders of full-blooded merinos demonstrated to the small farmer that his dreams could be realized. He did not stop to reckon how he could pay for the best Hammond, Rich, or Atwood stock. For him, wool growing was a stage on the way from self-sufficient farming to commercial agriculture. For half a century he had sold his surplus livestock, grain, dairy products, and wool. In the coming decades he would increasingly emphasize dairying.

The Vermonter, instead of being a crop raiser or woodsman with a few animals, was first of all a livestock tender. He spent a good deal of his time in barn and pasture and raised crops mainly to feed his animals. At least three-quarters of his marketed produce was live cattle, horses, swine, sheep, meat, dairy products, wool, tallow, and skins. He continued to sell relatively small amounts of Indian corn, oats, wheat, and rye, and his hay production was increasing. A new market for potatoes was beginning to develop in the starch factories of the northern counties, and the cultivation of hops was spreading in the same region. The Scottish farmers along the Connecticut in Caledonia and Orange counties from the beginning were productive dairymen; the butter from Ryegate and Barnet had a high reputation. More and more farmers were growing apples in the Champlain Valley and along the lower Connecticut. Back in the mountains of every county except in the southwest, and especially on the northern frontier, potash was still a by-product of settlement.

---

[12] Ibid., 31. Italics added.

[13] See, for example, C. W. Wright, *Woolgrowing and the Tariff* (Boston: Houghton Mifflin, 1910), 53, 155, 320-326; Mark A. Smith, *The Tariff on Wool* (New York: Macmillan, 1926).

The chief forest products, however, were rough timber, cordwood, maple sugar, and homemade shingles. Custom sawing had declined, especially in western Vermont, ever since the Albany market had opened with the Champlain-Hudson canal. Loggers continued to clear-cut the forests. The superb original stands of white pine and hardwoods were virtually gone, and a few timid voices began to call for conservation.[14]

The large-scale producer of any one of these items—and each product had its specialists—could usually afford to transport his own goods and save teaming charges. One might see, wrote a Hartford historian, "on a winter's day, as many as thirty two-horse teams . . . en route to Boston, each team being driven by its owner. . . . The farmers . . . then made annual trips to Boston." A load cost about thirty dollars each way between Woodstock and Boston, and varied with weight and distance. The small farmer with debts at the store paid them off in kind. "Farmers would get in debt during the year," wrote George Barney of Swanton, thinking of the thirties, "and then have to pay in wheat at 75c to $1 a bushel, corn 50c, oats 25, butter 10 to 12c per pound."[15] When the storekeeper had accumulated a load of one to two and a half tons, he hired a local teamster to carry the produce by ox-drawn wagon or sledge to Boston or a port on the western water route, Burlington, Whitehall, or Troy. A smaller quantity of goods was rafted down the Connecticut to Springfield, Massachusetts, or Hartford, Connecticut.

These loads paid for the molasses, sugar, salt, fish, whale oil for lamps, tea, coffee, tobacco, iron, and building materials brought back from the seaports. The demon rum, which formerly bulked large, was being exorcised by the temperance movement, and Western flour began to pour in through Whitehall.

Freighting by wagon was slow, and even the steam-driven lake boats were sluggish. But set against the somnolence of an earlier generation, circulation of goods and people was brisk and their numbers large. In the near anarchy of the woods, most men had been debtors, held back by nature, their habits, and their debts. Now, although the myth of the freeholding farmer as the backbone of the republic had a firm and widespread hold, over half the farms carried mortgages,[16] and the

---

[14] E.g., Nathan Hoskins, *A History of the State of Vermont* (Vergennes: J. Shedd, 1831), 16-17.

[15] Hemenway, *Gazetteer*, 4:1131; annual teaming: William N. Tucker, *History of Hartford, Vermont, July 4, 1761 - April 4, 1889* (Burlington: Free Press Association, 1889), 346; freight costs: Adams, *Prices and Wages*, 41-42.

[16] Clarence H. Danhof, *Change in Agriculture: The Northern United States, 1820-1870* (Cambridge, Mass.: Harvard University Press, 1969), 82.

village aristocracy, in league with a few rich farmers, spoke the decisive words. The next Vermont generation would see the valley villages expand and mesh with the cities. Who then would speak with authority?

Burlington Harbor, ca. 1848, by J. H. Hills from the breakwater. Engr. by De Lay Glover, Boston (identified by staff of Boston Public Library). Letterhead in photograph collection, Special Collections, Bailey/Howe Library, University of Vermont.

2. Burlington in 1840: An Inland Port

The most populous town in Vermont attracted travelers on the grand tour that included Niagara Falls, Montreal, Lake Champlain, and the seaports of the seaboard. Let us imagine we have found the journal of one visitor and read how he described the town where he spent a few days.[1]

Burlington, Vermont. Friday, June 26, 1840. I was not prepared for the glories of the sail along the broad lake after the wild smuggling and uncultivated look of the country near the U. S. border. Nor did we expect the man-of-war precision with which Captain Richard W. Sherman managed the rapid and orderly transfer of passengers and goods at each port. Commands are transmitted by bell signal, not by vulgar shouts as in many British ports. The stewards are numerous and all dressed in neat, clean, fancy uniforms. The customs officer merely asked if we had anything to declare and did not open our bags.

This pretty town was aglow in the setting sun as the steamboat *Burlington* passed Sharpshin [now Rock] Point from Plattsburgh. From the unfinished breakwater the dwellings on the slope above the three long wharves showed spots of white clapboard, red brick, and yellow through the foliage. Northward from the docks the shoreline rises to a bluff behind which a steeple and a square, gray, limestone belfry mark the northern extent of the village. The woods meet the water beyond. Crowning the crest of the hill, the tin dome of the college building is a beacon landmark for miles, and eastward the green fades into the hazy blue of Camel's Rump [now called Camel's Hump or Couching Lion] and Mansfield Mountain. We turned to drink in the sunset and the Alpine aspect of the Adirondacks piling up toward the southwest. The approaching steamer *Whitehall* was framed between Pottier's [now Shelburne] Point and Juniper Island, and two sloops

---

[1]Footnotes for the many details appear in an earlier version of this chapter, "An Inland Port: Burlington, Vermont in 1840," *New England Quarterly* 44 (December 1971): 635-649. David J. Blow supplies more details and pictures in his *Historic Guide to Burlington Neighborhoods*, Lilian Baker Carlisle, ed. (Burlington: Chittenden County Historical Society, 1990).

made for the harbor on the dying breeze.[2] A crowd of hotel runners competed for our patronage, and we soon found our baggage and ourselves in a carriage for the brisk drive up the slope to the American Hotel on Court House Square. Landlord Ira Shattuck, the stage man, served a generous table to upwards of fifty transients and boarders.

Saturday, June 27. The hubbub attending the departure of the Montpelier stage woke me before dawn, but I had another nap before the boy came to rouse me and remove my pot. Walking down to the waterfront, I found it already busy with loading and unloading: pigs being wrestled up the plank, country men with other livestock, a heavy dray of window glass lumbering down the slope of Water Street, and fishermen back from an early morning catch of walleye, perch, and bass for the boardinghouses.

I found my man and attended to my business. Bustling as these lake ports are on arrivals and departures, there is plenty of time for talk. Thomas H. Canfield, a young clerk in a store seven miles out the turnpike, checking a shipment at Follett and Bradley's, wholesalers, obligingly answered my questions.[3] Burlington has been booming since the Northern Canal linked the lake with the Hudson Valley in 1823, he told me. As the port of entry since 1822 for the Customs District of Vermont, with a lighthouse on Juniper Island and the new federal breakwater, it has no peer on the Vermont shore. Plattsburgh, across the lake, is still larger, but he expects Burlington to forge ahead.[4] It already has the largest volume of lake trade, nearly a million dollars gross. Burlington's market area includes the whole upper half of Vermont, which is still growing. "They're

---

[2] Ogden J. Ross, *The Steamboats of Lake Champlain, 1809 to 1930* (Albany, N.Y.: Champlain Transportation, 1930), 61-71, describes the sister ships *Burlington* and *Whitehall*, 1837-43.

[3] Thomas H. Canfield, "Discovery, Navigation and Navigators on Lake Champlain," in A. M. Hemenway, *Gazetteer*, 1:656-707.

[4] New York and U.S. census figures show major lakeport growth, 1830-50:

	Whitehall	Burlington	Plattsburgh
1830	2889	3226	4913
1835	3076	—	4426
1840	3813	4271	6416
1845	3954	—	6095
1850	4726	7585	5618

loading that wagon with flour for Littleton, New Hampshire," he said. "Most of the upper Connecticut Valley can get Rochester flour cheaper this way than from Portland."[5]

Whitehall, the gateway to the Champlain Valley, is also a funnel for emigrants from the hill country or Europe. Mr. Canfield introduced me to Elam Comings, just back from Oberlin College, who had nothing good to say about the lake-canal junction. According to this prim and pious youth, Whitehall is filthy, poorly laid out, congested with travelers. Every canal boat is overcrowded with noisy, profane, intemperate trash. Sleep was impossible in the ten-by-twelve-foot cabin, jammed with over two dozen travelers. Whitehall's harbor was clogged with boats emerging from the locks or jockeying to be first into them. To save shifting cargo, some of the canal boats are equipped to sail on the lake and ship their masts when they reach Whitehall. Burlington merchants are preparing a fleet of such "long boats" for the 1841 season.[6]

Canfield said Peter Comstock of Whitehall runs the Red Bird stages between Albany and Montreal and a fleet of canal boats to Troy. During the winter his four-horse coaches carry the mails to Vergennes thrice a week. Since 1831 he has been the principal partner of the leading lake freight line, the Northern Transportation Company, recently sold to James H. Hooker of Troy, who has heavy interests in Hudson River transportation. Comstock wanted to get into the lake passenger business too, but it is expensive to build a steamer to compete with the Champlain Transportation Company. This "Old Line," chartered in 1826, bought out Comstock's and other rival ferries and created a monopoly in 1834. It bought him out again in 1838, when he started to build the *Whitehall*.

The common people do not like the monopoly; it caters to the so-called aristocracy. I hear that when President Van Buren was here last summer he declined an introduction to the steamboat captain. "I know Sherman. He thinks the world is a steamboat and he is the captain." During the recent Canadian Rebellion, Patriot sympathizers blamed the line for the defeat of Robert Nelson's troops at Napierville. It ferried British troops from St. Johns to Nelson's rear. Temperance people

---

[5]On Burlington's hinterland, see "The Journals of Henry A. S. Dearborn," *Buffalo Historical Society Publications*, 7 (1904): 155, entry for October 7, 1838.

[6]See the journal of Elam J. Comings, May 9-10, 1836, quoted in Robert S. Fletcher, *A History of Oberlin College* (Oberlin, Ohio: The College, 1943), 2:539; David Wilson, *Life in Whitehall During Ship Fever Times* (Whitehall: Inglee and Tefft, 1900).

disapprove of the bars on the boats. Opposition seems strong enough to pass a bill taxing steamboat stock in the next legislature.[7]

Sailing vessels far outnumber the five steamboats on the lake: the two passenger queens, two canal tugs, and the old *Winooski*, the Burlington - Port Kent ferry. Well over a hundred sloops, schooners, sailing rafts, and canal boats collect and distribute produce at the docks of nearly every shore town. Archibald W. Hyde, Collector of Customs, told me that his 1838 returns listed sixty-seven Vermont-owned vessels totaling 4,250 tons. With the vessels registered on the New York side, the total lake tonnage must be double that.

I spent the afternoon getting acquainted with some of the merchants and professionals who make Court House Square the center of the village. Some of the sidewalks are bricked, more are graveled, and there are short stretches of paved street. Paths cross a circular green, enclosed with a painted railing and bordered by trees. Nearby streets are also well-shaded. Store steps project into the sidewalks, and wooden awnings shade the small-paned shop windows. As in other New England villages, the common is at the crossroads, where Shelburne Street meets Main Street. One axis leads from the docks up the hill, to become the turnpike to Montpelier at the college green. The other is the north-south highway from Middlebury, bending eastward to cross the Winooski River and continue to Canada.

Samuel Hickok, whose home and three-story brick store occupy the southwest corner of Court House Square, told me that the original settlement of Burlington Bay hugged the shore. He was the first trader to move up to the courthouse, to forestall customers coming from the interior. The Mills family run the bookstore, the Democratic weekly *Burlington Sentinel*, and the post office in Mills Row, east of the American Hotel. Postmaster Ephraim Mills, who gets $732 a year for part-time work, boasted that the post office's almost $3,000 gross income last year was by far the largest in the state. Whig patrons of the post office complain of its run-down condition, and, as always, of its service. If Harrison is elected, Whigs expect to replace Mills with the editor of the Whig *Free Press* and move the post office office north to College Street, near the paper and Huntington's bookstore. The latchstring of their Tippecanoe log cabin, built in the square for the Whig convention, is still out; I did not investigate whether hard cider is still available. Thursday's Whig

---

[7]Ralph Nading Hill, *Contrary Country*, 2d ed. (Brattleboro: Stephen Greene Press, 1961), 142; Burlington *Free Press*, 23 August 1839; clergyman in Middlebury *Vermont Observer*, ca. November 28, 1843; *Vermont Laws* (1840), 15-17. Lewis Hayden described discrimination against his black wife by Captain Davis of the *Saranac* in the *National Anti-Slavery Standard* of 22 July 1847.

BURLINGTON IN 1841
(Pop. 4,012)

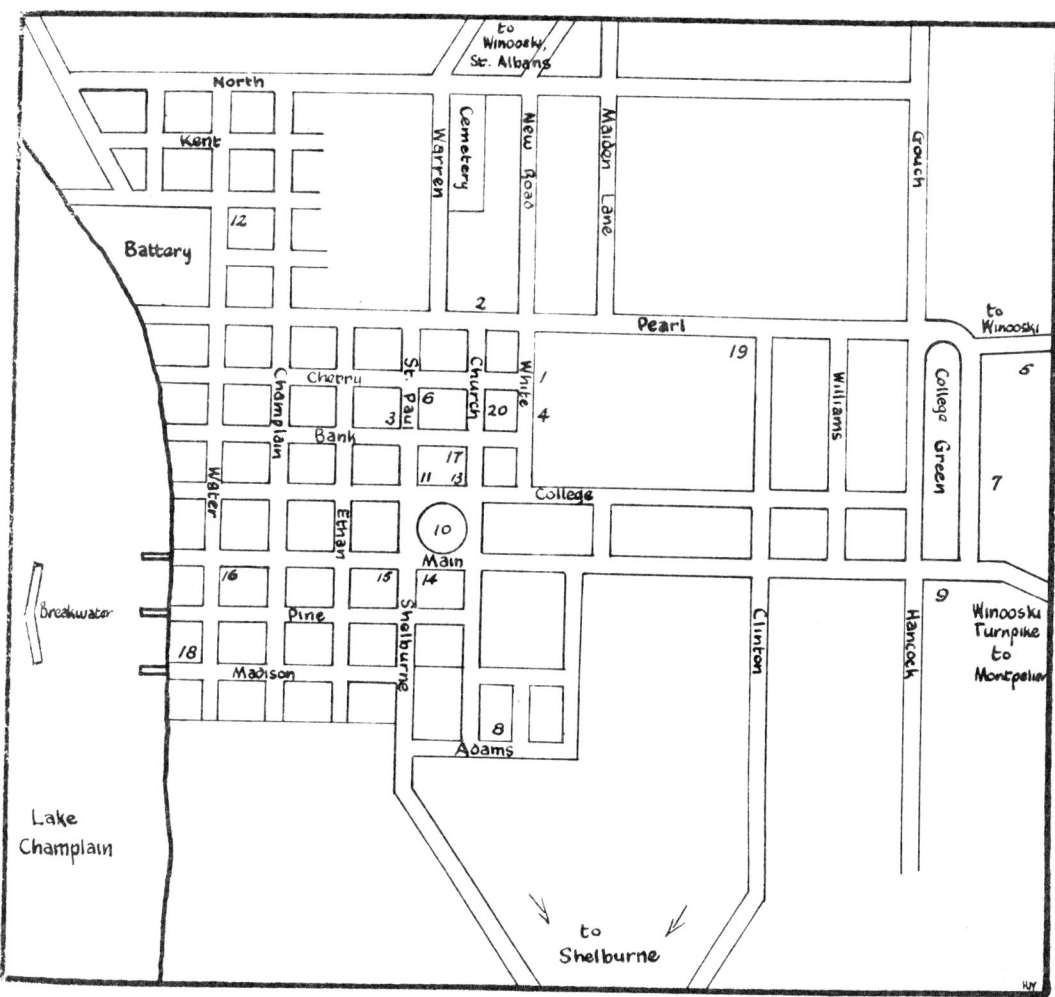

1. First Calvinistic Congregational Church.
2. Unitarian Church.
3. St. Paul's Episcopal Church.
4. Methodist Chapel.
5. Baptist Chapel.
6. St. Mary's Roman Catholic Church.
7. University of Vermont.
8. Burlington Female Seminary.
9. Medical College.
10. Court House Square.
11. Farmers' and Mechanics' Bank.
12. Glass House of Smith and Wilkins.
13. Howard Hotel.
14. American Hotel.
15. Franklin Hotel.
16. Jenner's Hotel.
17. Bank of Burlington.
18. Exchange Hotel.
19. Pearl Street House.
20. Chittenden County Jail.

Burlington in 1841. From Zadock Thompson, *History of Vermont* (1842), pt. 3, 39.

parade and convention trampled and littered the square and the main streets. Besides the four hotels on the square, a dozen men do business there, with several lawyers, such as ex-Congressman Heman Allen, town representative Don Carlos Baxter, Democratic leader David A. Smalley, and George P. Marsh, drawn there to be near the brick courthouse on the east side. The town divided with the county the three thousand dollars it cost to replace the courthouse that burned in 1828. The county clerk, sheriff, and juries have rooms on the ground floor below the courtroom, and the town uses the basement for its March and September meetings. The Roman Catholics have permission to use the town room on Sundays while they rebuild St. Mary's after a fire.

Sunday, June 28. A gloomy day with thunderstorms. I went to the Unitarian meetinghouse, for which Church Street is named, on the axis of the business street but buffered by a block or more of dwellings. The clock below the belfry and lantern in its tall steeple keeps time for the business community, well represented in its society. These liberal businessmen raised $23,000 in 1816 for a Boston architect to design and build the edifice and buy an organ. Unitarianism centers in Boston, the commercial hub of New England, and the largest of four Vermont Unitarian churches presides over Vermont's commercial capital.

A break in the clouds as we came from the Rev. George G. Ingersoll's service persuaded us to stroll back along White Street, which parallels Church Street and is named for the white Congregational house of worship built in 1811, which burned down a year ago. The Congregationalists were emerging from a wooden chapel and inspecting the progress of work on the new building. I recognized Henry Hickok, who had changed my money yesterday at the Merchants' bank. He introduced me to George P. Marsh of the building committee. They plan, he said, to use the renowned choragic monument of Lysicrates in Athens, also known as the Lantern of Demosthenes, honoring a dramatic chorus, as a unique bell tower. The building will symbolize the classical bond between the church and the University of Vermont faculty, which worships and holds its commencement exercises here.

Next south on White Street is a small Methodist chapel built within the decade, which cannot make up its mind whether to be Gothic or classical: its Gothic gables point toward the Episcopal, while its round arched windows agree with the Congregationalists next door. Turning toward the lake we braved the watchers at the windows of the county jail and the loungers across the street at Burdick's inn, Church and Cherry. On the next corner west they are planning a large Romish church building; a block south is St. Paul's Episcopal, which gives its name to the street and proudly proclaims in Gothic limestone its minority status in Vermont.

After dinner we engaged a carriage for the afternoon. The sun now steamed the washed leaves, fences, and walls of dwelling, shop and garden as we sped down College Street, enchanted by the blue lake at the foot of the hill. Back up Water Street, showing by rut and rubbish the signs of a freight route. The Battery bluff offers a magnificent panorama, which we were scarcely allowed to enjoy, because idlers insisted on telling us all about the British attack during the War of 1812.

The people who work in the glasshouse live near the Battery. Frederick Smith, one of the managers, spoke sanguinely about the prospects of the twelve-year-old venture in producing window glass. With a Whig tariff he expects to triple last year's output worth thirty thousand dollars, and increase the work force from forty to over a hundred. But the glassblower showing us around disagreed. "Charcoal is cheaper near the Adirondacks," he said.

We drove between recently planted rows of locust trees to North Street, a country road east of Champlain Street, and then into the new road to Winooski, which proved too muddy. The town built it so that freight wagons can avoid the hill up Pearl Street and the precipitous descent to Winooski Falls. Wyllys Lyman, George P. Marsh, and John N. Pomeroy stand to make money developing Maiden Lane [now North Union Street]. School district figures already show the village growing northward.

For a town sensitive to the tides of trade, with forced sales and foreclosures advertised in every newspaper, Burlington is building as if hard times do not exist. Heman Lowry, the census enumerator for Burlington, told me that nearly a hundred were employed as masons, carpenters, or in household furnishings during the past year, and nearly half the new houses were brick. People must be prosperous to afford a brick house costing upwards of $1,500 when a frame dwelling could be put up for about $500.

Pearl Street, named for a militia colonel and local magistrate who once lived at its head, dips past Maiden Lane into a broad ravine, crosses the wooden bridge, and at the house of University of Vermont president John Wheeler, corner of Clinton [now South Willard], enters another settlement of some seventy-five houses focusing on the north end of the college common. The new Pearl Street House, a phoenix hotel rebuilt after a fire, has plenty of room for freight wagons using the Winooski Pike. Tailor, millinery, and barber shops, one or two stores, and even an engraver cater to the college trade, but the college green is declining as a commercial center. Thaddeus Tuttle's 1809 store has long been just a dwelling. The last building has been cleared off the green, a fenced, turnstiled and graded hayfield ready for the scythe. Baptist Deacon Benns is having a fire sale and moving to Church Street. They say the Baptists will give up the chapel he built for them out the road to the Falls and build on Court House Square.[8] The trend toward dwellings supplanting shops near the college will continue. President Wheeler is talking with architect Ammi Young about designing him a new brick mansion south of College Street.

We passed the home of the Reverend James Marsh, professor of philosophy and former president, its apple orchard sloping to the east and south, an old yellow house built for the preparatory department in the 1790s. Three plain, tin-roofed college buildings face College Street, which ends at the green. The heavy enrollment of the past five years has filled North and South Colleges and overflowed into the town. Under the dome are the chapel, library, and classrooms. At the south end of the green, the two-story medical building has housed scientific apparatus and classes since 1834, when the medical department failed. The mercantile and professional community has always recognized the college's economic value, and at each financial crisis has invested in buildings and books. Many laborers, Papists, and Democrats find fault with the Puritan professors for urging neutrality during the Canadian Rebellion and for their other Whiggish doctrines. By and large, however, the community is proud of its college.

Fields come close to the green along Hancock [or Tuttle, now South Prospect] Street. At the break in the Main Street hill Thaddeus Tuttle, once-wealthy land speculator and merchant, built a Federal style brick mansion framed by fencing, its western parlor view protected by acres of slope. Governor Cornelius P. Van Ness, its next owner, entertained General Lafayette here in 1824. The Hon. and Mrs. Heman Allen, who moved in when Van Ness was appointed Minister to Spain, pretentiously named it "Grasse Mount" for the French admiral, le comte de Grasse in our Revolution. To own a mansion like this is the dearest dream of many a coming businessman. Nowadays the town aristocrats prefer the classical revival style of John S. Potwin's house built some ten years ago on equally spacious grounds below Clinton [Willard] Street. Except for the few blocks south of Main Street, we had toured the edges of the gridiron of streets that encompass three-quarters of the town's population.

Tea at Mr. George Perkins Marsh's, across from the Unitarian church. His knowledge is amazing, especially in the fine arts and languages. Two years ago he published an Icelandic grammer in Burlington. His library is a perfect wilderness of about five thousand volumes and the finest collection of engravings I have seen in the States. Tomorrow he promised to show me the works of the Burlington Mill Company at Winooski Falls, in which he has invested.

---

[8]See John E. Goodrich, "The College Park," *The University Cynic*, 10 (March 30, 1893), 180-183.

Monday, June 29. This morning Mr. Marsh drove me to the Falls over the new, level road, half a mile shorter than the road over the hill; dry and dust-free after yesterday's showers. The mills here have a checkered history, although they occupy excellent water privileges. Here the Winooski—or Onion, as is it is more commonly called—breaks through a weak point in a ridge rising abruptly on each side, dropping over two ledges, the lower providing a thirty-seven-foot head. Its flow is regular, for it drains a tenth of Vermont. Timber has been sawed here since Ira Allen's choppers cleared Burlington's cover of pine. Logs now come from Underhill and Bolton—also charcoal for the glass house and the smithies. In the early days they also ground grain and gypsum, made linseed oil, carded wool, fulled homespun, and forged bog iron. Nothing is left on the Burlington side, after the fire of '38, except Moses and Guy Catlin's rebuilt flouring, plaster, and saw mills.

Across the covered bridge, in the town of Colchester, the industrial village is developing a factory complex like those I saw in southern New England. Its central feature is the six-story brick factory, with its tremendous overshot wheel, its long wooden tenements for spinners and weavers, and half a dozen other buildings. Burlington businessmen invested $130,000 to build what is one of the three largest mills in Vermont, with the newest machinery, but Marsh says it has steadily lost money.

Unlike so many small woolen mills on side streams, the Burlington Mill Company competes in the national market. Instead of taking what the wool grower clips and returning cloth, the company advertises cash for wool. Instead of bartering cloth for wool raised in the surrounding hills and peddling the surplus, they ship to a New York jobber, in competition with British imports and Merrimack domestic woolens. With all the risks of a new enterprise, they cannot afford to try new weaves such as the fashionable doeskins and cassimeres, yet there is less future in their standard broadcloth.

While the mill loses money, the village of Winooski Falls gains. It already has almost as many people as the rest of the town, including Colchester Center, which has the post office, the town hall, and new Methodist and Baptist churches. At the Falls are more inns, stores and mechanics' shops than at the Center; also the Congregational meetinghouse built last year. Upstream from the woolen mill the foundry and machine shop of Guy Edwards makes cast iron fencing, textile machinery, and other castings.

The stuffs in the examining room had first-class quality. Several certificates of merit adorned the walls, but gold medals meet no payrolls until translated into sales. The employees, Agent Sidney

Barlow said, are mainly Yankee girls saving until their young men come back from the West to marry them, and a few stranded Irish immigrants and French-Canadian hands released after the harvest. They can't compete with Lowell wages. Whenever they hire someone with skill and experience from downcountry, they prove unstable, intemperate, and temporary. None of the hands knows enough about the work; none of them stays long.

Except for the Catlins' mills at the Falls, Burlington's manufacturers are off the square, on good roads leading inland or to the wharves, and close to where the workmen live, near Water and lower Pearl streets. The only producers with more than a strictly local sale are Farrar & Wait's pottery down Pearl Street from the Unitarian church, the glass house, and the boat builders. The pottery made $7,000 worth of stoneware and earthenware last year, and steamer repairs plus the sailboat business amounted to $69,800 for the shipyard. The shops use charcoal, hand, and horse power and can be located anywhere. The village's only metal workers above the level of blacksmith are near Water Street. C. M. Varney makes guns and also advertises as a whitesmith, gold and silversmith, die sinker, cutlery maker, and machinist.

This evening I heard an indifferent concert of the Tippecanoe Band and Chorus at the courthouse, but met interesting people. Professor Theodore F. Molt of Burlington Female Seminary and organist at St. Paul's played some pleasing pieces of his own composition on a locally built piano. He studied with Czerny and Moschelles. I met Dr. Bernhard J. Heineberg, with Molt's family among the few Germans in town, and Zadock Thompson, a walking encyclopedia of local knowledge. He has published a small gazetteer, a literary monthly, schoolbooks on geography, history, and civil government, and is about to publish a large repository of useful and scientific information about Vermont.

I mentioned seeing on the Battery yesterday afternoon a young Negro matron with a white laboring man and four little yellow children. Such miscegenation meets little prejudice here—just the prejudice between Yankee and foreigner, rich and poor. The well-to-do concert patrons hire the French, Irish or Negroes as servants and helpers, expect them to work hard for little, learn quickly, and not stay long. John Thompson's is the only Negro family enumerated in the Burlington censuses of 1830 and 1840. Isham Loney, the black barber by the Howard Hotel, Mr. Thompson said, recently published his rhymes in the local *Free Press*.

I asked about the foreigners. They are numerous near the lake where tenements rent cheap and landlords let them double up, but you find them all over town. Mr. Thompson thought there were as many as a thousand of French Canadian or Irish origin in town: day laborers, domestics, a few artisans, and two innkeepers. They have been filtering into the Champlain Valley for a long time, especially since the canals opened. As country people they have preferred to take up farms on the Islands or along the lakeshore as far south as Addison. Poor, hitherto deprived of the chance to go to school, called clannish because they naturally seek their friends and relatives for help, they have come, just as the Yankees came earlier, to better their lot.[9]

Most of the throng at the concert had brought lanterns, and I was grateful for lighted company on the uncertain footing of the square. I was surprised at how few had carriages; almost none had coachmen. I recalled Mr. Thompson's saying there were about 350 horses, including those belonging to farmers and the livery stables, in the whole town. That means less than a hundred private families in the village with a horse. On the other hand, there are almost as many pigs as people; even the poor immigrant can keep a hog.

Gardening is part of the way of life here. A recently rural people are still thriftily providing part of their own subsistence but they also devote some leisure to adorning the comfortable space around their dwellings with floral beauty. Today the scent of sickled grass and June flowers made me almost forget the village odor of outbuildings and street manure. "Burlington is known by its fruits," said the printer Chauncey Goodrich when Mr. Thompson told him only Woodstock and Calais exceeded Burlington's $5,000 worth of orchard products last year. They raise the popular Fameuse (pronounced "Fay-mews") apple from Quebec and other hardy strains.

I find the domestic scale of the village modest and homogeneous. Burlington's even growth for over fifteen years provided steady employment. This brought experience and confidence to the master carpenters, building in a style fashioned almost entirely without benefit of architect or village plan. To be sure, there are two resident architects: Henry Searle, designer of the new Congregational church, and Ammi Young, who came from Lebanon, New Hampshire, ten years ago. While their work lends a touch of coastal sophistication, especially up the hill from the ravine, the builders, thumbing their Benjamin, treat wood surely and brick with restraint. If they err it is to satisfy their clients' pretentions to elegance.[10]

---

[9]In 1820 Vermont had 935 foreign-born; in 1830, 3364. See U.S. Department of State, *Statistical View of the Population of the United States, from 1790-1830* (Washington, 1835), 38. The 1840 census did not record nativity.

[10]Asher Benjamin, *The Practical House Carpenter* (Boston: 1830) and many other versions between 1798 and mid-century; Lawrence Wodehouse, "Ammi Young's Architecture in Northern New England," *Vermont History* 36 (Spring 1968): 53-60.

Burlington is a busy inland port, in touch with New York, Boston, and the British Empire. The profits of commerce make it, in spite of the shabby blocks near the wharves, a jewel among New England country towns.

* * * * *

Our imaginary diarist's view was oriented toward the lake. Without Champlain Burlington was only one of thirteen major trading places in a network of stage and freight wagon routes. The thicker mesh in the lower Connecticut Valley reflects denser population and heavier trade. The thirteen towns, which geographers call "central places" because of their concentration of services, were by the contemporary census definition "urban" because each had more than 2,500 people.

After Burlington, Montpelier led the five towns with a population over 3,000, mainly because of its trade and traffic. The frosting on its cake was the patronage of four or five hundred legislators, lawyers, and lobbyists coming for the October and November sessions of the General Assembly. Bennington was second highest in bank assets and tax base, with a thriving iron industry and other manufacturing. Next came Woodstock, whose architecture today still reflects its pre-railroad prosperity. A shire town of the most populous and richest county in Vermont, Woodstock had inventive mechanics and a diversity of mills. Its Vermont Medical College and other "literary" institutions lent prestige if not large numbers to its other assets. Middlebury had a similar blend of manufacturing at the falls of Otter Creek, trade, courthouse business, and culture in Middlebury College and its feeder academy.

Ranked below were many villages with the same mixture in smaller proportions. Windsor, for example, an established village before statehood, had afforded extra profits to the fortunate entrepreneurs using the cheap convict labor of its state prison. From Middlebury and Hartford south, the large towns of 1840 had been well developed villages when Vermont entered the union. A generation more of village life meant a stronger tradition, with the kind of conservatism based on money longer possessed or spent for comfortable homes and public buildings.

Major segments of the main roads connecting these central places had been built as privately chartered turnpikes from the 1790s to the War of 1812. But people hated tolls worse than taxes. They won many exemptions; they built "shunpikes" around the tollgates; they knew the gatekeeper; they sued for damages from accidents caused by ruts and potholes. As people moved into the valleys from the hills where they had first settled, towns took over roadbuilding and maintenance, and the turnpike companies with high roads, losing traffic, abandoned them to the towns. The cost of maintenance forced others to do the same. Three pikes crossing the Green Mountains in the south, all chartered before 1830, lingered into the railroad era: the Searsburg from Bennington to Brattleboro, the Stratton from Sunderland to Newfane, and the Green Mountain from Shrewsbury to Bellows Falls. Only a few pieces of main line charged tolls in 1840. Town roads (there were no state roads) were repaired by the taxpayers, the amount of their labor set by town officials. In mudtime they sang,

> For now it ain't passable,
> Not even jackassable,
> And those who would travel it
> Should turn out and gravel it.[11]

Fights over road repairs were only equaled by fights over fences to keep livestock out of the highway and the farmers' fields, and fights over bridges, especially those between towns.

The roads that provided the leading villages with mail service each weekday, along with freight and passengers, were remarkably similar to today's trunk lines. The Boston-Montreal stage entered Vermont at Hartford (now White River Junction) and approximated the route of Interstate 89 to Burlington and the Canada line, with a night stopover at the state capital, Montpelier. Nine post roads started there, and travelers had the choice of seven public houses.

Westward to Burlington the Winooski Turnpike aimed at a water gap called Bolton Notch, the easiest crossing of the Green Mountains. Eastbound traveler Henry Dearborn called it "the most remarkable road I ever passed," because he seemed to be going down grade right up to the mountains.[12] Indeed, Montpelier's Pavilion Hotel was scarcely two hundred feet higher than the college buildings in Burlington.

The principal Albany-Montreal post route was by steamboat from Whitehall to St. Jean. When the lake was closed, the route was west of Lake Champlain, like Interstate 87. A westside highway served southern Vermont, like present U.S. 7, via Burlington, Vergennes, Middlebury, and Rutland to Bennington, where it crossed the present route from Albany via Brattleboro and Nashua to Boston. Heavier traffic originating outside the state also used the two other main routes across

---

[11]*Walton's Register and Farmer's Almanac* (1844), 22. For background on early nineteenth-century roads and roadbuilding see William M. Gillespie, *Manual of the Principles and Practice of Roadmaking: Comprising the Location, Construction, and Improvement of Roads (Common, Macadam, Paved, Plank, etc.) and Rail-roads*. 1847; 10th ed. Cady Staley (New York: A. S. Barnes, 1871), and Frederic J. Wood, *The Turnpikes of New England and Evolution of the Same Through England, Virginia, and Maryland* (Boston: Marshall Jones, 1919).

[12]"Journals of Henry Dearborn," Buffalo Historical Society *Publications* 7 (1904): 155.

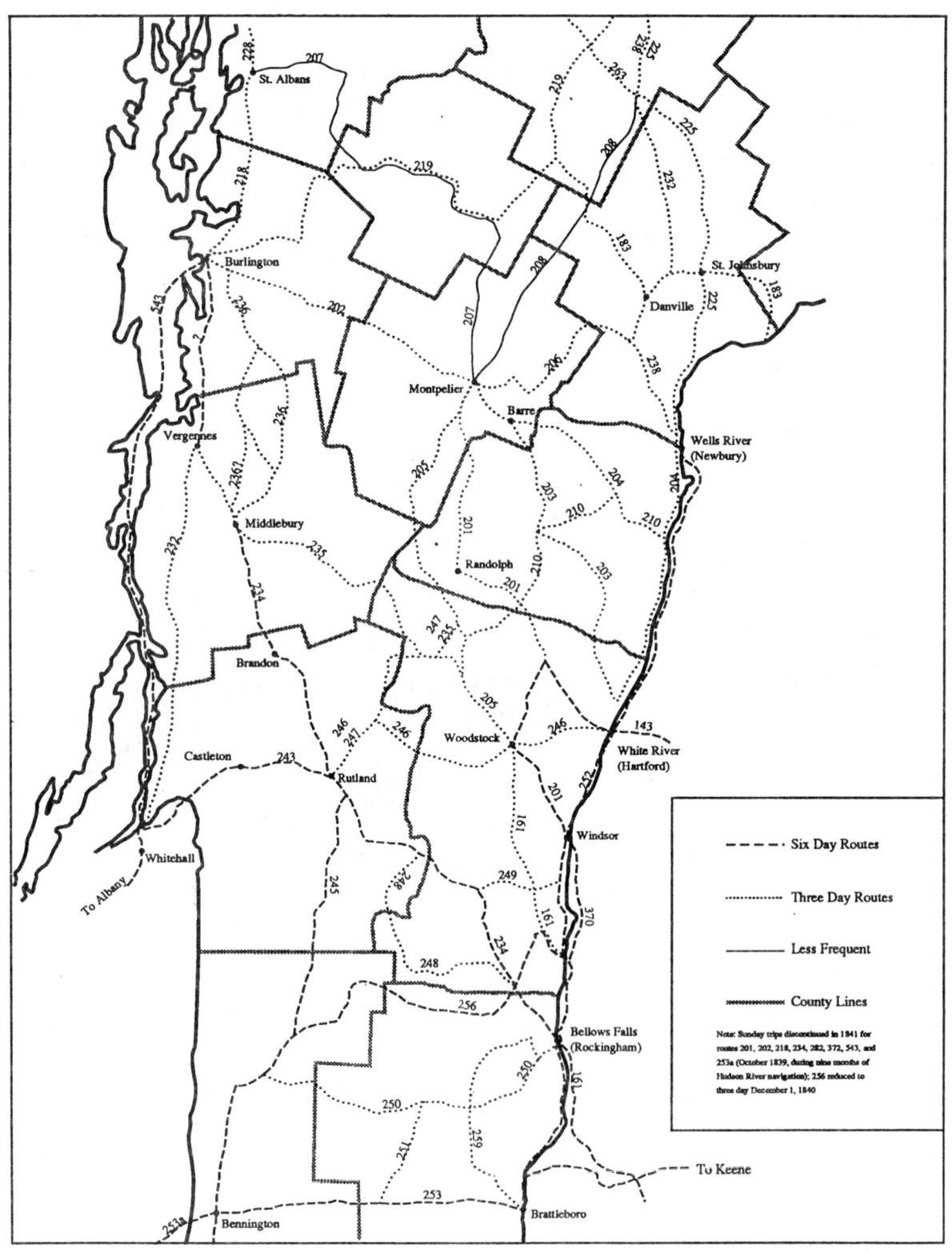

Vermont Post Roads, 1837-1841. Data from the postmaster general's Register of Contracts, in the National Archives, on Map No. 14 in G. Woolworth Colton, *Colton's General Atlas* (1857).

the Green Mountains south of Rutland. These highways made important crossroads at Chester, Springfield, or Bellows Falls, where a long covered bridge was built in 1840. Twenty Connecticut River spans, including this one, charged tolls in this period.

The Connecticut River highway (now Interstate 91) then served alternately the towns on both banks as far as Haverhill, New Hampshire, and Wells River. By contract scheduled to take thirty-two hours for the 183 miles from Hartford, Connecticut, to Haverhill, the trip took many hours longer in bad weather.

The gaily gilded and painted Concord coaches, an improvement of the 1820s, used two or three pairs of horses and changed them often in the hills, seeking to maintain their five or six mile an hour speed. Like the train whistles of the next generation, bugles blared arrival in a village, a welcome sound to taverners and riders alike. Charles Eldridge, an itinerant miniaturist, described what was probably the smoothest road in the system, from Springfield, Massachusetts to Brattleboro:

> Fatigued from the jolting, jouncing, squeezing, stewing confinement of an all day's ride, . . . broiled by the sun and [squinting from] . . . the dust, we were glad to pile our bones in bed. . . . But the snoring of our neighbors [a dozen in the tavern ballroom] presented an appalling obstacle.[13]

He had not enjoyed the advantage of riding in the fresh air on top of the baggage outside.

---

[13]In his "Journal of a Tour Through Vermont to Montreal and Quebec in 1833," Vermont Historical Society *Proceedings* 2 (June 1931), 58.

3. The End of a World and the Dawn of Industrialism

Adventist William Miller predicted the end of the world in 1843, and in a sense he was right. The world of farms and small villages scattered evenly over the hills—the world that sent its produce by wagon and water to the seaports and received its visitors from those ports by mail stagecoach and lake steamer—*was* coming to an end. The millenium so yearned for through free trade with Canada, canal transportation, merino sheep, household manufacturing, silkworm culture, or whatever utopia, failed to come. The new means of grace and hope of glory was the power of steam, already applied to boats, and soon to carriages and mill wheels. The railroads and their mill villages held the hope of the future.

"The Dawn of a Brighter Day" emblazoned on a rippling banner in the parade of some twelve thousand Whigs for "Tippecanoe and Tyler too" in Burlington on June 25, 1840, struck the state convention's keynote of revivalistic enthusiasm and expectancy, both for this election year and for the coming generation. The tail of the procession was still starting from the courthouse eight abreast when the head returned from a dusty, two-mile march around the borders of this largest village in Vermont. The colors, the county flags, the blurting brass bands, the tears flowing freely during four hours of spellbinding oratory launched a campaign that secured a Whig landslide that fall.

The mottoes boxed the compass of views and appealed to all kinds of Vermonters, but emphasized "Conservatism, the Sheet Anchor of Our Republic" (carried by the New York State delegation).[1] The reporter also noted the following signs and banners: Give us no more *experiments*; but give us *protection* (Lamoille County); Show us the better currency (Williston); Her walls cannot be thrown down by blasts from the Dutchman's [President Van Buren's] horn (Jericho); The public land, fair play and no gouging (New York); All farmers, all Whigs (Jericho); Mechanics' union; no reduction in wages (Rutland County); Old Orange; Old Tip; we'll try (Orange County) [then a Democratic stronghold]; Harrison and reform; one presidential term (Washington County); No slippery elm juice here (Enosburg); *Genuine Democracy*; Van Buren's cognac don't pass in Enosburg;

---

[1] See full coverage in the *Burlington Free Press*, 3 July 1840.

Hard cider, preferred to *hard times* (Addison County); and Let the people teach these palace slaves to respect Log Cabins (Essex County).

One reverend observer claimed that the frenzy was not from imbibing and assured the voting public there was "no profaneness, no intemperance, no games, no wrestling, horse-racing."[2] But Middlebury College students who attended without permission were expelled. The same Congregational chronicler noted moral sentiments, nonsense, jokes; a wagon carrying revolutionary veterans; among the log cabins, one drawn by twelve "superb greys" accustomed to hauling freight wagons from Brookfield to Boston.

Charles Paine of Northfield was launching his campaign for governor in 1841 by providing this log cabin symbol of the new Whig Party, optimistically calling itself "The Star That Never Sets." The cabin was the size of a schoolhouse, twenty by ten feet, built of peeled logs, with a bark roof, paper-covered windows, with buck horns on one gable end and a coonskin on the other. It created such a sensation that years later, farmers' wives dated local events by its passing.[3] They served hard cider at the door to all who cheered for "Old Tip."

Paine led the movement to span the state with a railroad during the ten years after he retired as governor in 1843. Although thousands of laborers built the railroad, Paine put the pieces together, reaped temporary rewards, and suffered for failures he was responsible for as president of the Vermont Central. Those failures, however, were inherent in the early system of railroad financing and building.

Paine was born in 1799, the fourth child of wealthy U.S. Senator Elijah Paine (1757-1842), who became one of President Adams's Federalist "midnight judges" of 1801, on the U.S. District Court for Vermont. Elijah held on to the office until a few weeks before he died, he said, to be sure a Whig would succeed him.

With Elijah Paine's passing went old pioneer Vermont. An immense crowd attended his plain funeral that May Day Sunday, 1842, at the rarely filled Congregational church in East Williamstown. If he lay in state in an open casket (and the newspapers did not describe the occasion), the mourners would have viewed a bald, six-foot, heavy-set body with a Roman profile,

---

[2]Ibid.

[3]Charles Paine (b. 1830, the governor's nephew), typescript "Memoirs" [1898, see its p. 100], 8, in Vermont Historical Society. These reminiscences are the chief basis for the rest of the story of Elijah and Charles Paine. See also Ezra S. Gannett, *The Useful Man: A Sermon Delivered at the Funeral of Hon. Charles Paine. at Northfield, Sept. 1, 1853* (Northfield: Woodworth and Gould, 1853).

in the clothes of a style Paine might have worn when he delivered the first Harvard Phi Beta Kappa address in 1782, or as one of the commissioners negotiating the Vermont settlement with New York in 1790: small clothes (trousers drawn at the knees, and long white stockings over gouty legs), long-tongued, large-buckled shoes, white ruffled shirt and white lawn cravat, to go with a silver-buttoned, high-waisted jacket of broadcloth or velvet.

Based on what we know about the judge, I imagine the usual dissonance between what the mourners must have said and what they thought (in brackets):

I remember he built the first sawmill and gristmill between Randolph and Montpelier, on the brook just over the Northfield line. [*Williamstown and Northfield proprietors paid him three or four hundred acres for those rude, short-lived contraptions in the very last place you would choose for a mill now.*]

He was a public benefactor. He offered two thousand dollars if the University of Vermont would locate in Williamstown, and even when Ira Allen bid higher, he gave money to the university and to Dartmouth College [*and they gave him LL.D.'s*]. He built a turnpike for ten thousand dollars some twenty miles from East Brookfield to Montpelier, opened it in 1803 and made it public in 1820. He had to replace the original bridge at Main Street, Montpelier, five times [*but he chased every toll*]. The stage driver and post rider stopped regularly at his door [*although some say they did not long patronize his pike*]. He was postmaster as long as I can remember [*with the franking privilege and the office on his property. But his daughter Caroline did most of the work since she was widowed and returned from New York to take care of her father. They say she has applied to succeed him, but we'll get the office moved to the Center now.*]

He paid his debts punctually. He believed in the sanctity of contracts. One time he rode till midnight to meet a deadline. [*As he would ride to catch a debtor leaving town. If you could not pay when due, you had to work it off with interest, repairing his turnpike, shearing his merinos, or haying and harvesting his broad acres at times a man most needed to work on his own farm.*]

He helped Northfield by investing forty thousand dollars, they say, in a broadcloth mill below the Center during the Embargo and now hiring nearly two hundred. [*It was not much of a concern until young Charles took it over in 1823. Charles, not the judge, made it one of the three largest woolen mills in Vermont.*]

We will miss seeing him in his front pew, which he faithfully occupied when not absent holding court, morning and afternoon, rain or shine, for nearly forty years. As a good steward he sympathized with the slave, was a leader of the Vermont Colonization Society from its founding, and preached temperance to his hired hands. [*He both served and drank liquor and even required his little grandsons to drink Madeira with their dinners. He sniffed inordinate amounts of snuff; as an irascible old man, he tended to make mountains out of molehills. He had an affair with his wife's sister—what other reason would have caused his wife to leave home soon after her youngest was weaned and not return until her husband's death?*]

Now the large family is scattered, and soon the farm and stock will have to be sold to divide the estate between the six children and their numerous progeny. Like the folksong about grandfather's clock, his favorite mount, Old Bay, "stopped short, never to go again, when the old man died." No more will he ride over his land, checking on the work. No more will we hear him holler "Yo-hoy" to call the men from the clearing a mile away. We will not see his like again.

As the judge epitomized the dying age of homespun and self-sufficiency, his son Charles typified the enterprising businessman of the new age dawning. The other children entered professions in New York or Boston, although two widows returned to be housekeepers in their father's Williamstown house. Charles, who was not interested in the book study necessary for a profession and liked to manage people, became the developer of the Paine family's local interests.

As landowner and representative of the leading family in the area, Charles Paine served Northfield as lister, selectman, town representative, and moderator of town meeting, 1822-33. Even his move from the hills of Williamstown to the valley in Northfield was symptomatic of the times. He climaxed another decade of work for the Whig Party with two terms as governor, perhaps to show his father he, too, could win high office, or because a governor's prestige and statewide connections would help promote his railroad.

When the General Assembly chartered the Vermont Central in 1843 over vehement Democratic minority objections, the governor could lobby for it, having retired from office at the beginning of the session. Only the Central charter contained perpetual tax exemption as long as its profits were under ten per cent; only the Central charter omitted the usual provision for legislative revision.[4]

In his second inaugural address, Paine was as dubious as everyone else as to whether a train could ever cross the Green Mountains. After all, a raft of railroad projects during the 1830s had come to nothing. Returning from the Whig National Convention in Baltimore by way of Boston in the spring of 1844, however, Paine was confident that the railroad would be built while his greeters were still incredulous.

The following August he sent the first surveying party, including his fifteen-year-old nephew and namesake, into Williamstown Gulf. (Forty years later the younger Charles Paine recalled only that the fat landlord of the Gulf tavern, when he needed mutton, simply shot a sheep on the steep hillside, instead of chasing it.) They stayed only long enough to "demonstrate the very difficult character of the pass" and moved on to the section from Montpelier Junction to Richmond.[5]

The first notable strike in Vermont history, known as the "Bolton War," occurred during the building of the Richmond section in July 1846. Two hundred pick-and-shovel Irishmen, without pay since they started work in April, walked off the job three miles east of Huntington's tavern in Jonesville. The angry laborers threw "impediments in the way of mail coaches . . . and with violent language and demeanor had attempted completely to prevent the free use and occupation of the road by the public."[6]

When the first money had come the week before, the subcontractor used it to pay what he owed for food and supplies. He escaped the threats of the laborers and brought back cash for part of the payroll. The laborers then held the contractor of the division hostage pending his partner's producing the rest. Meanwhile, the local sheriff arrested the strike leaders, who were rescued by their men. Then the sheriff called in Burlington's non-Irish Light Infantry and volunteer fire company, who, unlike the local posse, had not developed sympathy for the unpaid strikers. Faced by this Fourth of July "army" and persuaded by a Roman Catholic priest, the men released their hostage and dispersed, except for the dozen jailed in Burlington. Many never received their

---

[4]*Acts and Resolves Passed By the Legislature of the State of Vermont, At Their October Session 1843* (Montpelier: E. P. Walton & Sons, 1843), 43-50. Title varies; hereafter cited as *Vermont Laws* with date.

[5]Charles Paine (b. 1830), "Memoirs", 57-77, covers his experiences in the counting-room of his uncle Charles's woolen mill and with the survey crew of the Vermont Central, 1844-46.

[6]*Burlington Free Press*, 10 July 1846. The Bolton War is summarized in my article, "500 Miles of Trouble and Excitement: Vermont Railroads, 1848-1861," *Vermont History* 49 (Summer 1981): 133-134.

earnings. President Paine's nephew recorded only that "it was necessary to retrench" in the summer of 1846 "and all work ceased west of Northfield."[7]

The modern world of strikes, technology, and speed had invaded Vermont in 1849, when the locomotive *Governor Paine*, painted green and gold with red drive wheels, as garish as the Concord coaches it was running off the road, pulled the first train into Northfield, the railroad capital of Vermont. Liquor flowed all evening. Between midnight and dawn, someone decided that Governor Paine ought to be "notified." One of the customary privileges of common people in a village in those days was to interrupt the slumbers of the great to include them in a civic celebration. The governor graciously acknowledged the honor.

The first Vermont lines hoped to carry freight from Atlantic ports to Montreal and the Middle West and back. Vermont was part of the "underdeveloped" North Country, which could not support any line with only its own traffic. The speed, size, and complexity of railroad operation made the old precedents of stage coaching of slight value and of steamboating scarcely more pertinent. The enterprise was new, and every crisis called for innovation. The corporate form of organization for trade and manufacturing was new, especially in Vermont, and the large-scale, complex railroad operations required sophisticated management for which few models existed. Even the early experiences with short, flat, profitable spurs out of Boston and other ports misled Vermont promoters and Boston investors who furnished perhaps three-quarters of the capital for the two main Vermont lines. The Rutland and Burlington tapped Boston via Fitchburg, Keene, Bellows Falls, and Rutland to Burlington. The Vermont Central charter intended to provide a link between the line out of Boston to Lowell, up the Merrimack River and across the hills to White River Junction, Vermont. The Central used the White, Dog, and Winooski River valleys to reach Burlington. This enabled it to serve Charles Paine's Northfield and bypass Barre and Montpelier.

The Vermont and Canada Railroad was chartered in 1845 to build from a connection with the Central near Burlington to a connection with the Northern of New York (later the Ogdensburgh and Lake Champlain) near Rouses Point. The Canada controlled the franchise of a possible competing line through Grand Isle County and, by winning every negotiation with its connectors, dominated the only all-rail way around the Lake Champlain barrier. The Central and Canada also arranged to meet at Essex Junction, freezing Burlington and the Rutland out of direct access to the

---

[7]Charles Paine (b.1830), "Memoirs," 77.

through route. With a spur from the Junction through Winooski they fulfilled the letter of the charter requirement to reach Burlington.

Burlington merchants assumed that both Boston lines would come to Burlington, use steamers to cross the lake, and so on to Ogdensburgh from a New York port, while the Canada would connect the Rutland with Montreal. They did not see the inferiority of their water and rail route to the Canada's end run around the foot of the lake, which they failed to block. The Central, fearing that the Rutland might awaken to its need for a connection with the Canada, leased the Canada at an exorbitant eight percent of its construction cost annually, with the proviso that the Canada could run the Central if necessary to collect its rent. The Central soon failed, and J. Gregory Smith of St. Albans took charge of the system. First he moved the car factory from Northfield to St. Albans; ten years later he moved the rest of the shops, and once booming Northfield declined abruptly.

Early railroad construction was a bootstrap operation, with never enough capital, inadequate knowledge of the difficulties, and inherent hostility between the penniless Irish immigrants leveling the right-of-way and their Yankee bosses. Paymaster Daniel Wells described to Henry Sheldon his monthly visit to a shantytown on the Rutland near Ferrisburgh in the winter of 1848:

> I drove to a place in the forest, where nobody ever went, or goes except Railroad folks, when I found about 40 paddies at work & quite a settlement of Shantys. I had my horse put out & went into a Shanty, 6 inches by 4—where the goods are kept—& commenced posting up the paddies accounts, which occupied me until perhaps 8 o'clock. . . . I had a very polite & urging invitation to take some tea & spend the night among those *animals* congregated in the Shantys, but as I had in my possession 500 dollars . . . I did not feel safe to accept of their very polite invitation.

He paid them off the next day, at under four cents an hour after deducting company supplies and shanty rent.[8]

Catherine Driscoll Dillon, a beauty in her early twenties, followed the construction gangs. She kept a boardinghouse and grog shop on the Central, and moved northward with the crews on the Vermont and Canada, with whiskey always available after pay day.

---

[8]Daniel L. Wells to H. L. Sheldon, January 19, 1848; MS. in the Sheldon Museum, Middlebury.

The flood of immigrant Irish, on top of the dribble of French Canadians, diversified the Vermont of the 1840s. The sources and consequences of a prejudice such as the paymaster's are complicated. There is always aloofness between the settled and the newcomer, but the peasant Irish had a peculiar impact. They left hardship and oppression in the Old Country, had a hard trip across the ocean, and arrived with their prejudices against English-speaking Protestants intact.

Yet they expected things would be different in the United States. Jeremiah O'Callaghan, their principal missionary priest from 1828 to the establishment of the Diocese of Burlington in 1853, commented:[9]

> See the happy effect produced by the sound policy of the people [of the United States]. There all tribes and nations, blacks and whites, Turks and Jews, Greeks and Arabs, [live] in union and friendship. Arsenals full of arms; batteries in perfect order; peace without interruption; though there is no standing army, every man, to the age of forty-five, a soldier, and every soldier a citizen, ready, on the first call, to die for the common welfare. There are no cattle houghed, no White Boys sounding the horn, nor haggards in flames: because there is no portion of the people goaded into rebellion by the Orangemen or tithe-proctor.

He soon found a usurer in each Whig manager of a local institution and played the broken record of his obsession against banks and usury until his dying day. His eccentric, medieval passion against charging interest had blocked his finding a parish in Europe, but here an oddball priest who was willing and able to cover a lot of ground was better than none.

Long experience in Ireland, and O'Callaghan's incessant hammering on Protestant "false teachers," both in print and by word-of-mouth, framed an Irish mind-set and created an "Irish brigade" not only in Burlington, but wherever else clumps of Irishmen settled. Their experience on the railroad and in the quarry and mill confirmed their anti-Protestantism. It did not matter who burned the first Burlington Church of St. Mary's in 1838, or that Protestant "lords of the manor" gave land for a church and cemetery in several towns or let Father O'Callaghan use their buildings for Mass, or even that the priest was the most effective strike-breaker. In spite of the usually sincere

---

[9]Jeremiah O'Callaghan, *Usury; Or, Lending at Interest; Also, the Exaction and Payment of Certain Church-fees, Such as Pew-rents, and the Like, Together with Forestalling Traffick; All Proved to be Repugnant to the Divine and Ecclesiastical Law; and Destructive to Civil Society. . . .* 3d ed. (London: W[illiam] Cobbett, 1828), 116.

tolerance of alien ways by Yankee Protestants, the burden of poverty and adjustment fell on the Irish immigrants and they blamed the Whig bosses. The Irish were all Democrats.

The Quebecois were not Democrats, for reasons unclear, perhaps because of their hostility to the Irish. The *Burlington Free Press*'s sympathy for Father Ancé, when Bishop Benedict Fenwick of Boston sent him back to Quebec in 1843, sounds like divide-and-rule policy. French Catholics in Quebec were in the habit of managing the material aspects of their parish life and talking back to their priest. They had francophone missionaries in Burlington from 1835, and in 1850 Burlington's St. Joseph's became the first ethnic parish in New England. Unlike the Irish, they could walk home to their relatives north of the border if things got too bad. They were relatively more literate and more concerned for parochial schools. Most important, their language insulated them from both Irish and Yankee. A few were at least temporarily converted by revivalistic Protestants, but their basic reaction, if poverty did not require them to live among anglophones, was to form non-political enclaves. Nor did many Franco-Americans vote Whig and none spoke publicly for reform. They stayed out of politics.

The other new element on the religious scene was the Episcopal diocese of Vermont, established with the arrival in 1832 of Bishop John Henry Hopkins. A native of Ireland like Father O'Callaghan, he was as much out-of-step with his Vermont surroundings and an even more prolific pamphleteer. Even his election as bishop was by a seven to six vote of the clergy, the laity confirming. One wonders whether a dozen clergy in a score of parishes with a membership of 1,169 needed to be made into a diocese, when it had hitherto been cared for by Bishop Alexander Viets Griswold with the rest of New England except Connecticut. The attraction was an endowment of rent from lands reserved for church missions in every Vermont town chartered by New Hampshire. The Vermont legislature, while recognizing New Hampshire land grants, had asserted its right to use these funds (also New Hampshire grants) for schools. After a generation of litigation the courts ruled, as they had in the Dartmouth College case, that the state could not violate the previous arrangements. The bishop could count on part of his income from these glebe lands, and the rest from his salary as rector of St. Paul's in Burlington. Hopkins, a man of restless energy like O'Callaghan, was perhaps sent to the Vermont mission field where he would do the most good and be the least nuisance.

From almost underground status as Tories in the eighteenth century, Vermont Episcopalians had been diverted for decades by pursuit of this endowment, and had accommodated to the low church evangelical outlook of contemporary Protestantism. Hopkins changed all that. William S.

Perkins, rector of St. James Episcopal Church, Arlington, promoted revivalism. Bishop Hopkins rebuked and then removed him. Hopkins was convinced that the Church of England, American version, had a unique role as the preserver of the true Christian tradition in liturgy, polity, and theology. Of Presbyterian upbringing, he ran a book business in Philadelphia as a young immigrant, then operated an iron forge and furnace in western Pennsylvania, studied law and church history. Though his own denomination was dominant in the region, he chose on principle to ally himself with a struggling little group of Episcopalians. With the zeal of a convert he studied for the priesthood, was ordained in 1824 at Trinity Church, Pittsburgh, and participated enthusiastically in the conventions of his diocese. By the late 1820s he had found friends among the High Church party, who encouraged his ambition to rise in the hierarchy. He became assistant rector of Trinity Church, Boston, on hand when the new diocese of Massachusetts needed a bishop. He did not win that election, and again he chose the hard task with a small group, to build the diocese of Vermont. In his thirty-six-year episcopate, the number of communicants doubled.

This growth, however, occurred more because of what the Episcopal church stood for than through the persuasiveness of its bishop. Hopkins was not strong as facilitator or conciliator. He saw clearly what was right and stuck to that, alone or with a multitude. Some converts from the village elite, repelled by the bare, sermon-focused Congregational service, and the hard-line covenants, appreciated the rich sixteenth-century prose of the Book of Common Prayer, based on the medieval missal, the paraphenalia of the service (this yearning for more ritual sent others into Masonry), and the relaxed theology. Among these were Timothy Follett, Burlington merchant, and the family of Senator Dudley Chase of Randolph. What attracted Zadock Thompson, Burlington naturalist-historian, is not known. After teaching in his own private schools and editing short-lived magazines, he was ordained deacon and taught in Hopkins's school. Robinson Smiley, first Congregational pastor of Springfield, retired in 1825 and turned Episcopalian soon after, apparently disgusted with the methods of the revivalists. These recruits came before 1840; others like Governor Charles K. Williams, son of a Congregational minister, were attracted by what the English Oxford Movement stood for: veneration for the ancient Christian tradition, personal piety reinforced by traditional church liturgy.

The same tendency carried a few into the Roman Catholic church: the Barlows and Smalleys of Fairfield; William H. Hoyt, St. Albans Episcopal rector; in Burlington, Abby M. Hemenway, the Tuckers and Demings, and Collector of Customs Archibald W. Hyde. Orestes A. Brownson, Roman Catholic editor, is only one of many native Vermont religious leaders, like Joseph Smith, William

Miller, and Jason Walker who passed through a series of religious connections before finding a spiritual home. Sympathy for poor immigrant Catholics was important in the conversions of Brownson and Hyde.

Hopkins was not part of the Oxford Movement in America, although he sympathized with much that the movement stood for. He was not of the High Church party; he was usually a party of one. He did his own studying and published his own conclusions, usually at variance with the popular views of the day. He opposed the Anti-Masonic movement (some of his best friends were Masons), the antislavery movement, and the prohibition movement, while believing in the roots of their causes: Christian benevolence, Christian emancipation and care for blacks, and temperance. He believed the church should stay out of politics. He believed in education but not educational reform. His lifelong ambition was to establish a theological seminary to supply diocesan clergy and a school to train the laity for service. When he laid his first proposal before the diocese, it replied, "We can't afford it." He went ahead anyway and was soon bankrupt. Thereafter, never giving up, he went abroad to England or out-of-state to raise enough money to start again with the Vermont Episcopal Institute on the eve of the Civil War. His successor as bishop, William Henry Augustus Bissell, who taught in his first school, found him an autocrat.

Such a headstrong and talented man, freed by his intransigeance from full-time pastoral care of a sympathetic flock, had time to expend on a variety of creative activities. He published a book on Gothic architecture (1836) and tried to persuade vestries to build according to his plans. He fostered church music through the publication of *Twelve Canzonets* (1839). Desperate for money, he and his children created and colored lithographs of Vermont flowers and landscapes. He poured forth a steady stream of polemical publications—eighteen titles totaling over seven hundred pages in the 1840s—and participated vigorously in the deliberations of the American House of Bishops. By seniority, and not by popularity, he became Presiding Bishop in 1863. Having long refused to take sides on the slavery issue, he held his denomination above the fray and together when the Civil War divided other denominations. Like so many versatile Vermonters, his contributions were to the world.

Like Hopkins, most Vermonters had a central concern for schooling, but they disagreed on both what and how to teach. Words flowed in abundance during the 1840s on the issues of discipline, attendance, length of terms, better schoolhouses and equipment, centralized supervision, uniform textbooks, and teacher training. The Vermont system of education continued with little change, however, until long after the Civil War. In other words, while the new age of urban industrialism had dawned for the village businessman, the sun of school reform would not penetrate the clouds of rural habit for another generation.

The old way of learning the basics of one's vocation by child labor continued. If a family decided that one child should learn a trade, he (more often than she) was sent to someone, preferably a relative, friend, or neighbor, to learn how to use specialized tools and materials. Young women might work cheaply for an experienced seamstress or milliner, but the formality of an indenture for dressmaking, schoolkeeping, housekeeping or the male crafts was no longer thought necessary. Printing was one of the few trades still learned by formal apprenticeship.

Learning by doing what the master of the shop or the mistress of the house required was enough to learn, except what was learned in play or at the district school. Most of the play was already educational, although the reformers wrote about teaching with toys and games. Boys more often had such store-bought gifts as knives, skates, or guns, and a girl's most treasured possession might be a manufactured china doll, but many playthings were homemade. Sleds, traverses, and toboggans were for both sexes, and so were most games at school and parties at home. Tag, crack the whip, "pum-pum-pull-away," jump rope, hopscotch, snowball fights, and similar active games occupied the time before school and at recess. Indoors at home were taffy pulls, cornhusking, apple paring, quilting, and similar practical frolics and dances. Bundling (going to bed with your sweetheart, clothed) presumably continued in the backcountry, and so did a high rate of prenuptial pregnancies.

Rites of passage for women have not been described. They were probably associated with the rituals of early marriage and, as the age at marriage rose, with the activities connected with leaving home. For the adolescent male they consisted of at last being able to go hunting with the men, or taking part in a militia muster. The young bucks helped themselves at the barrel of rum supplied by their elected captain, chosen partly because he could afford to buy it. Then they were allowed to ridicule the serious business of learning to defend their country, by making a mockery of the manual of arms.

Basic literacy and figuring were taught in the common schools, with upwards of ten districts in the more populous towns. They were called common schools because they were meant for everybody, but they were neither compulsory nor entirely free. If families decided to spare the children's labor, they provided them with any textbook they could find in the house or at the local store. Families shared the burden of "boardin' 'round," feeding and housing the teacher for a period in proportion to the number of children they had in school. The teacher was a dependent included in family activities and under surveillance, like the hired hand, or the poor relation's child learning to keep house, and the boy learning a trade.

Schools represented the extremely decentralized base of the power pyramid in rural New England society, which admitted the new railroad technology and the immigrants but voted against change in education. "The School Meeting in District 13," in the story by Rowland E. Robinson presumably modeled on the author's own Ferrisburgh district, drew eight males from the sixteen dwellings in the two-mile-long district. A raccoon family crossing the road outside diverted the meeting from its small amount of postponable business.

The agenda of a school meeting included arranging for firewood, for a boy from a nearby house to start the stove each winter school morning, and to fix the sequence of boarding around. Its most important business was to hire a teacher for the minimum wage, never called a salary, who could not only "learn" his scholars, but also rule them and inculcate the values held by the community. Vermont writers on schoolkeeping, from Samuel Read Hall to Hiram Orcutt, emphasized the conservative meaning of "keep": to restrain, regulate, manage, provide the framework for "teaching the young idea to shoot" at the known target. And yet the system turned out mechanical inventors and men of original ideas like George Perkins Marsh and John Dewey.

Scholars in the common schools proceeded at their own pace, according to their motivation, ability, and application to the tasks assigned. They learned the three R's with some spelling, geography, speaking, and proper behavior. If the teacher was capable and interested, a scholar who had mastered the basics might do more advanced work.

Most teachers were single, in their early twenties, and went on to other work after a few terms. They lived in families, which served both to control their behavior and provide their social life. Their preparation consisted of "completion" of common school work with enough proficiency to satisfy the district prudential committee, elected by the district school meeting. A few college students "worked their way" by teaching Vermont winter schools during their long vacation. Most of some 3,250 Vermont teachers, however, had not even spent a term at a grammar school or academy, much less attended or graduated from college.

Young women, a majority of the teachers by 1850, were cheaper, and first invaded the schoolroom for the two-month summer term, when the older, and presumably more unruly, boys were busy with peak farm work. The schoolmaster was less often replaced by a woman for the two-month winter term beginning soon after New Year's Day. He was assumed to be able to bully the older boys, now free from everything but chopping and chores, if not with threats, then with violence.

Corporal punishment, common in the home, was expected from the teachers. They used a ruler, a sapling whip, or whatever was handy. (The Community Church of Island Pond in the 1980s, attacked for child abuse, was following the norm of an earlier age.) The teacher usually administered the "lickin'" before the whole school, at the beginning of the day after the "crime" was committed and judged, like the public hangings of the previous generation. People tell stories of pupils ganging up on the master (never the marm, although she also wielded the stick). The teacher who could not subdue them by might, manipulation, or psychology was not long for that district. "Barring out" of the schoolhouse and other practical tricks on the teacher have perhaps been played up because they were sensational and exceptional, yet Windham County Superintendent James Taft treated "breaking up the schools"—which I assume to mean driving the master away by violent pranks—as a common disturbance in 1848. He blamed the parents for using their children to get rid of the teacher.

Typical of the competitive learning atmosphere was the "spelling school." It brought teachers and their star pupils together from nearby districts and had social elements of flirting and being on best behavior in a different place. The "singing school," on the other hand, taught by a specialist, emphasized the opposite qualities of cooperation and harmony. Learners won prizes for memorizing and so prevalent was rote learning that many a lad and lass learned whole books by heart. This system produced in 1840 the second highest literacy rate in the twenty-six states: 469 literate whites over twenty years old for every one who could neither read nor write. A rural society wanted no more.

The reformers wanted a great deal more. They wanted teachers trained at normal schools in educational methods, or at least at spring or fall institutes with a few days' lectures. They wanted to keep teachers longer by paying them better. They wanted uniform texts, blackboards, outline maps and globes; well-ventilated, evenly heated schoolhouses, with playgrounds off the road, good drinking water and clean outhouses; better statistical reporting; less truancy when farmers were tempted to keep children home for haying, harvesting, herding, or logging. They would depend less on rules, more on judgment; less on corporal punishment, more on persuasion. They still believed in church-related schools, but in view of the fact of religious pluralism, they would settle for "moral" education, with the King James Bible read daily. They interpreted the statistics of intemperance and crime as proportionally higher among Roman Catholic immigrants and assumed that only in a generalized Protestant atmosphere could they abolish ignorance and vice.

The recommendation of Governor Silas Jenison, piously reiterated by his successors and in a prize-winning essay by Pittsford's Thomas H. Palmer, launched a dozen years of reformer vehemence beyond the perennial call for better schools. The narrow passage of the 1845 school law had been coupled with repudiation of the state's obligation to restore the school fund established in 1825 by a six percent tax on bank profits and "borrowed" in 1833 to help pay for building a statehouse. At the height of the school reform movement in 1847, abolitionist Daniel Pierce Thompson published a tract in the form of a novel, *Locke Amsden; or, The Schoolmaster*. Aiming to exemplify the arguments of the reformers, it demonstrated that the teacher who adopted their program could move off the farm to the village, marry the mill owner's daughter, go to Congress, and raise educational standards. Led by Governor Horace Eaton, also State Superintendent of Common Schools, the reformers kept claiming victories but were defeated by Vermonters' fierce localism and the cost of school reform. The General Assembly abolished Eaton's county superintendents in 1849, and after Eaton retreated to a professorship at Middlebury College, refused to fund his successor after one year. The reformers, however, did not expect change to come quickly, as in the storybook. They wanted a "system of supervision" by state, county, and town superintendents who could gradually make these "improvements" as people were persuaded.

With close to 100,000 exposed at some time during 1840 to common schooling, and three-quarters as many by 1860, less than 4,000 attended academies. These higher schools prepared not so much for college as for the professions. Informal apprenticeships in law or medicine usually followed. With a tutor such as the local minister, or at the academy, one might begin Latin and Greek and "the higher branches" including mathematics, all deemed essential into the twentieth century for divinity and law. Seminary was a finishing school for all of its female and most of its male students. There were separate schools for each sex and coeducational schools in which social contacts were strictly limited. Justin S. Morrill, after a term each at Thetford and Randolph academies, chose storekeeping when he had a chance to keep school. Although satisfied that he chose business over a profession, he always regretted his lack of a "liberal" education.

The colleges in the North Country, even Dartmouth in Hanover, New Hampshire, and Union in Schenectady, were small, poor, and struggling for students. Norwich University, Middlebury College, and the University of Vermont enrolled a little over two hundred students in any one term. One Vermont resident in a thousand was somewhere in college during 1839—a higher ratio than any other New England state's. Many chose college because hard times discouraged starting to farm or going into other business. The competition of too many academies and colleges cut the costs and increased scholarship aid, especially for those studying for the ministry. In the West were enlarged opportunities for clergy, editors, lawyers, and other vocations, which would soon be called professions. For Protestant ministers, more jobs opened as agents for tract, Bible, Sunday school, and other evangelical institutions. The foreign mission field expanded, and its high overseas death rate made for rapid turnover.

Many students were older and more serious than today's late adolescents, because of having to earn money for college, or not being released from family farm obligations until they were twenty-one, or hearing a late call to the ministry. As mature men knowing their career goals they were less comfortable with the customary role of the college, *in loco parentis*, treating students like children. They often concentrated, in the little time they had free from study and recitation, on self-government and self-improvement in secret, social fraternities. The college library met faculty needs; the fraternity library, in the tradition of the earlier literary societies, reflected student interests. Weekly fraternity meetings during the term were exercises in Roberts' Rules, debate on current or perennial issues, exposition, and humor. The pious formed prayer groups, and converted youths taught Sunday schools.

The occasional violence that boiled over on American campuses may have related more to younger boys, enjoying freedom from career pressures, or to the larger fact that at the dawn of urban-industrial America, youth had lost deference to traditional authorities. For example, one spring night, the blaring of tin horns brought University of Vermont's President Wheeler and Professor Benedict to the corner of the Burlington campus near the Pearl Street tavern, to order the boys to bed. In the lanternless darkness, President Wheeler hit the ground. Two seventeen-year-olds were expelled, one a son of Bishop Hopkins.

The Manning affair at Middlebury College, 1837-38, a case of extreme student satire and insubordination and faculty over-reaction,[10] manifested a crisis that nearly destroyed the Congregational college. The town pastor and the college president promoted revivalism; their attitude displeased the state Congregational establishment, which began to look with more favor on the University of Vermont. Under a few loyal teachers like Benjamin Labaree and Ezra Brainerd Middlebury raised enough money and students to survive as a less intensely religious college.

Norwich University, under its founding president Alden Partridge until the mid-forties, struggled against the popular peacetime aversion to the military. Two of its professors tried to revive

---

[10] See David M. Stameshkin, *Middlebury College*, 131-133.

interest in the militia and in their college by publishing *The Citizen Soldier* (1840-41), but June training was a joke and the legislature abolished it, requiring only an annual audit of arms. The new president, Truman Ransom, resigned in 1847 for a colonelcy in the Mexican War and died leading an assault on Chapultepec, but only one "Vermont company" volunteered. Most Vermonters opposed "Mr. Polk's War" as part of a plot to expand slave territory.

The historian, like the Fates, measures and cuts off periods from the seamless garment of time. While the Vermont countryside seemed to lie in afternoon shadows, with the sun of the rural way of life lowering, it would take more than another century before urban dwellers occupied surviving farmhouses like hermit crabs, and nearly all would recognize that they lived in an urban world. Only the rhetoric would survive. Figures of speech are illogical reference points. On the same landscape, from another perspective, the first gray light of dawn was breaking on an unbelieving world: the possibility that technology could support an urban civilization. The forties were as full of contradictions as sunset and sunrise. Sheep kept grazing on the hills; Yankees and sheep kept leaving for greener pastures, while foreigners and cows began to replace them. Lake Champlain trade brought prosperity to shore towns, especially Burlington; when the trains came, Burlington lost much of its backcountry market. The fireworks of revivalism fizzed out; majority Protestantism, bleak as truth and apparently motionless, held on while minority Episcopalians gained in the villages. Of all the hullabaloo of reform, school reformers shouted loudest and won the least.

More movements were in the bud before 1850, which flowered in the fifties. In economic development, granite, marble and slate quarrying, textiles, metalworking, woodworking, and special, patented products boomed many villages. Political habits formed in the Jacksonian era shaped the coalition contests up to the Civil War. The country press, ultimately the agent of urbanism, was the principal medium in these contests and reflected the villages' first adjustments toward joining a railroad-industrial society. And overriding all these changes, rising emotions over the distant wrongs of slavery distorted every decision. Let us examine how one small corner of the Union faced the impending crisis.

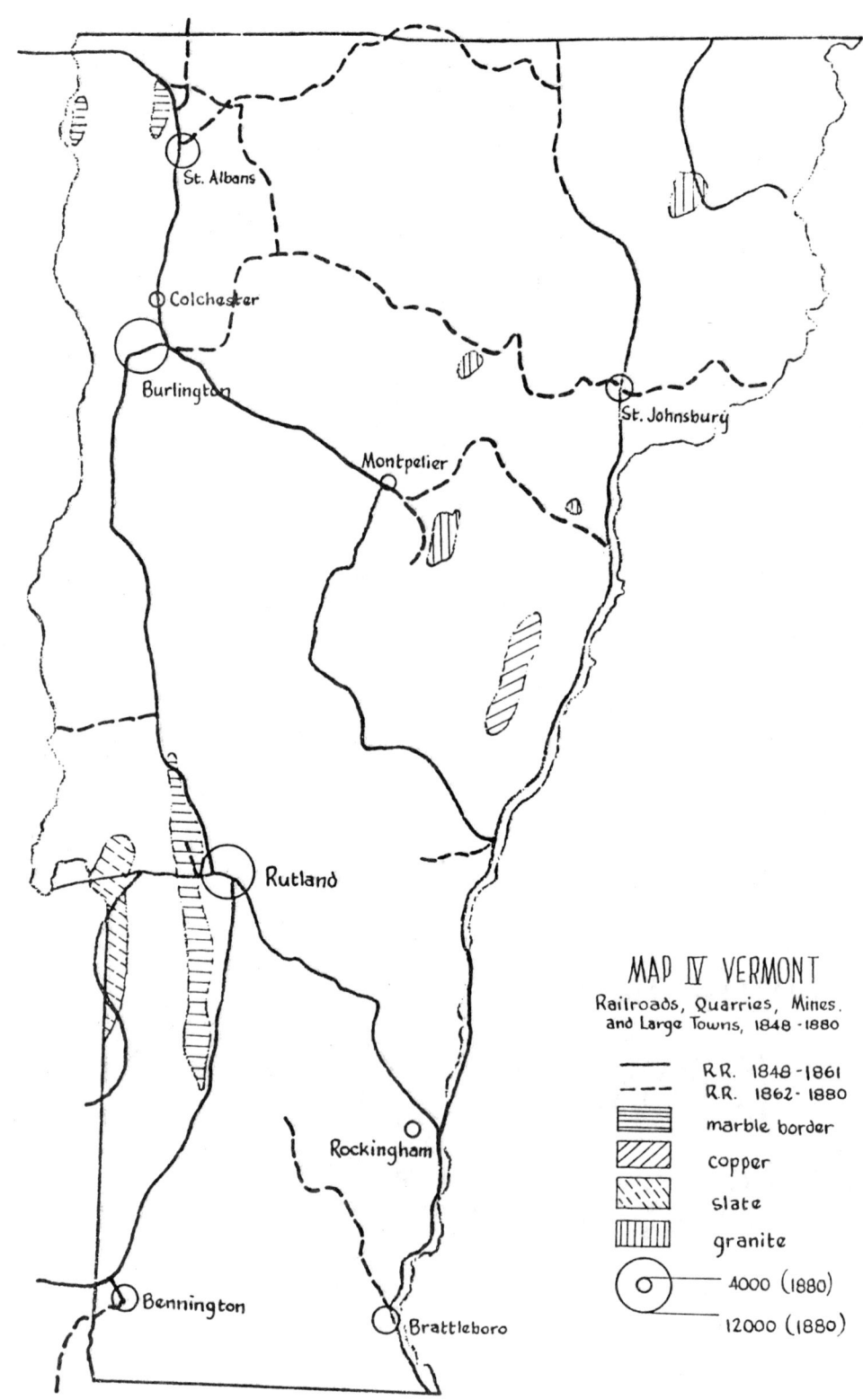

Vermont Railroads, Quarries, Mines, and Large Towns, 1848-1880. Adapted from W. J. Wilgus, *Transportation in Vermont* (1945), Figs. 3, 10.

4. Village Industry

The wild picturesque waterfalls . . . will be deformed by the ugly presence of mills . . . the beautiful pastoral life of the inhabitants will give place to oppressive factory village life . . . the din, conflict and degradation of manufacturing and mechanical business—the golden equality which now exists, will precipitate into rigorous forms of caste, of capitalist and laborer, corporations and operative dependants—labor will become more and more disgraceful, and the conflict of duplicity and fraud will . . . widen into general strife. Vermont will be no more the Evergreen State, for a false society will have blasted its beauty and dried up the blood of its vigor and prosperity. Ten years will not have passed ere the citizens of Vermont will be surprised at the social revolution which their railroad system will have wrought . . . so long as railroads are held as private property, they will be powerful agents in the production of national wealth, whilst they will degrade and impoverish the masses.

John Orvis, utopian socialist, Ferrisburgh
Harbinger 5, June 14, 1847

Town proprietors planned from the beginning to provide gristmills and sawmills for their neighborhoods, and these, with other neighborhood industry, multiplied on the innumerable little falls of the North Country. This chapter is about the fortunes of villages whose mills expanded beyond the local market as part of the shift to a national economy in the generation before the Civil War. It implies the story of other village mills and shops driven out of business by the same forces that brought in superior and cheaper products. By the end of the period, a few manufacturers had freed themselves from the falls by using steam engines, and coal to fuel them began to come from Pennsylvania.

Colonial New England started manufacturing early, in spite of British policy reserving fabrication for the mother country. Arnold Toynbee's *Study of History* suggested that the pressure of a moderately demanding environment stimulated processing of raw materials at hand. The widespread presence of small amounts of iron and even some copper, with plenty of wood to be burned into charcoal for furnace and forge, encouraged settlers having some acquaintance with English industrial technology to exploit the deposits. The Protestant and especially Puritan work ethic turned those idled by winter into making things and searching for ways to use the resources God had provided them. They did not think first of enriching their dress, their homes, or their meetinghouses with costly ornament bought with their surplus. Their penchant was to put to work the capital saved from the fisheries, forests, or fur and foreign trade. A clever millwright could make the waterwheels for the basic grinding of grain and sawing of timber. The owner of the water privilege could invest his profits in other milling. The Allen family of Litchfield County, Connecticut, dressing deerskins at Cannon Falls on the Housatonic, forging iron at Salisbury, and Ethan's mining lead in Northampton, Massachusetts, exemplified this urge to exploit what was available.

Alexander Hamilton based his *Report on Manufactures* (1791) on what he saw already developing in New England and the Middle States. Manufacturing meant power: power to be independent of foreign industrial countries; power derived from denser, more diversified population providing a broader tax base and higher real estate values; power from the profits building an infrastructure of communication and government and a superstructure of culture.

The leaders in the Vermont settlement process, holding these Hamiltonian ideas, looked for mill sites and bog iron while most of the settlers looked for fertile soil. While Ira Allen's *History of Vermont* (1798), in its promise of abundant ores, was the pipe dream of a real estate promoter in prison, it did relate to what happened in the quarter century after Vermont joined the Union. In western Vermont ironworks developed at Swanton, Sheldon, Westford, Bristol, Vergennes, Middlebury, Salisbury, Shoreham, Brandon, Pittsford, Fair Haven, Tinmouth, and especially Bennington. Matthew Lyon started the iron industry of Fair Haven in the 1780s using ore from Moriah, New York, above Port Henry. A glass house on Lake Dunmore in East Middlebury prospered and then went bankrupt in 1813; they burned copperas (iron pyrites) in Cuttingsville, cut marble for gravestones at Middlebury, and many other towns had their hopeful developers.

This small-scale extraction of ore and stone, however, did not build villages. Men moved into the woods where the mineral was, erected their crude engines, housings, and huts, and processed the material while the ore was rich enough, the price was high enough, or until it was worked out. Then the woods gradually took over the hollow frontier. It was hollow because pioneers did not fill the land between the mine or furnace site and the earlier edge of settlement. Industry in the back hills of Vermont's Connecticut Valley included stone and mineral works such as Tyson's Furnace in Plymouth, Guilford's slate quarries, and Grafton's soapstone. Its mills mainly processed wool and woolens.

Waterpower was a perennial resource for a succession of uses. Proprietors offered land bounties for starting mills, not just to serve loggers and grain farmers, but to attract settlement. At that state of hydraulic technology, brooks served better than great falls. James Whitelaw's 1810 map of Vermont shows most of the mills on side streams. Millwrights learned to harness some of the power of the Otter, Winooski, Lamoille, Missisquoi, and Connecticut, but sites the size of Bellows Falls, compared to the middle-sized falls of the Black River at Springfield, were just too big to handle.

Windsor County was full of these modest-sized water privileges. The Green Mountain backbone marked its western border. With settlement uninhibited by the Revolution, much of its land passed the initial clearing stage early, and that included a broad band of hills dissected by the White, Ottauquechee, Black, Williams, and West rivers. Carding and fulling mills, sawmills and gristmills, forges and foundries along these streams found a stable market in its settled farmers. They enjoyed a thicker network of roads and turnpikes than elsewhere in the state and could raft their produce down the Connecticut. From 1800 past 1860 it was the most populous Vermont county and probably the richest in real and personal property. When the railroads arrived along three edges of Windsor County in 1848-49, none of its mill villages was more than a ten to fifteen mile teaming from access to the railroad-made national network.

Before we look at the number one county's number one industry, Windsor rifles, in its number one village, we need to understand the role of the railroads in making and marring the fortunes of Vermont and Windsor. The railroad, the first large-scale, integrated industry in the United States and the largest Vermont enterprise until well past 1900, reoriented everything it touched, and it touched nearly everything. Railroads wanted long hauls; local traffic generated only about one-fifth of the Central's and Rutland's freight revenue for fiscal 1857-58. For a few years under the Reciprocity Act of 1854, heavy Canadian traffic to and from Boston crossed Vermont, especially for bonded goods exempt from tariff.

Railroads triggered tremendous changes. In less than a decade, by 1855, over five hundred miles of single track crisscrossed the state. The huge investment, amounting to $26,000,000 in construction alone, paid few dividends and was an almost total loss, but the managers manipulated the rail lines to their profit, and the lines themselves remained as long-term improvements. Most

of the money spent to get started benefited English and southern New England suppliers of rails and rolling stock, but several millions stayed in Vermont for land damages, wages, salaries, and buildings.[1]

When railroads sold stock in Vermont they promised that real estate values would double. For those along the tracks that promise often came true. In the 1850s the total value of Vermont farms increased one-third—from $63,000,000 to $94,000,000—according to the federal census, and village values rose even more. Near the tracks people noticed more paint and tidiness, less household manufacturing, less barter, and more cash transactions. Where the railroads followed the stage routes the unearned increment benefited the owners in already important centers. Speculation was rampant where villages rolled their centers downhill to the depot, as in Rutland and Bellows Falls, or shifted from one center to another within the town, as in Danby, Essex, St. Albans, Newport, Barton, Newbury, Hartford, and Randolph. South Royalton grew in five years from two sets of buildings to a hundred houses. Jonas Wilder retired from the superintendency of the Rutland and Washington Railroad in 1858 with a contract to supply that line with fuel. He bought woodlands around West Rupert and started a store to supply his choppers and teams. Prospering, he added a shoe shop, a miller's room and a tin and stove shop, and ran the post office. He grossed fifty thousand dollars a year—big business for a country store in a depression—and eventually collected most of his bills. Island Pond was created out of the woods when the Grand Trunk came through Brighton in 1853.

The landscape changed, as we can see in the paintings of James Hope of Castleton, in the earliest stereo views, and in contemporary lithographs. Construction thickened near the new depots, the depot hotels, and livery stables. You could tell where the railroads were by the telegraph poles, the daring wooden bridges, and the plumes of smoke from the locomotives.

Accidents, in terms of passenger miles or in proportion to the labor force, were probably no worse than were suffered in other industries or by earlier carriers, and the public felt that nothing could be done about them. "To publish them all would crowd out everything else," wrote the editor of the Middlebury *Register*, December 7, 1853. Railroad Commissioner George P. Marsh urged full reports and investigation and was not reappointed.

---

[1]"A Route to the Lakes," in Edward C. Kirkland, *Men, Cities, and Transportation: A Study in New England History, 1820-1900* (Cambridge: Harvard University Press, 1948), 1:159-191, sets Vermont railroad history in broader context. Bassett, "Vermont Railroads," 140-153, discusses early railroad operation and its by-products.

Loss of life and limb began during construction and continued through the period. Inexperienced bosses and men blew themselves up in blasting. Clumsy derricks loading stone or hoisting timbers dropped their loads on workmen, and gravel diggers dug their graves in cave-ins. Since much of this construction was cheap, hurried, and wooden, it broke, burned, or rotted. Accidents resulted from jerry-built and soon rickety roadbeds. Bodies paid the price of mechanical errors, penny pinching, and superficial inspection. Boiler explosions became engineers' nightmares. A faulty switch placement sent an engine through the Otter Creek bridge at Whiting. Happily the couplings broke, saving the passenger cars. "Gross carelessness in the laying of the rails" threw a train off the track near Brandon. Bridge washouts and rock slides in cuts caused frequent derailments. When part of the machinery of a passenger locomotive broke near Whiting, the fireman, already skittish from having been pulled from an overturned engine a few days before, jumped to his death. The Boston-bound mail train derailed near Clarendon when a drive wheel came off, and a passsenger car rolled over three times. Conductors, brakemen, and passengers were crushed between cars. Not every locomotive had a cowcatcher to fend off livestock and drunks straying onto the tracks. On top of a freight at night a man had no "tell-tale" dangling rope signal warning him to duck before going through a tunnel. Accident compensation for passengers, more common than for workmen or shippers, was rare. Courts usually assumed, "Let the traveler beware."

The telegraph permitted early warning of unforeseen changes in schedule, but it was not used for safety until 1852 in Vermont. The Rutland's northbound train, stuck in a snowbank east of Rutland, was scheduled to meet the southbound train at Middlebury. Passengers persuaded the Middlebury telegraph operator to wire the superintendent in Rutland. He sent back instructions to proceed to Rutland, thus accommodating local and New York passengers. Rules required waiting in Middlebury, and the fearful engineer would not move until the telegraph man agreed to ride in the cab with him.

Rail passengers, although frequently given free rides or half fares at first, did not find early rail travel comfortable. Tickets were for one short line only, until the invention, claimed by Jonas Wilder of the Rutland and Washington, of the coupon ticket for all the lines from origin to destination. The Central added sleeping cars in the summer of 1859 and gradually the overnight stop at Northfield, St. Albans, or Rutland disappeared. There was still a great deal of waiting for trains. Burlingtonian E. J. Phelps's classic "Lay of the Lost Traveler" (1865) about connections in Essex Junction caught the spirit of non-cooperation between rival lines, apparently deliberate in their planned inconvenience. Railroads became common carriers of disease: Ellen White of Thetford had smallpox in Boston and spread it to a dozen others by going home before she was well.

Both the village industrialist and farmer counted on the railroad to bring them iron, buffalo robes, goods from warmer zones, and manufactures, and to move their products quickly and cheaply. Whatever the difficulties of adjusting to a novel mode, most local shippers chose the cars over wagons and boats for their stone, ore, lime, lumber, cheese, butter, and livestock. By 1851 the Passumpsic was carrying lumber and masts, and rafting on the Connecticut dwindled. In the early fifties more Vermont cattle and sheep reached Boston slaughterhouses than from any other New England state and in better condition than when they had been driven for weeks. Then in the late fifties the vagaries of rates, the barrier of the Berkshires, and the lack of a railroad bridge across the Hudson at Albany brought middle-western hogs and cattle over the Rutland to Boston. "A drovers' Saloon car has been fitted up," reported the *Rutland Herald* on April 13, 1857. The St. Albans car factory built some twenty cattle cars for this trade in 1859.

Local freight had to be stimulated with low rates. Jonas Wilder as agent for the Central gave away a few barrels of lime from the Underwood lime kiln near Essex Junction to Massachusetts builders and bleacheries. The Central soon had shipments worth a thousand dollars a month and Underwood added six kilns. Wilder set a low rate for lumber from Burlington to points from Manchester, New Hampshire, to Boston, and helped build Burlington as a lumber depot. Wilder adopted refrigerator cars for butter in 1851, enabling farmers to ship fresh butter for higher prices throughout the warm weather. The St. Albans depot shipped about a million pounds in 1851 and 2,700,000 in 1858. Cheese production increased statewide from half a million pounds in 1851 to two million in 1860. Thus by helping to market dairy products and meat in the cities, the railroads speeded the shift from wool growing to dairying.

Windsor was the leading village in Windsor County, more populous than Springfield until 1860 if we include West Windsor, separated in 1848. President Timothy Dwight of Yale viewed it in 1797 and 1803 as the ideal country town, in touch with the centers of civilization, comfortably balanced between the bucolic and the urbane. Its convicts distinguished it in 1840 from a score of villages.

Since 1807 when the state prison opened at Windsor, requiring hard labor for convicted criminals, the prison superintendent had contracted for a variety of work: cooperage, basketry, shoemaking, carriage making, blacksmithing and gunsmithing. The prison produced only a thousand dollars worth of guns in 1840. It is easy to exaggerate the importance of this cheap convict labor, poorly motivated and in limited supply. However, Enoch Cobb Wines, reporting on American prisons to the State of New York in 1866, asserted that prison wages were one-third or one-quarter of the going rates, practically all the contractors got rich, and states ran their prisons on the proceeds without supplementary appropriations. Hard labor might be viewed only as punishment or as rehabilitation, sometimes sending the ex-con into the world with self-respect and a useful trade.

Jabez Proctor, father of Redfield, the marble mogul, and on the Governor's Council, 1822-26, thought convict labor so worthwhile that in 1830 he moved the machine shop of his National Hydraulic pump factory from Proctorsville and established it, with a new stationary steam engine, in Windsor State Prison. Besides this early emancipation from waterpower, the company was one of the first shops outside of the arms industry to manufacture interchangeable and, therefore, replaceable parts. It also established something of a cost-accounting and office records system. The sale of a pump to the City of St. Louis demonstrated the transportation and exchange difficulties of out-of-the-way Windsor. National Hydraulic's man had to superintend the slow installation process, and for pay he had to take western land. Recognizing these handicaps, the company sold its basic patent to Fales & Jenks of Providence, Rhode Island, which used the improvement for a century.

Guy Hubbard, historian of the machine tool industry in the Windsor-Springfield region, found a sort of genealogy, not only of managers but also of inventors and inventions, in the story of how one thing led to another at Windsor.[2] Nicanor Kendall, son of a blacksmith, married the daughter of Proctor's inventive partner, Asahel Hubbard, invented a safe underhammer lock for a squirrel rifle, which left the top of the barrel clear for sighting, and contracted for prison labor to make it.

Enter Richard Smith Lawrence, a Chester native who gained experience with men and metal in the machine shops of upper New York State before returning at twenty-one to Windsor relatives in 1838. Because he put a peep sight on his uncle's Pennsylvania rifle, he was hired in the prison gun shop. He worked his way up to superintendent in six months and to a partnership with Kendall in a decade. Through a pump salesman in New Orleans the rifle shop got a large order from the Republic of Texas and, as the Mexican War loomed, won a bid early in 1845 for ten thousand rifles delivered in three years, at $10.90, ten cents under the nearest competitor. With capital augmented

---

[2] Guy Hubbard, "Leadership of Early Windsor Industries in the Mechanic Arts," *Vermont Historical Society Proceedings* (1924), 157-182, based on a broader, illustrated, and more detailed account, "The Development of Machine Tools in New England," reprinted from *American Machinist* 59-61 (July 1923-September 1924): various pagings. Joseph W. Roe summarizes in *English and American Tool Builders* (New Haven: Yale University Press, 1925), 191-192, 186-188, 283-285 (Lawrence's reminiscences).

by a new partner, Samuel E. Robbins, a retired Boston lumber dealer living in Windsor, they bought land, built an armory, hired the best machinists in the Northeast, and added a good deal of free labor. They finished their contract in eighteen months and secured another for fifteen thousand rifles. They lost a quarter-million dollars in an unwise venture into railroad car building, but continued the profitable small arms business.

Windsor continued to impress the world, although in the early 1850s the management recognized the disadvantages of the Windsor site for large-scale manufacturing and built a Hartford, Connecticut, plant to handle a Sharps contract for fifteen thousand rifles and carbines. Robbins & Lawrence received honorable mention at the 1851 London Crystal Palace exhibition for its display of U.S. Army rifles. Each day the rifles were taken apart, the pieces of the different rifles mixed up and reassembled, to show the merits of interchangeable parts. England had no national armory and its arms were custom built. With the onset of the Crimean War, a royal British commission inspected the Windsor works in August 1854 and closed a contract for $44,360 worth of its machine tools to make the 1853 minié rifle at a new Enfield small arms plant.

The following March, Robbins & Lawrence accepted what proved to be an impossible contract for twenty-five thousand Enfields, complete with bayonets, at $15.50 each, to be delivered on a monthly schedule for a year beginning June 1856. The company received a £20,000 advance and would suffer a penalty of five dollars for each rifle not delivered on schedule. Robbins accepted the contract, knowing the expense would far exceed the profits, because he expected huge contracts to follow. He epitomizes the bullish spirit of the years before the Panic of 1857.

The difficulties surpassed his greatest fears. Lawrence asked for sample rifles, but no two samples were alike. He asked for a set of accurate gauges, but these, made of hardwood and originally accurate to within a sixty-fourth of an inch, were warped in transit and useless. He had to build his own master gun. Steel gauges, hardened and oilstoned, were fitted to the parts, and accurate jigs and fixtures, twenty years ahead of their time, built around the parts. Preparations intended to take three months had taken nine.

From December 1855 to May 1856 the new machinery in the new shops at Windsor and Hartford made 640 rifles a month. Then the Pennsylvania sawmills supplying the black walnut for gunstocks shut down on account of drought, yet production rose to two thousand rifles a month. Meanwhile the Crimean War ended and the British rescinded the tardy contract, with Robbins and Lawrence owing $73,000 on the money advanced and $73,000 in penalties on 14,600 rifles not delivered on time. The creditors foreclosed. Robbins organized the Vermont Arms Company to make rifles and a new sewing machine, but soon sold out to Lamson & Goodnow, who were making scythe snaths in the prison.

The men trained by Lawrence and his master mechanics at Windsor and their inventions, both mechanical and institutional, exerted a vast influence on machine-based industry the world over. The machines that Henry D. Stone, Windsor superintendent, installed at Enfield were copied all over Europe. After 1849 the company sold more and more drills, millers, and especially turret lathes to the world metalworking industry and continued to invent. Stone improved Blanchard's gunstock lathe and rifling machines; Lawrence invented an edging machine and the lubricated bullet. In style these machines were breaking away from the cabinetmakers' architectural patterns toward what J. A. Kouwenhoven has called the modern vernacular.[3] Office systems kept tab on each machinist and each product. "Bell cards," schedules maximizing work by daylight by minutely adjusting the times for starting and stopping work, regimented employees. A "Resin Gas Plant" lighted the shops at night.

A year after the bankruptcy, the shops reopened under lease to make guns and sewing machines on a smaller scale.[4] While they were closed Windsor mechanics found other jobs elsewhere and brought Windsor ways with them.

Other metalworkers and toolmakers in Woodstock, Springfield, Brattleboro, Bennington, Fair Haven, Brandon, and smaller villages suffered severe, sudden changes from exposure to the national market and to the national business cycle. (See table, p. 58.)

Textile mills held on in the hills while a few expanded. The five largest accounted for forty-three percent of the total value of Vermont woolens produced in 1860.

---

[3] J. A. Kouwenhoven, *Made in America: The Arts in Modern Civilization* (Garden City, N.Y.: Doubleday, 1948), 15-52.

[4] The census of 1850 showed Robbins & Lawrence capitalized at $160,000, hiring 155 men, and using $60,150 worth of materials to make 9,500 rifles worth $114,000, 120 railroad cars worth $54,000, and machinery undervalued at $13,000. Lamson & Goodnow at the prison used fifty men to make 100,000 forty-cent scythe snaths, while the Hammond & Draper foundry produced three hundred tons of castings. In 1860 the survivor firm of Lamson & Goodnow reported the same scythe snath operation at the prison, also hiring forty men to make 3,500 sewing machines worth $50,000 at the armory. No report on gunmaking.

Vermont Metalworking, Machinery, Tool and Instrument Shops*
(Value of product in thousands of dollars)

1850

Firm, Location	Employees	Values	Type of Product
Robbins & Lawrence, Windsor	155	181	rifles, machinery, railroad cars
E. & T. Fairbanks, St. Johnsbury	225	161	scales
Vt. Central R. R. Co., Northfield	—	—	railroad car shops
Champlain Transp. Co., Burlington	104	120	steamboats & repairs
D. Taft & Co., Hartland	20	59	agricultural tools
Granger, Hodges & Co., Brandon	100	50	furnace & foundry
Royal Blake, Brandon	50	48	furnace & foundry
Conant, Briggs & Warren, Brandon	30	45	railroad cars
Conant & Howe, Brandon	50	40	furnace & foundry
Lamson & Goodnow, Windsor	50	40	scythe snaths
Brooks & Bros., New Haven	18	30	edge tools
Leonard Barney, Bennington	12	30	foundry

1860

Firm, Location	Employees	Values	Type of Product
E. & T. Fairbanks, St. Johnsbury	250	530	scales
Vt. Central R. R. Co., Northfield	136	268	railroad car shops
John Howe & Co., Brandon	—	125	scales
Lamson & Goodnow, Windsor	40	42	scythe snaths
"	55	50	sewing machines
	95	92	
Brandon Iron & Car Wheel Co.	70	32	railroad car wheels
"	7	25	fire brick
"	10	12	mineral paint
"	6	8	paper clay
" (foundry—worked 4 mos.)	6	—	pig iron used in car wheels
	99	77	
Davey & Nichols, Fair Haven	32	65	rolled iron, nails
W. C. Smith, St. Albans	30	60	foundry, mowers
Estey & Green, Brattleboro	25	44	melodeons
Shedd & Walker, Burlington	8	40	tinware
Bowman & Mansfield, Rutland	20	39	castings, machinery
A. J. Fullam, Springfield	12	35	stencil tools
Eagle Square Co., Shaftsbury	40	35	steel squares

*This and subsequent tables in this chapter are compiled from the copies in Vermont State Library, Montpelier, of the manuscript Schedule III, Manufacturing, of the 1850 and 1860 censuses.

Vermont Woolen Mills, 1850-60
(Capital and value of product in thousands of dollars)

Village	Firm	Capital	Male	Female	# Emp.	Product
Winooski	Burlington Mill Co., 1850	250	150	300	450	400
	Harding & Brother, 1860	400	190	150	340	500
Pownal	R. Carpenter, Jr., 1850	12	12	5	17	35
	" 1860	130	85	85	170	300
Cavendish	Fullerton & Derby, 1850	60	37	30	67	125
	F. C. Fullerton & Co., 1860	135	50	45	95	175
Ludlow	Ludlow Woolen Mill Co., 1850	35	9	9	18	17
	Ward & Buffum (Harding), 1860	65	45	40	85	150
Woodstock	Solomon Woodward, 1850	70	26	24	50	72
	" 1860	146	36	47	83	e150
Proctorsville	Smith & Balcom, 1850	30	40	40	80	96
	George L. Balcom & Co., 1860	50	40	40	80	120
Cambridgeport	Granite Mfg. Co. (idle), 1850	—	—	—	—	—
	Solon Perry & Co., 1860	50	23	12	35	108
Bennington	H. E. Bradford (hosiery), 1850	—	—	—	—	—
	" 1860	20	30	60	90	100
Gaysville	Hobert & French, 1850	3	2	2	4	2
	" 1860	40	20	23	43	98
Bridgewater	W. H. Lemmex, 1850	—	—	—	—	—
	" 1860	40	22	20	42	20
Bethel	D. F. Faulkner, 1850	10	18	18	36	82
	" 1860	40	15	15	30	80
Quechee	Ottauquechee Mfg. Co., 1850	26	15	15	30	41
	Joseph C. Parker, 1860	30	20	20	40	80
Reading	Prosper Merrill, 1850	8	11	8	19	21
	" 1860	50	25	18	43	75
Quechee	Dewey & Spaulding, 1850	25	18	16	34	35
	A. G. Dewey & Co., 1860	75	21	25	46	71
Gaysville	Merrick Gay, 1850	4	8	9	17	11
	" 1860	20	20	20	40	70
Waterville	John Herron, 1850	36	32	19	51	82
	Wells & Herron, 1860	14	22	15	37	64
Saxtons River	George Perry & Co., 1850	50	21	14	35	39
	Farnsworth & Hoit, 1860	38	20	14	34	60
Danville	Benjamin Greenbanks, 1850	9	9	4	13	19
	" 1860	44	23	23	46	56
Barnet	George Greenbanks, 1850	12	11	9	20	26
	" 1860	33	15	13	28	52
No. Montpelier	A. W. Wilder & Son, 1850	4	4	4	8	5
	H. A. Little, 1860	65	15	16	31	52
Middlebury	Davenport & Nash, 1850	25	35	15	50	60
	Davenport & Clay, 1860	28	20	9	29	50
Chester	Thomas Sawyer & Son, 1850	12	7	9	16	19
	J. F. & T. R. Sawyer, 1860	25	12	9	21	50
Putney	James Keyes, 1850	25	13	13	26	35
	" 1860	9	13	13	26	50
Springfield	Village Falls Mills, 1850	11	7	5	12	26
	Holmes, Whitmore & Co., 1860	20	17	17	34	50

eEstimated.

In 1860 all forty-six mills, the most widespread and in their total product the largest Vermont manufacturers, hired 2,073 workers, fifty-eight percent women. The top twenty-four, listed above, had only fifty-two percent women. This suggests that the larger mills hired more immigrant families, with men and boys given preference. Vermont's woolen mills reported a total output worth $2,938,000. Four Vermont cotton mills made wadding, sheetings, and prints worth $178,000 in 1850. Five in 1860 emphasized prints and increased their production to $263,000, with half again as many employees. Here and there were a few large processors, like the Winooski grist and flour mill, tanneries and shoe factories, paper mills, potteries, and woodworking.

Two types of development in the 1850s showed the diversity and durability of Vermont industry. St. Johnsbury became a village dominated by the scale maker, E. & T. Fairbanks, the largest company in the state. Stone working, with supporting industry, made Rutland town and county the fastest growing in the state, with a total set of products worth much more than Fairbanks scales.

The marble industry of the Rutland district best typifies the characteristic cutting edge of Vermont's nineteenth-century manufacturing and its connections with political, social, and technological forces. The new cities wanted marble public buildings, and the newly rich of the cities wanted marble mantels, table tops, and other elegance. Small quarries, not all of them listed in the census, subsisted on a steady market of marble gravestones, with only slate as the ignoble competitor.

Leading firms won orders for monuments advertising growing towns and successful families. Manley Brothers of Dorset sold a six-hundred-dollar memorial for Charles Paine to Northfield in 1856. The Rutland Marble Company raised and Larkin G. Mead carved fourteen tons of Ethan Allen for the new Vermont statehouse in 1859. Marble deposits were extensive, accessible, and of high quality, making monopoly hard to achieve among the myriads of starters. The tangled skein of rail projects, each lobbied through the legislature, each offering cut rates to quarries, each fighting for the best connections, had to be worked out before dependable transport at steady tariffs could serve the industry.

An ancient marble-sawing technique, rediscovered in the Berkshires, was brought to Middlebury about 1802. Soft wrought-iron blades moved across the block with sand as abrasive and water as cooler. As the marble industry expanded, Davey's Fair Haven rolling mill met virtually the whole marble mill demand for saws. By 1841 the Freedley quarry in Dorset had substituted hand channeling for wasteful blasting and wedging the blocks apart at the seams. Channeling consisted of lining up a row of laborers who pounded holes with long chisel-ended iron drills until the block

Vermont Quarries, Stone Mills and Mines
(Value of product in thousands of dollars)

1850

Firm, Location	Employees	Value	
Hydeville Co.	76	84	marble quarries in Rutland & Castleton; slate quarries & milling in Castleton
Sheldons, Morgan & Slason	40	78	marble quarry, mill
William F. Barnes, Rutland	50	45	marble quarry, mill
William Y. Ripley, Rutland	17	30	marble mill
Vt. Copper Mining Co., Vershire	75	30	copper ore
Jackman & Sherman, Castleton	16	30	marble mill
	274	297	

1860

Firm, Location	Employees	Value	
Rutland Marble Co., Rutland	150	300	marble quarries
Hydeville Co., Castleton	42	146	stone milling
Sheldons & Slason, Rutland	200	141	marble quarry, mill
W. Y. Ripley & Son, Rutland	15	127	marble mill, &c.
Adams & Allen, Fair Haven, Rutland	76	114	marble quarry, mill
Ira Cochran, Dorset	22	80	marble quarry, mill
Sherman, Hawley & Adams, Rutland & Fair Haven	68	75	marble quarry, mill
Holley, Fields & Kent, Dorset	85	70	marble quarry, mill
Vermont Marble Co., Rutland	55	65	marble quarry, mill
Clement & Gilmore, Rutland	20	50	marble mill
Eagle Slate Co., Poultney	100	42	slate quarry
Ira Sykes, Dorset	6	32	marble mill
E. D. Selden, Brandon	40	30	marble quarry, mill
Sutherland Falls Marble Co., Rutland	47	30	marble quarry, mill
	926	1,302	

broke off. Bowman & Mansfield's Rutland foundry and M. F. Douglass on the Arlington-Shaftsbury line made a lot of these drills. Horses or oxen on sweeps furnished the power for the derricks, introduced in 1848, to raise the block to a rollered block boat dragged to the railroad or mill. Only a few saved the millers' profits by sawing their own blocks with woodstocked steam engines at the quarry. The rest used the power of muscles and water only, although William F. Barnes kept a mechanic working to invent a steam drill.

By 1853 marble fever was epidemic in Rutland County. Imagine the excitement of blasting and carrying off the cover of dirt and rock on your barren sheep pasture and finding out whether the underlying marble was worth a fortune or you had just thrown money down the hole. Nobody bored first and tested the cores. Quarries could count on the cheap manual labor released by the completion of the main Vermont rail network. Three rail routes competed to carry the stone: via Castleton and Whitehall (1851), via Poultney and Eagle Bridge (1852), and via North Bennington (1853). The tendency of the merchants, millers, and landowners who speculated in marble land was to hold on to it and not to develop it faster by inviting outside capital. Half of the Rutland firms in 1861 were run and apparently owned by those who had before 1851 opened most of the quarries and sawed most of the slabs. They stayed on at least to sell their improvements, usually after the Civil War. Rutland marble properties, according to its tax lists, rose from $113,864 in 1849 to $262,270 in 1861.

The story of H. H. Baxter and the Rutland Marble Company shows how hard it was to corner the marble business and how closely marble and railroads were associated. Baxter, in charge of railroad construction from Bellows Falls and Bennington to Burlington, was according to the *Burlington Free Press* of 10 December 1850, "*about* the best contractor ever to manage spades and gunpowder." He returned to Rutland in 1854 at age thirty-seven with money made building the Cleveland and Toledo Railroad and organized the Rutland Marble Company with his former Rutland Railroad associate Thomas H. Canfield and New York bankers. Baxter's firm bought the old Barnes quarry, a known producer, and made new openings in West Rutland. His firm hired more labor and made more money before the Civil War than any other out-of-state venture. It built company tenements and provided company stores and, like its competitors, supplied stables and smithies for its draft animals, and shops for sharpening drills, mending machinery, and splicing the long hoisting ropes of the derricks.

Deepening quarries caused more accidents from breaking tackle or sudden rockfalls. Whether because of these, the reported wage dispute, general feelings of bad treatment, the deepening depression, or spring fever, most of the West Rutland quarriers went on strike in April 1859. Could some of the strikers have been in the "Bolton War"? Had others worked for Baxter on the Rutland Railroad right-of-way? According to "Hibernicus" of Wallingford, writing to the Boston *Pilot*, (quoted in the *Rutland Courier*, 8 April 1859),

> The men have been ill-used—seldom get any money, but had to take store-pay. They were charged one-third more than anywhere else; they were promised sixty-five cents per day for the winter, and ninety cents for the summer; but they received only fifty cents for the winter. The bosses cast stones at them when they would raise their heads to take a moment's rest. They made them work longer hours by changing the time.

Sheldons & Slason's Marble Quarry, West Rutland, in Edward Hitchcock and others, *Report on the Geology of Vermont* (1861), plate xxxvi.

During the previous winter, "when we were injuring our health in those quarries," wrote a striker in the 29 April *Courier*, workmen had to pay thirty to thirty-six dollars for a miserable house, four dollars a cord for punky wood, and fifty cents a bushel for potatoes. Some were forced to pay others' debts, to trade at the company store or lose their jobs, to work for one company only or leave town.

Animosity focused on Baxter, the rich man from away, worth $290,000 according to the 1860 census. It was "work all day for sugar in your tay—drill ye terriers, drill" in Baxter's quarry as it had been on Baxter's crews. He had bought the old state fairground north of the East Village, well apart from common folks, and built himself a sumptuous gas-lit palace. The Clifford girls, his Irish servants, could tell how the rich carried on there. Newspapers described the mansion with mixed envy and civic pride, but it symbolized to the Irish quarriers the class of sharp, unfair dealers with whom they had always fought. Father François Picart of St. Bridget's tried to keep his flock fed, housed, and united. Four companies evicted four hundred men, but the tenants of William F. Barnes, who paid a dollar a day and kept operating, took in the strikers.

By June 1 the strike was over with no sign of concessions. Two months later the priest presided at the organization of the Quarrymen's Benevolent Association, to raise among able workmen the expenses of sickness, disability, funerals, and widows; to eradicate intemperance; and to promote employer-employee good feeling. Before Christmas Baxter abandoned the deepest quarry and Bishop de Goesbriand transferred Picart to Milton.

Cold figures from the census and tax lists show the shape of the booming marble business. In 1850 over three dozen firms from Manchester to Brandon reported capital of $286,000. In 1860 there were only a dozen firms left south of Rutland, and a dozen recorded in the Rutland area, the twenty-four capitalized at $1,160,200, more than three-quarters invested in the Rutland area. The 1850 census recorded 404 men and eleven women paid $113,500. Ten years later they hired 945 laborers for $293,000. The 1850 report listed over a million feet of slabs or blocks sold for $414,000. In 1860 they disposed of nearly two million feet of marble products worth $835,000. The Dorset-Danby marble district had gained slightly while the Rutland district had grown from two to four times its size in 1850, in spite of the depression of 1857-60.

The new slate business of western Rutland County and adjacent New York towns repeated the cycle in marble: initial enthusiasm, debt incurred in development, flooded markets (first in school tablets, then roofing), curtailment of unprofitable lines, reorganization and stabilization. One new product that helped carry slate through the depression was marbleized or enameled slate, introduced by Boston stockholders about 1855. Marbleized slate and cast-iron looked like the genuine article and cost only a fraction as much. Unlike the marble business, slate was early and thoroughly taken over by out-of-state capital. The villages of Fair Haven, Poultney, Castleton, and Granville, New York, grew on the stone business.

St. Johnsbury of all Vermont villages best showed the distinctive features of the railroad revolution of the fifties. In 1840 thirty-eighth in population (1,887), it soared to fifteenth in 1850 (2,756), even before the railroad arrived, and seventh in 1860 (3,469). Situated beside the sleepy Sleeper's River, with little waterpower, it early turned to charcoal, then to stone coal. E. & T. Fairbanks of St. Johnsbury was already Vermont's largest industrial employer in 1850 and second only to Windsor's Robbins & Lawrence in value of product.

Erastus Fairbanks, eldest of three brothers, had the intensity that drove his scales to the top. He studied law enough for business purposes and trained as a storekeeper. When his brother Thaddeus received a patent for a platform scale, Erastus put himself at the head of the Connecticut Valley movement to provide a freight outlet by rail. Once the third and operative charter of the Connecticut and Passumpsic Rivers Railroad had passed in 1845, Fairbanks became its principal stock salesman in Vermont. "I have never associated with any visionary enterprise," he wrote Ira H. Allen of Irasburg, arguing for investment in his line.[5] The Passumpsic raised $300,000 in northeastern Vermont and $700,000 in Boston, and began construction from White River Junction to Wells River in 1846.

Fairbanks managed the line to serve his scale works and his town. The Passumpsic bonded for half a million to build the next twenty miles from Wells River to St. Johnsbury, 1849-50. When the stockholders voted in 1854 to resume building northward, Fairbanks resigned his presidency, but thereafter a member or agent of the family continued on the inside. The Fairbankses joined the rest in wanting to finish a through route to Montreal and beyond, but not at the cost of profits. The village reaped the trade advantages of being the terminus for at least five years and won legal business when it took the county seat from Danville in 1856. With construction money in sight the Passumpsic started building to Barton in 1857 but waited out the depression and did not reach Newport until 1863. It paid small but steady dividends, got along without a telegraph line alongside until the Civil War, added a Pullman car in 1872, and continued to burn cheap local wood until 1882.

---

[5] 8 September 1845, in the Wilbur Papers, Special Collections, Bailey/Howe Library, University of Vermont.

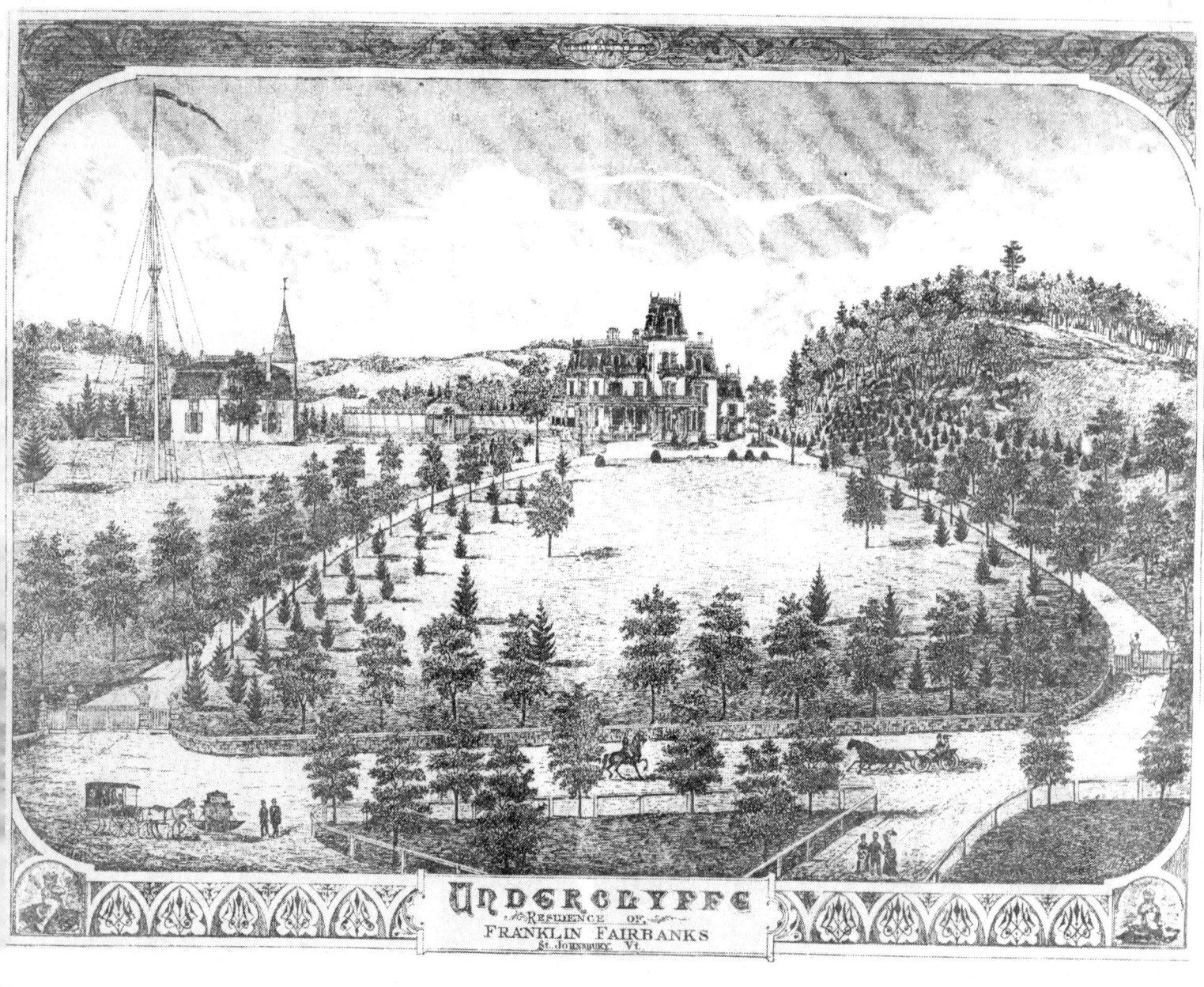

Underclyffe, Residence of Franklin Fairbanks, St. Johnsbury, from 1872 to his death in 1895. From F. W. Beers, *County Atlas of Caledonia, Vermont* (1875), 61. Compare mansions of H. Henry Baxter off Grove Street, Rutland, and J. Gregory Smith off Congress Street, St. Albans, referred to on p. 64 and p. 192-193.

The Fairbanks family represented many facets of Vermont's mid-century years. Thaddeus kept inventing improvements throughout his long life, but other Fairbankses had a measure of his mechanical talent. Erastus was the business manager. Joseph, the youngest brother, shouldered his share of the business but was also a school reformer, Governor Horace Eaton's right-hand man. Joseph "sent out hundreds of pages of letters and press articles on almost every theme of current importance" from farming and science to home life, temperance, slavery, and Sabbath observance. After Joseph died and Erastus became so ill the family feared they would lose him too, the partnership incorporated in 1859 with Erastus's three sons, Horace, Charles, and Franklin, among the corporators—another step into the modern age.

Erastus shared the intense Congregational piety of the whole family. As the rail layers approached St. Johnsbury in November 1850, he castigated in the local *Caledonian* the Passumpsic contractor for working his men on the past two Sabbaths. He had never allowed any work on Sunday. It "has outraged the moral feelings of the community," he wrote. St. Johnsbury leaders were still clamping down on balls and circuses after the Civil War.

The Fairbanks philosophy of benevolent paternalism worked in the relatively homogeneous population of Yankee mechanics sharing the Whig-Congregational ideals of the first family. The scale factory did not need large amounts of unskilled immigrant labor and did not encourage, although it did not try to exclude, Roman Catholics. The parish of Our Lady of Victory had a resident priest in 1858, and a church was built in 1860 for eighty families. The car shops were moved to Lyndonville in 1867, which was already and continued to be much more Democratic than St. Johnsbury. The Fairbankses ran the town by common consent because their enterprise kept the home fires burning. They operated a company store from 1851 but it had several competitors. St. Johnsbury was not a company town, for there was other industry. No labor troubles were reported, although scale factory wages declined from an average $480 a year in 1850 to $402 in 1860. Perhaps the skilled jobs, which might have provided labor leadership, were well rewarded.

Fairbanks Scales excelled its many competitors in advertising and salesmanship. The firm established agencies in Boston, Albany, New York, Philadelphia, Chicago, and St. Louis, and itinerant salesmen throughout the country and Canada. Its best persuaders were medals and citations from trade fairs, and the scales themselves. A five-hundred-ton canal weighlock at Albany was probably the largest scale built in the nineteenth century, and Americans favored the biggest. From canal and railroad behemoths down to mint and postal models sensitive to the fraction of an ounce, the scales heralded accuracy for the coming age of precision. The firm advertised scales used in Europe, Mexico, Cuba, Venezuela, Bolivia, Peru, Argentina, Brazil, and China. William H. N. Prince, Rio de Janeiro agent in 1861, wrote the home office, "I have been obliged to purchase a dress suit costing $24 . . . to wear at my audience with the Emperor. I shall probably never wear it again. Shall I add this suit to the bill?"[6]

A local competitor loomed in the late fifties: John Howe & Co. of Brandon. Howe, an early promoter of the Rutland and Burlington Railroad, acquired in 1850 with two other Boston capitalists the old Conant-Sprague furnace and foundry. He moved to Brandon, added woodland for charcoal and mine openings producing lignite, kaolin, yellow ochre, manganese, and umber, as well as the brown hematite iron ore. He made castings and car wheels, but also fire brick, paper filler, and paint. Brandon paints, celebrated in William Dean Howells' *Rise of Silas Lapham*, covered red barns, factories, and federal lighthouses all over the country. Howe was good at using by-products and also at acquiring patents for products that would use his castings.

His most important patent was by Frank M. Strong of Vergennes and Thomas Ross of Rutland in 1856. They doubled the life of the scale by resting the platform on chilled iron balls instead of the knife edge used in the Fairbanks scale. By 1860 Howe had won away from Fairbanks thirty-two first premiums at exhibitions and incorporated his scale company separately from his Brandon Iron and Car Wheel Company.

The success of both scale businesses, compared with the railroad interests of Howe and others, reflected national economic conditions: railroad construction nearly stopped while trade, requiring scales, was recovering. The stability of Vermont villages through the adjustments required during the hard times of the late fifties and after rested on trade, the diversity of many small shops, the mobility of skilled labor, and the perpetual tinkering of many mechanics.

It would take a fat book to list all the Vermont inventions that paid off. Those that "failed," like the 1819 sewing machine of John Knowles of Monkton, Thomas Davenport's electric motor of the 1830s, and the steam automobile of John Gore (1835), which scared Brattleboro horses at twelve miles an hour,[7] would run to many volumes.

I give some examples that made big differences. In 1854 the Vermont Central shop in Northfield introduced an 1838 patent lengthening the life of railroad ties by treating them with zinc

---

[6]Quoted in Fairbanks, Morse & Co., *Pioneers in Industry; The Story of Fairbanks, Morse & Co.* (Chicago: The Company, 1945), 33, 34.

[7]The selectmen banned it from town roads unless a boy ran ahead blowing a horn. See Mary R. Cabot, comp. and ed., *Annals of Brattleboro 1689-1895* (Brattleboro: E. L. Hildreth, 1922), 211, 307, 640-641.

chloride. They made railroad car chairs on a patent by John Howe. Howe also owned an automatic coupler and a car wheel patent. Reuben Daniels of Woodstock, a prolific inventor, made a ragpicker for A. G. Dewey's shoddy mill in Quechee. The Brothers brothers in the Winooski woolen mill invented a burr crusher enabling the firm to use cheap Argentine wool and to keep going through the depression. Windsor had its revolutionary rifle improvements, while Springfield prosperity depended partly on D. M. Smith's bank lock, lathe dog, and spiral clothespin; Davidson, Parks & Woolson's shearer, H. F. Crain's "spino-abdominal supporters and trusses"; Frost's scythe snath; Gilman's pump; J. C. Loveland's scissors sharpener; Fullam's stencil tools. Lemuel Hedges, a Windsor cabinetmaker, patented a double circular saw in 1842, as well as a divider basic to the production of Shaftsbury's carpenter's square industry and the Stearns rule factory in Brattleboro. Jacob Estey's melodeon business with a pair of key improvements was beginning to emerge above its Brattleboro competitors, but remained a small and uncertain branch of pipe and pump manufacture and cabinetmaking. Brattleboro machinists worked on papermaking, mowers, steam engines, lathes, planers, die sinkers, and other objects too numerous to mention.

Bennington, Vermont's third largest town in 1860, had a mix of small mills similar to Springfield's, stretched along the Walloomsac and Paran Creek. Most notable in requiring a distant source of some raw materials and an extensive market, with always the need of patents to keep ahead of the competition, were the powdermills and potteries, mainly shut down by the depression. The market for explosives depended on railroad building, quarry opening, and war, none of which was booming toward the end of the decade. Yet in spite of a field littered with bankruptcies, both managers and laborers could switch lines and continue. While firms and investors lost, the villages of the southwestern region kept growing. The same pattern obtained in the villages of the other industrial regions.

5. Village Business and Social Conditions

How did people who served the village industries view the industrialism that was pushing up the valleys? They looked for the opportunities it offered, chose one, or if the chances seemed poor, they left if they could. Innkeepers, chambermaids, and grooms where the stage used to stop; stage operators and drivers as stagecoaches lost passengers and mail to the railroads; woolen millers who could not afford the new machinery for the kind of cloth in fashion, and their operatives, who stayed only a few years anyway; iron and copper miners when the price went down or the ore gave out—all were ready to try their hand at something else, somewhere else. In a mobile society, where practically nobody had lived more than half a century in the same place and most people moved every few years, home was where the heart was, an unrealizable dream. They expected to move on. Those at the top were better able to dig in, buy at the bottom of the market, call on family cohorts and other networks, and pull still farther ahead. But the mighty could also fall hard, like Charles Paine of the Vermont Central and Samuel Robbins of the Windsor rifle factory.

The first choice was to try a new business or new work nearby. A tavernkeeper who could not have traders and drovers for clients could sometimes specialize in spas. Watering places in Vermont, taking their cue from Saratoga, were as old as the century, but those in Clarendon, Panton, Sheldon, and Highgate expanded in the 1840s, thanks to pleasure travel by lake steamer. They held on and expanded even more in the next quarter-century, thanks to pleasure travel by rail, too.

The water-cure fad brought Dr. Robert Wesselhoeft from Boston to Brattleboro, where he treated 563 cases from 1845 to 1848, according to his annual reports. His regimen was one of the natural reactions to heroic orthodox medicine that powdered, puked, blistered, and bled. The German method that Wesselhoeft followed prescribed early rising, baths, drinking lots of water and not stimulants, mild outdoor exercise through the 'sylvan dell' along Whetstone Brook, and a lively variety of social entertainments. After the founder's death in 1852 two successors vied for the increased patronage. The Wesselhoeft plant, worth some thirty thousand dollars in building, waterworks, sheltered promenades for bad weather, carpeting, canaries and *objets d'art*, attracted patients and boarders from every large city from Montreal to New Orleans. "There they stand," wrote Samuel Bowles, editor of the Springfield (Mass.) *Republican*, at the peak of the 1854 season,[1]

> two comfortable-looking piles of boards and shingles, bristling . . . against one another on the same street, with their generous piazzas of a summer afternoon thick with babies, pretty women and pale men. . . . there is considerable rivalry between the 'establishments.' . . . The village is very gay from such an irruption from the cities, and the 'establishments' expend part of their rivalry in attractive dances, theatricals, tableaux.

In 1855 the Brattleboro water cures sent missionaries to lecture on hydropathy, and Clarendon Springs experimented with a resident physician and baths. The Brattleboro establishments survived the hard times after 1857, one adding Swedish calesthenics and starting *The Water Cure World*, edited by their Dr. C. R. Blackall, in April 1860. They continued past the Civil War as resort hotels.

Other resorts began to appear on Vermont's principal lakes, a comfortable carriage ride from a depot, but village hotels such as the Island House at Bellows Falls, the Newbury House, the Bardwell and Berwick in Rutland, the several in Burlington and Montpelier, did a larger business because they could serve both businessmen and tourists.

Contemporaries correctly expected the railroads both to redistribute and to increase tourist traffic. Erastus Fairbanks urged Ira H. Allen, Orleans County capitalist, to subscribe for Passumpsic stock in a letter of September 25, 1845, because the line, once connected to Stanstead or Sherbrooke and Montreal, would divert much of the pleasure travel to and from Lake Champlain and Niagara Falls. The state geologist argued that "our magnificent scenery may be a source of pecuniary profit [not to be boxed, bottled, or shipped]. . . . If by descriptions of . . . our scenery [in my final report], amply illustrated by *good* engravings, we can make our scenery better known, travelers from abroad will more frequent our State."[2] When the General Assembly eventually authorized that "final report" by Edward Hitchcock and his assistants, it was entitled *Report on the Geology of Vermont: Descriptive, Theoretical, Economical, and Scenographical* (Claremont, New Hampshire: Albert D. Hager, 1861) and included thirty-eight lithographs and 365 woodcuts.

---

[1] Quoted in Brattleboro *Eagle*, 11 August 1854.

[2] Charles Baker Adams, *First Annual Report on the Geology of the State of Vermont* (Burlington: Chauncey Goodrich, 1845), 59. Note his use of abroad to mean out-of-state.

The railroads not only redistributed travelers but also housing and public buildings. Those first to know where the tracks and depot would be and with enough money to buy land near them profited most. The Rutland real estate boom was the strongest of the many in other growing villages. With a net four thousand newcomers during the 1850s to house and supply, not a building season went by without the din of new construction. The selectmen laid out eighteen new streets for residences between 1852 and 1856. In the peak year of 1853 some two hundred dwellings went up, as well as the permanent depot, shops, stores, and factories. Carpenters could buy a lot for two hundred dollars, build a house for five hundred, and rent it for a hundred dollars a year. The shortage made the poor pay the highest rent for the worst housing. In 1851 the Rutland Land Company bought the 150-acre farm of Moses Strong in "Nebraska," across the tracks, and had disposed of the subdivision by 1854. The incomplete assessors' records tell of the sudden influx of 1849-51 and 1855 and an almost as rapid exodus in 1857-58, checked by institutional building before it affected real estate values:[3]

	Polls	Value of Bldgs.	Grand List Total
1848	457	160,435	12,117.45
1849	480	168,216	11,797.59
1850	480	185,692	12,223.08
1851	691	—	13,110.89
1852	1165	265,053	15,854.31
1853	—	—	17,079.63
1854	—	—	—
1855	1193	432,501(1)	16,960.58
1856	1575	—	—
1857	—	—	—
1858	1195	—	—
1859	1050(2)	—	—
1860	1230	661,594	22,542.60

[3]Derived from the MS. Tax Records in the Rutland City Hall. Since the grand list was recorded in the spring the shifts represent activities chiefly of the previous year. (1) The title beginning in 1855 is "Value of Buildings and Quarries," but marble properties are not included here. (2) The decline in polls from 1858 to 1859 was affected by the organization of a poll-tax-exempt militia company.

Bank loans facilitated this rapid Rutland growth, as with development in other towns, but few have paid attention to the state's banking history.[4] In the beginning people thought only hard money, which you could test by biting, was safe. The Vermont State Bank, chartered in 1806 with branches in Woodstock and Middlebury (and later briefly in Westminster and Burlington), was ordered to close in 1813. It provided much needed and safer circulation of currency, but suffered losses from bad paper money issued by out-of-state banks. In the decade from 1818 until 1827, ten private, commercial banks started in the principal trading centers: Windsor, Burlington, Brattleboro, Rutland, Montpelier, Danville, St. Albans, Vergennes, Chelsea, and Bennington. Governor Jonas Galusha, although he signed the first bank charters, was suspicious of bank notes as paper money and the effect of banking on rural economy.

Yet by 1840, after three years of depression, Vermont had seventeen banks with total assets of $2,638,193, most of them in the largest villages. Their directors and officers continued to be leading wholesalers, manufacturers, shipping managers, and landowners. Farmers in those hard times resented this interlocking power and registered their protest by voting for "Smilie and Bank Reform," raising the Democratic vote to forty-five percent in 1842. The Democrats did not reach that height again in over a century. Banking expanded: by 1850 twenty-seven Vermont commercial banks had $5,800,000 assets. The year before, seven mutual savings banks reported deposits totaling only $149,000. Small depositors gave up higher interest and depended on trustees to manage their deposits wisely. At least their savings were safe from the burglaries frequently reported in the papers. The rural habit of hiding cash at home was going out of style.

In the scramble to make discounting profits during the flush times of 1848-54 banks earned their share of public criticism. Lucius E. Chittenden of Burlington lampooned the bank lobby in a mock session of the General Assembly, *Magna Carta of the Moosalamoo Bank*, a manuscript of which survives in the Special Collections of the University of Vermont's Bailey/Howe Library. The "free banking" law of 1851 allowed banking associations to do business without a charter, but within nine years all the banks taking advantage of this law were out of business.

---

[4]The following sketch is based on William P. Dillingham, "Banking Interests of Vermont," in William T. Davis, ed. *The New England States: Their Constitutional, Judicial, Educational, Commercial, Professional and Industrial History* (Boston: D. H. Hurd, 1897), 3:1472-1488, and Frederick P. Smith, "Evolution of State and National Banking Supervision in Vermont," (senior thesis, Department of Politics, Princeton University, 1937), copy in Special Collections, Bailey/Howe Library, University of Vermont, by a later president of the Burlington Savings Bank.

Bank troubles arose from several sources. They had tied up too much money in securities or Western mortgages (on farms, village real estate, timberlands, and railroads). Then some banks issued too much in bank notes, in proportion to their cash on hand or in city banks. This made them vulnerable in times of panic. They often lent too much to single individuals, especially to their own officers. And with Vermont bankruptcies totaling half a million in 1857 alone, they suffered from loans unrepaid. Although in 1857 the notes of seven Vermont commercial banks were heavily discounted in Boston, all but two recovered. Banking Commissioner Daniel Roberts concluded in his 1855 report, with some exaggeration, that the legislature had been deaf to all commissioners' proposals. Little was done after the Panic of 1857 except to prescribe inspection of closed and insolvent banks.

The struggle for money, power, and prestige among bankers was an undercover fight among a few that rarely erupted. A group headed by William Y. Ripley, Center Rutland marble miller, petitioned in 1851 for a second Rutland bank, but was headed off for ten years. The position of cashier was a sure road upward, unless one succumbed to the temptation to embezzle, as in the case of Homer Hubbell, long with the Missisquoi Bank of Sheldon, who vanished in 1865 with $75,000 (according to a St. Albans correspondent in the *Montpelier Watchman*, 4 January 1866). The list of new ventures and the figures for banking operations reflect the villages' economic growth beyond the upheavals of the late 1850s, and the population and commercial trends of the decade. Burlington, Rutland, and Brattleboro banks did over a quarter of the business shown in these totals (in thousands of dollars) from the bank commissioners' reports.

	Capital	Circulation	Specie	Deposits in City Banks	Notes Discounted	Total Resources
1850	2,159	2,856	127	882	4,362	580,027
1853	2,914	4,795	186	1,241	6,686	8,756
1855	3,603	3,704	202	1,282	6,378	8,581
1858	4,042	3,015	178	843	6,171	7,975
1860	4,004	3,725	185	1,282	6,689	891,742

While banks provided security for depositors and spread risks for investors, insurance grew another hedge against the uncertainties of the times. Long present in seaport cities, fire insurance companies appeared in seven Vermont villages by 1860 (Bellows Falls, Brattleboro, Burlington, Woodstock, Chelsea, St. Johnsbury, and especially Montpelier). This change showed the new secular urban outlook. One did not submit to one's loss as the will of God; one took precautions through collective security.

A little earlier than savings banks, county mutual fire insurance companies organized to compete with the Montpelier Vermont Mutual and out-of-state firms underwriting Vermont properties since the 1820s. Insurance firms grew when other businesses were failing in the late 1850s, although there were ceaseless complaints, especially against fire underwriters. Their lawyers had the unpleasant responsibility of collecting assessments to meet damage payments. They threatened or instituted suit over damages to force partial settlement for losses and took refuge behind the fine print requiring, for example, the use of all *possible* (not just reasonable) diligence to save the property. In spite of more regulations almost every year, loopholes in this new business remained unplugged and policyholders unhappy.

Brattleboro hosted the first Vermont life insurance company, Vermont Mutual Life chartered in 1847, and the National Life Insurance Company, destined to become Montpelier's leading business, followed the next year. Seven incorporators were prominent national politicians like Henry Clay, enlisted to prove the enterprise was sound. The pattern of metropolitan enlistment of local capital and management was repeated here: Benjamin Balch of Massachusetts sold the idea to wealthy Vermonters. Albert L. Catlin of Burlington and Julius Y. Dewey, Montpelier physician, each subscribed $10,000 of the original $100,000 capital, with twenty-eight other stockholders. Dewey, president from 1851 to 1877, reduced his practice to examining prospective policyholders and promoted the business. Many prominent Democrats—David A. Smalley, Timothy P. Redfield, Homer W. Heaton, Oramel H. Smith, Paul Dillingham, and Charles G. Eastman—appear on its roster of officers.

National Life had a favorable press for it guaranteed eight percent interest to stockholders and twice distributed $100,000 to policyholders. Because actuarial prediction was very uncertain, National Life charged high premiums and paid only $121,000 in death claims through the 1850s. Half of these were to heirs of those who died during the California gold rush, nearly five hundred of whom were insured for extra premiums amounting to a third of a million. An 1849 law, broadened in 1856, permitted married women to hold life insurance in their own names. Up to the Civil War, National Life wrote some three thousand policies in fifteen states and Canada totaling about $3,750,000 and had 1,257 policies worth nearly two million dollars in force in October 1860. It doubled its assets between 1854 and 1860. It invested mainly in Vermont real estate mortgages;

otherwise in bank and railroad securities, acceptance loans, notes, and from 1860, federal and Vermont bonds.

Village trade and services, which supplied much of the local capital for the new enterprises of the fifties, continued to flow in the same arteries, but circulation in the hills was sluggish. The characteristic country store sold or bartered a little of everything. For example, G. W. McGaffey of Sutton advertised in the 2 January 1858 *Danville North Star* "all kinds of Produce taken in exchange," especially potatoes for the nearby starch factories, while C. C. Brown of Cabot in the same issue sold hardware, hollow ware (cast-iron stoves and pots), ready-made clothing and groceries and "Wanted in exchange: Old Iron & Rags, Copper, Pewter, Brass, Wool, Pelts, Furs, and most kinds of barter." Even in the northern hills store-bought clothes were replacing homespun. Vermont households, which had made an aggregate of goods worth over six dollars per capita in 1810, made only twenty cents per capita in 1860.

Itinerant photographers continued to rent upstairs rooms and stay in town as long as they could sell pictures. Sometimes, where the legislature, a college or academy, or the size of the village promised steady business, this meant a residence of several years. F. Mowry maintained his Rutland business over six years, and moved into "new 3-story Daguerrean Rooms" in 1859.[5] A. F. Styles was "permanently located" in St. Albans, Burlington, and Montpelier studios in 1860, with skylight parlors and stereoscopic equipment.

What you could get at a drugstore gives you a glimpse of social customs and costumes. W. A. Bacon, "the celebrated Hair Oil general," ("16,000 bottles sold in 7 months") who moved to Rutland from Ludlow in 1857, also made and sold cooking extracts, inks, blacking, shaving and toilet soap and handkerchief perfumes. He dealt in books, stationery, toys and candy, and briefly published a gossip sheet. Pond & Morse, with one store up the hill on Main Street, Rutland, and the other near the depot in the Bardwell House basement, offered in 1855 "Chemicals, Surgical Instruments, Trusses, Physicians' Glass Ware, Abdominal Supporters, Lace Stockings, Shoulder Braces, Pessaries &c. Fancy Articles, Perfumery, Fine Cutlery, Musical Instruments." On the side they made Carhart patent melodeons in Poultney. They advertised the usual painkillers, including Burnett's cocaine, and in 1859 installed "a great curiosity . . . a Soda Fountain. . . . all kinds of

---

[5] *Rutland Herald*, 5 March 1853, 5 September 1856, 12 August 1859. St. Johnsbury's Gage, "the Old Dagereen," advertised stereo views in the *Brattleboro Eagle*, 10 February 1854.

Syrups and Soda water from the same 'nozzel'."[6] Store hours contracted: Burlington barbers and hairdressers agreed in 1856 not to open on Sunday; Rutland retailers decided on an eight o'clock closing in 1860.

Perhaps prohibition, enacted in 1852 and confirmed by a slim margin in an 1853 referendum, was partly responsible for the innovation. The tavern bar had been supplanted by the town liquor agency (sole dispenser of alcoholic beverages for mechanical, medicinal, and chemical uses only), the drugstores (dispensers of the same with patent medicine labels), the groceries (dispensers of "Maine Law beer"), the physicians (illegally except through the agent), and the surreptitious sellers of "rot-gut" including the taverns. Maine Law beer worked cures in Brattleboro. When served in a Middlebury restaurant, witnesses testified that it "looked, smelled, and tasted like strong Beer of the old rat soup kind," but swore it could not intoxicate. Fowle's Oxygenated Bitters, discovered by Dr. G. B. Green of Windsor, had testimonials of other Vermont doctors. Wolfe's Schiedam Aromatic Schnapps, "entirely free from the pernicious fusil oil" in grain liquors, claimed to correct the bad effects of swamp and limestone waters. These and other liquors were sold in "dry" Vermont, in villages big enough to have segregated neighborhoods where church temperance people did not often snoop. Even temperance men admitted that liquor consumption increased, especially among the young; that although many refused to deal in it, others made enormous profits from selling adulterated stuff concocted in New York cellars.

If the perspective shifts from changing opportunities in village stores, taverns, banks, and insurance companies to social problems somehow associated with these changes, the liquor problem was central in people's minds. The time-honored way to deal with the evils of alcohol was to preach at the rummies and their suppliers. Since the period of settlement, when Vermonters along with other Americans had been heavy drinkers, moral suasion and social pressure had gradually removed the preachers' drams, deprived harvesters and barn raisers of their rum, and closed stills. Doctors, with ether only gradually accepted as an anesthetic from the early 1850s, still used whiskey to dull pain.[7]

---

[6]Atwater's *Directory* (1855), 116; *Rutland Herald*, 20 February 1856, 11 March, 20 May 1859.

[7]The *Montpelier Watchman* (17 October 1856) reported chloroform used in an arm amputation by Dr. Alexander of Danville. Dentist Nathaniel Harris recorded in a Sheldon Museum manuscript dated 22 January 1858 his bad experience using local benumbing agents. In 1853, he wrote, "I bought the right to use Ether . . . from Doctor [William Thomas Green] Morton of Boston for Addison County." After he tested it, he let physicians use it. See my column in "Sheldon Museum Notes," *Middlebury Addison County Independent*, 24 October 1988.

In the 1840s a new anti-alcohol method gained favor, to use the local or state governmental power against those who had not been persuaded to abandon strong drink. In a period when enterprise free from government interference was an article of faith in Britain and America, a new reason for government interference with individual lives was added to the old ones favoring tariffs, bounties, and other benefits of state aid. The licensing law of 1846 required that each town vote annually whether to allow licenses to sell wine, beer, and spirits. Unless a majority *statewide* voted to license for general sale, county court judges could grant licenses for medicinal, chemical, and mechanical purposes only. "No license" won every year, and by a better than sixty percent majority except in 1848. These steady victories encouraged temperance people to campaign for state prohibition. Maine had adopted it in 1851; Vermont followed with a narrow legislative victory in 1852, spearheaded by the Sons of Temperance in Castleton, Rutland, Middlebury, Montpelier, and Woodstock. They circulated twenty thousand copies of the Maine law, won the approval of the Congregational state convention and the other evangelical denominations, collected over thirty thousand signatures to petitions, and imported out-of-state speakers. The act required a referendum the following winter, which the prohibitionists won by a 1,171 majority in a light vote, thanks to the votes of the large towns. The proponents explained that places like Rutland and Burlington knew the evils of intemperance. Some opponents charged that employers influenced their workmen to vote dry or stay home (the ballot was not secret); the industrial districts generally voted dry. The next year nearly everyone working for the U.S. Pottery Company of Bennington, according to the *Bellows Falls Argus* of 29 December 1853, signed the pledge. The company fined or discharged all who violated their pledges.

The reformers asserted that intemperance was the principal cause of poverty and crime, especially among foreign-born Roman Catholics. Catholic Bishop de Goesbriand himself preached against intemperance, and an Irish temperance society was formed. Yankees could displace their aggressions on some seventeen thousand Irish-born immigrants and five or six thousand more French-speaking Canadians. In 1860 over three out of five of these immigrants were in the Champlain Valley, although the Irish, when the railroad needed them no longer, were left stranded along the way, free to walk on until they found work. Burlington had eleven hundred Irish-born in 1850 and almost as many born in Canada—French, Irish, and a minority of Protestant British background. A 1907 classifier of the Montpelier census according to ethnic origin added the first two generations in America to the foreign-born. By that system eighteen percent of Montpelier village was of Irish or French Canadian origin in 1850 and twenty-four percent in 1860, a significant minority.

The presence of immigrants signified jobs, cutting the woods in the still-growing northeastern counties, at common labor in the commercial-industrial centers. Smaller numbers were skilled, along with a handful of professionals. In 1850 there seemed to be an excessive proportion of foreigners on relief. Burlington tended 973 foreigners, a number three-fifths of the total population. In the summer of 1849 a cholera epidemic peaked; Burlington, a port of entry for immigrants and cholera, had a dozen cases and built a pest house to isolate them, but the plague strained the relief budget.

Poverty was an ancient problem, sometimes solved by warning itinerants for whom the town did not feel responsible to move on, or by auctioning the poor to the lowest bidders. The poorhouse or poor farm was a relatively new solution based on new assumptions: that supervised work by the able-bodied poor could cut the cost of poor relief; that collective operation of a boardinghouse and farm is cheaper than scattering paupers among individual families; that minimum maintenance is incentive to stay out of or get out of the poorhouse. While some assumed that poverty was the pauper's fault, others were merciful regardless of the faults of the poor.

Reports emphasized both economies and comforts. At Brattleboro the 160-acre poor farm provided meat, dairy products, grain, fruit, and vegetables. Eight Franklin County towns economized by sharing a poor farm in Sheldon. Burlington spent $4,500 in 1859 for a new poorhouse, complete with two water closets for the old and infirm.

The poor farm was a general purpose asylum for those lacking care on the outside. Poor farms were dumps for perhaps three-quarters of the eleven hundred deaf, dumb, blind, aged, mentally ill, and mentally defective in 1850. A handful of deaf and dumb went to an asylum at Hartford, Connecticut; a few blind went to the Perkins Institute near Boston. The rest were either tended by family or friends at home or in poorhouses. The idea of asylum in America was not yet half a century old. On the positive side, it was intended to isolate "problems" so that they could be dealt with. On the negative, it was "out of sight, out of mind."

The Brattleboro Asylum for the Insane, opened in 1837, was a partial exception to this record of frustration and indifference. In 1861 Dr. W. H. Rockwell, superintendent since the beginning, reported that at last, with a hundred new rooms, something more than mere custody would be possible. The state contributed only a few thousand dollars. The towns sent a third of the inmates, yet paid less than half their cost. Families of patients wanted relief from their onerous responsibilities. As public awareness of the asylum increased, overcrowding was chronic. Under these conditions, little therapy occurred. As an economic enterprise, however, the asylum's annual reports show a staff of fifty running a bigger business than any machine shop, organ factory, or water cure in Brattleboro.

Brattleboro Asylum for the Insane Operations

	1850	1855	1861
Patients	328	394	438
State beneficiaries	143	143	138
Wages	$7,000	$10,500	$14,000
Supplies, provisions	$22,000	$28,000	$31,000
Repairs	$2,000	$6,500	$10,000
Furniture, bedding & clothes	$3,000	$6,000	$7,000
Total expenses	$34,000	$51,000	$62,000

Several other hospitals or infirmaries started before the Civil War but had comparatively few patients. A Burlington U.S. Marine Hospital, completed in 1858 for thirty-nine thousand dollars through the influence of David A. Smalley, Democratic Party leader, stood unoccupied until 1863, when it received Union soldiers. Talk of its recycling as a reform school ended when war broke out.

Vermont doctors practiced in almost every town, but their leaders congregated in the villages. Village physicians, including the few specialists, reactivated the Vermont Medical Society in 1841 and affiliated with the American Medical Association organized in 1847. While the country medical colleges at Woodstock and Castleton closed, the old Medical Department of the University of Vermont reopened in 1853 and granted a hundred degrees before 1861. Also in 1853 Montpelier and Burlington physicians petitioned successfully to improve the supply of cadavers and legalize their dissection, pointing out the need to achieve competence by the practical study of anatomy. From 1851 until they finally succeeded in 1856, doctors lobbied for a registration law recording vital statistics. Some have suggested that the 1846 law penalizing the performance of abortions was part of organized medicine's campaign to monopolize practice by excluding the "unorthodox" and the midwives.[8]

The prestige of the orthodox was not yet high enough to ward off the "quacks" and medical entertainers. Lecturers to "gents and ladies" privately and separately on the physiology of sex,

---

[8]See James C. Mohr, *Abortion in America* (New York: Oxford University Press, 1978).

"electric" doctors, Thomsonian apostles of steam baths and the sweat-producing lobelia, all promised "a rich feast of amusements, with valuable instruction."[9] The heretical medics flourished partly because they cured. In a state where over a third of the fatal diseases were respiratory, the regimen of walks, fresh air, baths, massages, and sensible clothing allowed the body to cure itself. The homeopaths, whose theory called for small doses, made the greatest gains during this period, forming their own medical society in 1855. Dentists, almost without exception working in the leading villages and periodically visiting patients about their counties, organized the year before.

People buried their dead in cemeteries, in the churchyard while it was important to be buried in hallowed ground. Over a dozen proprietary graveyard associations chartered in the nine years before 1861 chose scenic sites showing more thought for the view of a rural landscape than for religious connections. The slate and marble stones, with a bit of granite beginning to compete, no longer taught the mourner in sepulchral rhyme and weeping willow images the vanity of life. Terse names and dates, with size of stone proving family prominence in this world, marked the shrines. In 1849 the legislature voted five hundred dollars for a stone to be incorporated in the monument to George Washington in the District of Columbia, with a three-hundred-dollar supplement in 1851. In 1853 it chartered the Bennington Battle Monument Association; in 1856 the Hubbardton Battle Monument Association. People began hunting for Ethan Allen's grave, originally marked with a board, long gone, and the tide of opinion rose for a prouder granite pile and statue larger than life for the state's revolutionary hero. The Norwich University cadets had made pilgrimages to revolutionary shrines long before they were marked. Despite legislative injunctions in the charters that cemeteries be used for burials only, new ones were planned and served as parks.

Village improvement was an ambivalent nostalgia for the rural past and determination to tidy up for the urban future. Pollution had been tolerated when quantities were small and space was abundant. With congestion, eyes and noses were offended by rubbish, offal, and manure in the streets and back alleys. Wastes were buried, burned, thrown into a river or pond like the one in Burlington's ravine off Court House Square. Burlington and Rutland needed sewer systems, but the only action was a "pipe" dream: the Burlington Steam Draining Company, incorporated in 1859 by future Governor Frederick Holbrook, DeWitt Clinton Clarke, editor of the *Burlington Times*, and others, for "removing . . . night soil . . . deodorizing . . . and converting . . . into a dry and powdered

---

[9]See, for example, *Rutland Herald*, 27 August 1856. The advertisements do not explain what the electric treatment was—perhaps a mild shock.

condition, or disposing of it in its crude state, for purposes of fertilization."[10] Improvers remarked that the best sidewalk led to the cemetery. They wanted shaded walks upon which they would not wade or stumble. The tree was the pioneer's enemy but the villager's friend. The "May Day Movement" fostered by improvement associations in the late 1850s planted trees in public places and decorated parks with memorial sculptures and fountains. Students of the University of Vermont had pioneered in 1836 by fencing, grading, and planting elms and grass in its college park.

As with poverty and some illnesses, crime received the isolation treatment in county jails or the state prison at Windsor. The cities sometimes spilled their felons into the hill country. Bristol Bill, British burglar sentenced for transport to Botany Bay, in Australia, escaped and joined a band of swindlers in New York. Convicted of counterfeiting in Groton, Vermont, he assaulted the state's attorney and went to Windsor for ten years. Brothels, found only in centers and subject to sporadic raids, occasionally lost their working women to state prison. Five, including Emeline L. Ball, "the New Hampshire Racer," were convicted from Rutland in 1858. Rural society had not depended primarily on jail to discipline criminals, but villages began to want more than the constable, the posse, and the town crier to control their crowds and night wanderers. Only a small fraction of their charters or amendments in the 1850s referred to law enforcement (Burlington, Manchester, St. Johnsbury, St. Albans). Bennington had a squad of seven policemen in 1858, with major attention to vagrants.

Street lighting, the silent policeman, was nowhere installed, but a dozen towns incorporated gas companies and Burlington's was in operation by 1854, reporting to the next census a production of 240,000 cubic feet worth $9,000 with a $77,000 plant. Works in Montpelier, Rutland, Brattleboro, Woodstock, and Windsor followed. The 1855 law providing $2,500 to provide the statehouse legislative chambers with gas provoked the opposition to remark that lighting a match in the assembly room would do the trick. Industrial and domestic gas lighting increased fire hazards, but villagers looked on the bright side: they were modern improvements.

Block fires first taught village leaders the evils of congestion. The worst were in Windsor (1848, "half" the business section), Brattleboro (1852, $80,000 damage, and 1857, over $200,000 damage), and Bellows Falls (1860, "half" the business section). When village buildings had enough space around them, bucket brigades might quench the blaze, but business blocks, even when ordinances required masonry construction, could be saved only with better equipment, tighter

---

[10]*Vermont Laws* (1859), 113.

organization for rapid action, and a dependable water supply. Hardly a year went by without the enactment of fire prevention laws defining fire districts, concentrating authority in fire engineers to own fire stations and buy fire engines. Already exempt from poll taxes and militia duty, volunteer firemen were further exempted from jury duty and all but highway taxes. Some companies disbanded and, still supported by private gifts, served in municipal fire departments.

Usually after a holocaust the old water tubs on carriages were replaced by better equipment, sometimes steam fire engines costing upwards of eight hundred dollars and weighing a ton. Horses still drew the engines, but instead of depending on the brawn of two score young men pumping furiously, steam now powered the stream that the crew aimed at the flames. Rutland's 1857 engine house was built opposite Merchants' Row a few months after a bad fire there. Burlington's new Ethan Allen Company No. 4 bought the first steamer for a thousand dollars in 1858, causing the rival Boxer Engine Company No. 3 to buy a bigger one, which took prizes all over the state for the heights or lengths it could throw water. Rivals were sometimes more interested in winning than in extinguishing the fire, for a fire provided the most exciting show in town, with the colorful carriages, the clanging bells, the shouts, the crowds from miles around helping or getting in the way, the chances for loot in the confusion. After the fire was out, the companies socialized at their annual banquets, balls, oyster suppers. They paraded in bright uniforms and enjoyed their junkets to state contests rivaling state fairs for crowds, drunks, runaway horses, cornet bands, lemonade, and evening fireworks. Fire losses, however, continued to be stupendous, because of inadequate water supply. Some village patrons gave up their hydrants in disgust and went back to equally unreliable cisterns.

People more and more recognized fire, water supply, crime, sickness, and even poverty to some extent, as problems that human effort, rightly ordered, could solve. But there was no labor "problem," because most people thought conditions of labor were fixed beyond human control. The best way to improve labor conditions, opined the *Montpelier Watchman*, 14 April 1853, was to diversify the economy with manufacturing. The press and the Whigs were sure that strikes were wasteful, useless, and unrighteous. The vote safeguarded labor's right to fair pay, according to Charles T. Russell's 1855 oration at the Brattleboro state fair. Labor could regulate corporations by its representatives in the legislature.[11] Servants, mechanics, common laborers, the Irish let go after the railroads were built had an employment problem, but they solved it by going elsewhere and

---

[11]Charles T. Russell, *The Enfranchisement of Labor: an Address Delivered Before the Vermont State Agricultural Society, at Brattleboro, Vt., Sept. 14th, 1854* (Middlebury: Register Book and Job Office, 1855).

finding another job. A strike was so rare it was worthy of note. Newspapers reported only the Bolton War of 1846 and the 1859 marble strike in West Rutland.[12] The *Rutland Herald* of 9 March 1855 noted more as a joke than a news item that the washerwomen of Brattleboro had struck for seventy-five cents per dozen pieces. "Go it, suds!" it cheered.

In fact, the cheerful attitude was not just newspaper boosterism, but permeated village society. After a fire, business rebuilt. If something broke, there was money to fix it. If an institution failed, there were others to take its place. People were willing to try new ways, for the village itself was a new way to prosperity, the growing edge of a society whose losses were underneath or elsewhere.

---

[12] See above, pp. 35-36, 62-64.

6. Urban Culture: Arts, Schools, Churches, Families

The turbulence of new village life was like the common weather pattern of a movement of warm air pushing over cold air and precipitating a storm. The turbulence was complicated, because urban-industrial ways collided with the old ways of near subsistence settlement, layered over a powerful heritage harking back through peasant clusters and Christian communities to old pagan stones that cannot be deciphered. The new ways also conflicted with the commercial patterns developed earlier in places like Woodstock. The village elite, moving between the seaports and their hometowns, made or imported the symbols and staffed the leadership positions. Ordinary people accepted, practiced, used, and sometimes venerated the new symbols and changed institutions.

The churches, the schools, and the arts were all affected. Let the story of music in mid-century Vermont ring the changes on the diversity of effects.[1] Village audiences came to hear secular as well as church music. Traveling musical companies competed with other kinds of shows. For two bits (children and sometimes ladies admitted at half price, the press free) barnstorming companies out of New York and Boston offered panoramas and dioramas of the Crimean War or the Holy Land, readings, comic dialogues, ventriloquists, magicians, gymnasts, contortionists, glassblowers, Wild Men of Borneo, Siamese twins, bell ringers, and concerts. Because audiences came for the novel and comical, the musical portion was secondary.

Minstrel shows and popular singers planned to reach the farmers when their work was light, from fall until the weather and the state of the roads interdicted getting to the town hall. An agent distributed posters and handbills in advance and arranged with the local weekly to give the performers a boost in return for advertising. People liked "cork opera" best, by white actors who blackened their faces with burnt cork and caricatured blacks in their song and dance. Pell and Mulligan's "Original Metropolitan Opera Troupe" would perform, according to the *Rutland Herald* of 30 December 1853, "burlesques, queer sayings, fancy dances, jigs, reels . . . Life in old Virginny."

---

[1]Discussion of village exposure to music derives from my article, "Minstrels, Musicians and Melodeons: A Study in the Social History of Music in Vermont, 1848-1872," *New England Quarterly* 19 (March 1946), 32-49.

"The Bards of Ossian" led by Ossian E. Dodge, a quartet consisting of an alto and three men, were likened to Samson because they brought down the house. Dodge sold subscriptions to the Boston *Literary Museum* and sometimes passed out a sheet of music to every female attending, to dress the house. The eccentric Norwegian virtuoso violinist Ole Bull came to Vermont, but Swedish Jenny Lind's American sojourn of 1850-52 passed it by. Most popular of vocalists were the singing Hutchinsons, well-known in Vermont by 1847, and frequently returning to antislavery conventions and other reform gatherings. Cultured Boston looked down on them. "Music in Boston is at its lowest ebb, until the music-loving population flows back from the mountains and the sea-shores," wrote John Sullivan Dwight.[2] "The 'Hutchinson Family' are singing to their crowds in the new Tremont Temple."

Highbrow artists, whose winter concert season was in the cities, arrived at villages along the railroads between May Day and September, when the fashionable were at spas and hotels. Colleges set standards by hiring the best chamber groups out of Boston, such as the Germania Band and the Mendelssohn Quintette Club, to perform contemporary works (Donizetti, Flotow, Verdi) as well as baroque music at their commencements.

With encouragement, one of their members would stay behind in a town as a musical jack-of-all-trades, providing leadership for local amateurs. J. B. Holmberg, advertised as "one of the best Clarinettists in the world," came from Sweden with Jenny Lind in 1850, played in Middlebury quadrille and cornet bands, and later scraped up a living as a violinist, music dealer with H. L. Storey in Burlington, private teacher, and instructor of cornet bands. Housewives still hummed the old folk tunes, but they wanted their daughters to be able to get through a modern piece or two on the piano and aspire to play for hymn singing. Musicians opened doors to urban gentility, yet were as suspect as the teachers of French and dancing. Russell B. Walker, after a few weeks in Rutland, published his card in the 15 July 1853 *Herald*: "Particular attention paid to the improvement of manners, stoops corrected, gaits improved, the polite accomplishments of the social circle, etiquette of the street and ballroom taught, making dancing as it should be, an innocent and instructive recreation."

The early career of George A. Mietzke shows how an unknown foreigner, like Theodore F. Molt in Burlington a generation before, could establish himself as a professional musician in Vermont. Born of a musical family and briefly affiliated with the Prussian Royal Academy of Music in Berlin, Mietzke emigrated about 1858 at twenty-three and served as director of music at Castleton

---

[2]In *Dwight's Musical Journal* 3 (17 September 1853), 191.

Seminary. This cultural missionary from a center of the musical world could no longer depend on the patronage of European nobility and government subsidies. To survive in America he had to promote popular appreciation of music.

His letter in the *Rutland Courier* of 13 January 1860 outlined his musical philosophy. God has given almost all people some talent, which needs to be developed early in the public schools, Sunday schools, and in church congregational singing, he began, speaking like a Lutheran used to congregational participation in the liturgy. The church quartet is not called to show how superior its singing is, but to teach the congregation. He was already an American in advocating low prices for mass purchase. Public schools were not yet free, but he wanted the fees low for music classes. He wanted singing societies in every town, giving cheap concerts. He wanted people to love singing so much that they did not envy rivals' successes. He wanted young ladies to learn to read new pieces, so that they would not be bored with the few numbers they had memorized to catch the right husbands. He wanted the family to gather around the piano and not just dust it as a decorative symbol of class.

Once secure in Castleton Mietzke soloed on the violin at concerts of Mendelssohn Quintette members in Castleton and Rutland. "Alpha" in the 5 September 1858 *Rutland Herald* reported that Castleton "still . . . prefers sharpers and negro melodies to honesty, talent, and the music of Beethoven." He collected references and started teaching in Rutland at fifty cents a lesson. He helped found a Rutland Academy of Music, which performed a sacred concert in Castleton, Mietzke at the piano. After his first seminary term he toured the county during the February holidays, played for a 148-couple dinner dance at Barnes's Hotel, West Rutland, and helped prepare the Seminary chorus to sing parts of Haydn's *Creation*. He or his pupils sometimes played his own compositions. His marriage on 15 December 1859 to Nancy Mead of West Rutland in the Congregational church signaled his decision to settle in the area. Nancy taught and sang with him for several years. At the outbreak of the Civil War the Mietzkes moved to the North Granville, New York, Ladies' Seminary, where he continued to compose patriotic pieces, marches, dances, and songs, printed in Rutland, and sold by E. N. Merriam, book dealer and show agent.

Most Vermont academies and female seminaries had a married couple like the Mietzkes teaching voice, piano, and "thorough bass." Claude H. Clarke, principal of the St. Johnsbury Academy of Music, with experience in Boston and New York bands and orchestras, directed *The Flower Queen* in Montpelier in 1861 and stimulated music in the Fairbanks scale town for three years until he joined the First Vermont Cavalry in 1862.

Mietzke also competed with out-of-state organizers of musical conventions (now called festivals), gathering music lovers from a region to sing an oratorio or cantata and listen to a lecture on authentic voice production. Lowell Mason, Boston professional, came as early as 1840. His son recalled with embarrassment Vermont's "crudity of musical taste" when fife and drum, "the instrumental outfit of the town," escorted his father to the church. Actually, well before 1840 Vermonters were playing the usual basic strings, woodwinds, and brass. John W. Moore's *World of Music*, published with sheet music in connection with Moore's *Bellows Falls Gazette*, struggled along in Bellows Falls and Chester from 1840 to 1847 while Moore promoted Windham County conventions. Benjamin Franklin Baker, principal of the Boston Music School, sang the part of Goliath in the "Oratorio of David" at a Walpole, New Hampshire, interstate convention in 1853 and returned every few years from 1850 to 1865. George F. Root, New York composer and director of musical conventions all over the United States in the 1850s, directed his cantata, *The Flower Queen*, at Rutland in 1856, and the next year helped organize the Western Vermont Musical Association, which survived for eighteen years.[3] These city professionals, along with Isaac B. Woodbury and W. B. Bradbury of New York, composed the most popular church pieces and sold their own glee books and anthem collections at the meetings, with plenty of fresh tunes in each edition to keep up interest.

Reaching farthest down into popular culture were the cornet and quadrille (square dance) bands of the fifties. Brass bands had long played for June militia musters. With the revival of military training about 1855, back came the bands (at least thirty by 1860) to assist the musters and parades of the new companies, while the dance bands had new business at their soirees and balls. Rutland citizens subscribed for two band stands in the parks near the hotels, where a piazza audience could enjoy the concerts at a safe distance. In the winter, bands accompanied sleigh rides for an oyster supper in a neighboring town. The Burlington Cornet Band throughout the 1850s furnished music for lake excursions, gave concerts in the town hall and in the parks, and played for college commencement. Incorporated in 1858, it bought ten instruments for nearly a thousand dollars, and the next year played at Hubbardton for the anniversary of the Revolutionary battle there. Bandstands began to dot village greens and were a necessary feature near each fairground

---

[3] Its manuscript records, 1857-74, are in the Sheldon Museum, Middlebury. See also William Mason, *Memories of a Musical Life* (1901; New York: Da Capo Press, 1970), 25; Seth Shaler Arnold, "Diaries," for references, *passim*, to Moore and Windham County conventions; and numerous newspaper notices. A Connecticut River Valley Choral Society was incorporated in 1861; Vermont river town histories do not mention it.

race track. Bands met sometimes overpowering competition from the "steam organ," also called "mechanical band" or "automatodeon," which had appeared with circuses by 1850. In 1856 one was advertised at the Burlington state fair, said to play "Hail Columbia" loud enough to be heard ten miles away. Technological unemployment was already threatening the music trades.

Vermont's musical history in this period was part of the process of urbanization, an outgrowth of railroad development. The villages that prospered because of rail connections had the cash, the halls, and the potential audiences. Traveling musicians could reach them more cheaply and quickly than before. Railroads and steamers brought a trickle of immigrants: the singing Welsh in the slate region, the tune-loving Irish and French Canadians, and a few isolated Scandinavians and Germans. Equally important was the European influence on metropolitan culture, indirectly affecting Vermont. The German band, the German string ensemble, the foreign soloist, the native who had studied in Europe reinforced the instruction of local teachers.

Better transportation multiplied musical activity at home while increasing stimuli from abroad. More conventions benefiting from excursion rates expanded the market for all kinds of music, attracting first-class leaders. Performers entertained and stirred the sentiments, whether for religion, reform, militia training, or politics. A national popular musical vernacular was beginning to overshadow rural folk music.

The same refrain with different verses could be sung about architecture, sculpture, painting, and literature. In a turbulent period, machine-made wooden and cast-iron facades and decorations were both cheaper and richer in variety than the red and white purity of the artisan-crafted, homogeneous domestic architecture of the previous half-century. Successful businessmen preferred Italian villas, English parish churches, and experimental mixtures of shapes and colors.

In sculpture, Woodstock-born Hiram Powers moved to Cincinnati because there was no home market for his carving skills. He was clever at fixing things whether in iron, wax, or marble and invented sculpturing tools. Vermonters crowded to see one of the six copies of his "Greek Slave," a social phenomenon because it was a publicly exhibited nude and appealed to Greek revival and antislavery sentiments. But Vermont gave Powers no contracts for Revolutionary memorials, and Larkin G. Mead, Jr., thirty years younger, carved the statues of Ethan Allen in Washington's statuary hall and at the Montpelier capitol. Mead, also an expatriate, born of a leading Brattleboro family in touch with cultured summer visitors, was encouraged by Henry Kirke Brown, a water cure patron, studied under him in Brooklyn, and taught drawing at home until the Civil War.[4] Maidens in seminaries learned how to draw and watercolor landscapes and fashion dried flower wreaths and hair pieces, but no rich patron ordered murals, and most memorial statues were by out-of-state artists.

Probably a greater dependence on urban literature than on urban music and art could be shown, for libraries, small and private though most of them were, not only expanded but stocked contemporary writers. Vermont rhymesters poured forth their effusions in the press, but only the popular poets Charles G. Eastman and John Godfrey Saxe produced good light verse. Saxe's *Poems* (1850) had forty "editions" (most of them printings), and his wit was in constant demand around the northern lecture circuit.

The urban emphasis on verbalism—on skill in the use of words, especially words in print—as necessary to get ahead in this world was basic for school reformers. They started three short-lived school journals to pump their propaganda and showered letters on the sympathetic editors of the village press.[5] The rural districts continued cold to school reform, but John Sullivan Adams of Burlington, First Secretary of the State Board of Education (1857-68), could be pleased that villages made the most improvement. "Some of the best school houses are located in a few of the largest and wealthiest towns, as in Woodstock, St. Johnsbury, Windsor, Rutland and Bellows Falls," he reported after his first year, while picking out Burlington as having one of the worst. Important villages had inferior schools because of their rapid growth and overcrowding, or because Roman Catholic laborers were unwilling to tax themselves double, for town and parochial schools.[6]

Gross statistics seemed to show improvement throughout the state. Male teachers' wages rose fifty percent in the fifteen years after the school law of 1845 and females' pay doubled as more women were hired until they were doing three-quarters of the teaching at half the pay rates of the

---

[4]Mary R. Cabot, comp., *Annals of Brattleboro, 1681-1895* (Brattleboro: E. L. Hildreth, 1922, 2 vols.), 718-722; *Brattleboro Eagle*, 24 February 1854; A. M. Hemenway, *Gazetteer*, 5:152-153. About the Brattleboro water cures, see pp. 71-72 above.

[5]*The School Journal and Agriculturist* (Windsor,, 1847-49), published monthly by the editors of the Congregationalist *Vermont Chronicle*; *The Teachers' Voice and Vermont Monthly Magazine* (Burlington and St. Albans, 1853-55), edited by Zebina K. Pangborn and "Published with the sanction of the Vermont Teachers' Association"; *The Vermont School Journal and Family Visitor* (Montpelier and West Brattleboro, 1859-66), monthly "published by a Committee appointed by the Vermont State Teachers' Association."

[6]*First Annual Report* of the Secretary of the Vermont Board of Education (Ludlow: Rufus S. Warner, 1857), 20-21.

men. Still, teachers kept leaving the state, especially for Massachusetts where wages were twice as high. The poorly paid schoolma'ams left teaching for marriage or better-paying jobs as domestics, seamstresses, or dairymaids. Villages gave teachers more independence by not boarding them around and providing a salary that more than made up for the free board and room of the district school teacher. Villages attracted the pick of academy graduates and college students earning their way toward their professions. Villages more often kept the few long-term teachers who continued from personal or service motives. Villages more often had the fenced playgrounds, blackboards, dictionaries, globes, maps, clocks, and thermometers the reformers called for.

With more scholars per district, the villages initiated graded elementary schools and substituted tax-supported union high schools for academies. Brattleboro swept out its academy and district schools in 1842, followed by Windsor, Woodstock, Burlington,[7] and Vergennes by 1850 and six more towns by 1861. Support for the sixty-nine academies in 1859 came from the denominations or from endowments or because principals, like Hiram Orcutt, could attract enough boarding students.

Orcutt's career combined support for public education with successful private school administration at Hebron (New Hampshire) Academy, 1842-43, Thetford Academy, 1843-55, North Granville (New York) Ladies Seminary, 1855-60, Glenwood Seminary, West Brattleboro, 1860-66, then Tilden Seminary, West Lebanon (New Hampshire). He helped organize the Vermont Teachers' Association in 1851 and became editor and proprietor of its *Vermont School Journal* in 1861. He collaborated in editing a reader that sold seventy-five thousand copies. His two editions of *Gleanings from School-Life Experience: or Hints to Common School Teachers* (Rutland: G. A. Tuttle, 1858, 1859), full of moderately conservative common sense and non-sectarian Protestantism, was written for his teacher training classes.

The Episcopalians had failed to sustain Bishop Hopkins' school in the 1830s, but the undaunted bishop tried again before he had even paid off its $13,000 debt. For five years after 1854 he begged throughout his diocese and in eastern cities, raising about $30,000 in paid-in pledges, with some $5,000 more out of his own $1,200 salary and outside earnings. He added a little here and there from lecturing widely, substituting for Bishop Alonzo Potter of Philadelphia, and surveying the campus and lands of the University of the South (Sewanee). In 1860 he dedicated the Gothic

---

[7]The Burlington academy founded in 1829 was called "Burlington High School" but received no town support until the late 1840s.

building of the Vermont Episcopal Institute at Rock Point, Burlington, whose architecture he had inspired if not designed, and straightway started another drive for a girls' school.

Pluralism in secondary and college education expanded, with the weight of attention and activity on providing moral, nonsectarian programs. President Benjamin Labaree stabilized Middlebury College by downplaying the evangelical and Congregational hallmarks of its first thirty-five years, raising money, and attracting a young faculty, strong in science. Middlebury managed the appointment of its Professor of Geology, Charles Baker Adams, as first state geologist and saw the benefits of releasing the Rev. James Meacham, Professor of Rhetoric and English Literature, to serve in Congress, 1849-56. Perhaps such evidence of public service would challenge Burlington's priority as Vermont's university. Middlebury's graduating class rose to twenty in 1860, the highest since 1840, but hovered around ten for the rest of the century. The village could not grow as a college town with those small numbers. The University of Vermont prospered up to its semicentennial celebration in 1854, reopened its medical department, and added a separate library building, but was plagued with deficits and difficulties not overcome until the 1870s. Norwich University also ran, benefiting from its military specialty when war was expected or at hand, but Dartmouth across the Connecticut River usually had more students from Vermont (thirty to forty) than any Vermont college. Norwich began thinking of moving away from its severest competition to central Vermont.

Bishop de Goesbriand could not afford to think about higher education, even church-related academies, when his poor flock, he wrote a Breton bishop 18 December 1853, was "famished for the Word of God and the Sacraments." When they had enough priests they needed their own buildings, to free them from dependence on non-Catholics. The Irish flood of the late forties had overwhelmed Burlington priest Jeremiah O'Callaghan and his cohorts. Beginning at an age when most men of his period expected to give up control, O'Callaghan had traveled far and wide, served St. Mary's parish in two Burlington buildings, bought and started a parochial school, and held the fort for twenty years. But his eccentricities and combativeness irritated Protestants predisposed toward nativism. When the priest-pamphleteer had attacked the local Protestant clergy, the *Burlington Free Press* retorted that it was "perfectly right for an itinerant foreign priest to take upon himself the whole subject of politics—to preach it in the church, proclaim it at the corners of the streets, and publish his opinions to the world! Such are the monstrosities of the times." But "this reverend Paddy," the Whig editor continued, "according to his own showing, has thrice been spewed from the church and his native country as a shatter-brained disorganizer. That such an individual should find our religion, our laws, our institutions, and the whole frame-work of society wrong, is certainly not wonderful; and that he should content himself with simply denouncing our business men as cut-throats, our clergy as impostors, and our statesmen and legislators, as bribed and venal orators, indicates a degree of modest charity" equalled only by the Democratic *Burlington Sentinel*'s giving him space.[8] O'Callaghan did not moderate his attack over the years. "We had lately a fortunate escape from a vile faction of idlers who made a desperate attempt to get our village incorporated," he proudly reported to the *Boston Pilot*,[9] "for the exaction of heavy loads of fresh taxes. But they were defeated by the honest portion of the natives, and our Irish Brigade." It was time to bring order into the immigrant chaos and improve public relations, the Catholic hierarchy thought.

In 1853 it established the new Diocese of Burlington and chose Louis de Goesbriand to run it. The new bishop, born in Brittany, served his American apprenticeship in Louisville, Kentucky, and Cleveland, Ohio. He spent his first year in Vermont surveying the diocese, found temporary help in two French priests and five Oblates of Mary Immaculate, and then recruited a new team of young Irish and French clergy in Europe the following winter. In 1849 there had been three resident priests and three transients. De Goesbriand assembled nine priests and a deacon for his first diocesan synod late in 1855, at the peak of the nativist Know Nothing Party's influence, and by the outbreak of the Civil War there were fourteen settled priests, mostly under thirty-five years old. The older clergy against whom antipathy had built up were swept out. Their young replacements could reach the lost sheep and strengthen their resistance. The majority were francophone (seven Bretons) and most of the Irish had studied in Paris. The first synod established sacramental standards and registers, the use of a common English edition of the catechism, annual inventories, and episcopal control of buildings and the movements of priests beyond their parishes. O'Callaghan would have been unhappy that parish money now had to be banked.

A vigorous building program expanded diocesan property in the decade from eight church structures in five counties with a capacity of 4,600, worth $43,000, to twenty-seven in ten counties,

---

[8]*Burlington Free Press*, 13 October 1837.

[9]Quoted in the *Burlington Free Press*, 2 May 1853.

capacity ten thousand, value $110,000.[10] Even then the total capacity was only half big enough to shelter the nominal Catholics in Vermont. Nine-tenths of the churches built and the priests resident were in large towns and industrial centers, where they had gotten along in rented paint shops, schoolhouses, railroad shanties, private homes, or abandoned Protestant churches. Rev. J. B. Daly had used "the old 'Ball Alley' on Main Street" in Rutland. The Rev. Zephyrin Druon, who came from France a few months after de Goesbriand, bought or constructed chapels and churches in ten towns, often acquiring prominent sites, as in Montpelier next to the statehouse. In the major villages, too, were the only parochial schools founded before the Civil War: Burlington (1854, staffed by Sisters of Providence from Montreal), Rutland and West Rutland (1855), St. Albans and Swanton (1857), and Highgate (1858). Burlington had the only convent, with thirteen Sisters of Providence and fifty-one orphans reported in the 1860 census. The bishop hoped to climax these gains with a cathedral, but on his return in the spring of 1861 from a second trip to France he postponed building on account of the Civil War.

De Goesbriand early faced the problem of getting French and Irish to live peaceably in one religious family. Quebecois had had French-speaking priests in Burlington off and on since 1835, and in 1850 Bishop John Bernard Fitzpatrick had approved the establishment of St. Joseph's, the first ethnic parish in New England, in the care of Fr. Joseph Quévillon, the first settled French Canadian priest in Vermont. French Canadians conducted their own church business through *marguilliers*, members of a prudential committee called a *fabrique*. Bishop de Goesbriand aimed to centralize the care of property. For a man not yet forty to be telling elders of the *fabrique* what to do produced tension. The Canadians erred, wrote the bishop in his diary, when they bought an old store in Lowell for a church. Another group decided to have a building in Enosburg, "perhaps because I said I thought a chapel had better be nearer East Berkshire." He found the Canadians "very poor *in every respect*."[11]

He came to appreciate their loyalty when he dealt with the O'Hears and Hannas of Highgate. Catholics had settled in Highgate since 1824, bought a lot in 1849, and finished the Church of St.

---

[10]The 1850 and 1860 census tables in Schedule VI show capacity of Protestant houses of worship far beyond the number of adherents. A partial list of December 1858 communions in eleven Roman Catholic churches, however, comes within three hundred of the capacity of those churches in 1860 (typescript copies of Bishop de Goesbriand's diary in the St. Michaels College Library and Special Collections of the Bailey/Howe Library, University of Vermont, 12-13).

[11]De Goesbriand *Diary*, 4 (13 March 1854), 19-20 (10-14 June 1862); see also 12 (11 February 1858).

Louis by 1856. Fr. MacGowan of St. Albans had financed the pews by subscription, but did the parishioners have any property right in them? Of the twenty-six pewholders, all but four turned them over to the bishop in December 1854, in return for three dollars each, but threats of excommunication could not budge the rest. So de Goesbriand ordered the four pews taken out of the church with crowbar and force. His enemies called the sheriff, who jailed him for trespass, but parishioner Menard put up his farm to bail him out. Illness postponed the trial to April 1859, when the bishop, defended by Benjamin H. Smalley, a St. Albans convert, before Congregationalist judge Asa O. Aldis, was found guilty and fined $10.83 damages and costs. Roman Catholic law, said the judge, "has no force in determining what the right of these parties are" except by agreement. The Vermont Supreme Court heard the bishop's appeal in January 1861 and affirmed the verdict. It granted that the bishop had title to both land and building, but was only "trustee" for pewholders, who had sole right of possession and use for public worship. The bishop then used his ultimate weapon: he immediately interdicted the Church of St. Louis. No services were held in it until Nicholas Hanna and Thomas O'Hear capitulated in July 1865. The damage from the bitter fight left a deep wound; the parish did not recover enough to support a resident father until 1886.[12]

Catholic competition stimulated Protestants to build more churches and add members in the growing villages, although unrelated internal migration, evangelism, and prosperity accounted for part of the growth. The Congregationalists paid the best ministerial salaries in the state and sustained costly building programs in St. Albans, Burlington, Brandon, Rutland, Bellows Falls, and Woodstock in the decade from 1851. The other denominations followed suit. A few hundred Welsh who struggled and built in the slate region were the only substantial group of Protestant immigrants to Vermont in this period.

The religious revival of 1858, started among New York City businessmen, added the principal new active members not brought in by migration or emulation. With frequent and protracted prayer meetings, this Yankee labor-saving device of praying by steam, as one newspaper quipped, used the age-old call, "Are you saved?" Like the earlier revivals, it minimized denominational differences. It differed in three respects: it was a reaction to the excesses of reformers; it was depression-related; its less boisterous style appealed to young village businessmen. In a sense it was an inchoate fear

---

[12]My account of the Roman Catholics in this and other periods is based on the unpublished diocesan history by David J. Blow and William Goss, archivists of the Diocese of Burlington, which they have kindly let me read. They have used Vatican and episcopal archives that are not easy of access. See also Ronald C. Murphy and Paul Jeffrey Potash, "The Highgate Affair: Episode in Establishing the Authority of the Roman Catholic Diocese of Burlington," *Vermont History* 52 (Winter 1984): 33-43.

of the rising tide of anger and intransigeance leading to the Civil War. Instead of working in harmony to build Christ's kingdom, wrote John Cain in his *Rutland Courier* of 20 November 1857, "the churches have been . . . divided and paralyzed by side issues. . . . The human mind . . . can entertain but one absorbing question at a time." "Business-Men's Prayer Meetings" gathered daily at the Congregational "chapel" on West Street, Rutland, in the spring of 1858, and like all the other services, they were non-denominational. Adventists led by Elder Miles Grant of Boston capitalized on the ferment, apart from the "evangelicals."

The revival's institutional products were Young Men's Christian Associations, which died out during the Civil War and revived after. The purpose of the Rutland YMCA was "to promote evangelical religion among all classes . . . of this town, and especially among its young men; feeling the great value of concentrated efforts."[13] The Rutland group behaved like a fraternal organization and a lyceum. When Daniel Russeguie died of lockjaw the *Rutland Courier* (12 November 1858) mentioned that he belonged to the "Y" and would have a large funeral. The young men also heard ministers lecture on such subjects as the mythology of the ancient druids. Similar organizations appeared in West Rutland, Brandon, and Norwich (with a "Young Ladies Christian Association"), "continuing instant in prayer," as St. Paul wrote, acting as missionaries and tract distributors to districts bereft of access to pastors, and generally taking themselves very seriously.

Practically no Vermonters took women's rights seriously, among the myriad reforms that cried for their attention. Therefore it is amazing that Clarina Nichols, divorcee, woman editor of a Democratic paper and public speaker (albeit on the more popular issues of temperance and antislavery), should be allowed to address a joint session of the General Assembly in 1852 on issues of women's rights.[14] Except in a majority of schoolrooms, men governed. Even in common schools men controlled the appointment of teachers and, through the system of boarding around, ruled the schoolma'ams by family and community pressures. Mrs. Nichols spoke for a bill to allow women to vote in school meetings, a victory not won until 1880.

Mrs. Nichols belonged to a leading West Townshend family, the Howards, who came during the Revolution from the Blackstone Valley between Worcester and Providence. This area of Baptist and Quaker strength reinforced the Puritan penchant for nonconformity in its emigrants. In spite

---

[13] *Rutland Herald*, 8 April 1858.

[14] I take Mrs. Nichols's story from my sketch in *Notable American Women, 1607-1950: A Biographical Dictionary* (Cambridge, Massachusetts: Harvard University Press, 1971), 2:625-627.

of having only one year of formal education beyond the common school, she ran an academy in upstate New York while raising three children in the 1830s. Toward 1840 she left her Baptist preacher husband and in 1843 married George W. Nichols, editor and publisher of the Brattleboro *Windham County Democrat*. She was its editor for ten years, championing reform for a thousand subscribers.

In 1847 she won the sponsorship of State Senator Larkin G. Mead, Brattleboro lawyer and banker, for a series of laws expanding property rights for women. Her friend Daniel Pierce Thompson, editor of the reformist *Green Mountain Freeman* of Montpelier, secured her privilege to speak and canvassed all day to fill the gallery with sympathetic ladies.

She started with stage fright, continued tremulous, but received a stamping ovation, with favorable press comment for her womanly mien. She always took pains to present a wifely image, knitting en route to her speaking engagements, which multiplied in the early 1850s throughout the Northeast until she took her family to Kansas to fight for freedom. She carefully separated her image from that of the wild radicals. She quoted the Bible effectively, favored popular reforms, and told stories of her experience and observation of oppressed women. Her story in a feminist journal of a pair of robins sharing both housework and breadwinning skillfully used irony and humor.

The Nichols family as recorded in the 1850 population census of Brattleboro was a normal Vermont household. There was George W., 65; Clarina, 40, Birsa C. Carpenter, 19, her daughter by her first marriage; George B. Nichols, 6, in school, their only child; a twenty-three-year-old printer; and two young women, one Irish-born, presumably helping around the house or at the printing shop.

Other mid-century households might have other siblings or cousins, perhaps a couple recently married who worked in the family business and could not yet afford separate housekeeping. The total swelled with children of paupers or struggling widows, or those boarding while attending school away from home; the schoolteacher; the itinerant seamstress or tailor staying until all the family clothing needs were met, or even a wandering miniaturist or portrait painter, like James Franklin Gilman after 1872, creating a farm-and-family image in return for his keep. Yet in 1850 the average size of household for the 3,816 in Brattleboro was only 5.8. All these people down to the age of ten or less worked and produced.

Samuel Dow's scattered children maintained family ties by correspondence. Mary wrote home 31 May 1852 from Lowell, Massachusetts, "there is a pretty fellow in the Mill that they train me . . . I dont think of anything mor to tell you about him but I will tell you i have got a new dress and bonnet and gloves." By July she wrote again, both sick and homesick. Her last letter of 27 February 1853 asked for money to come home. She had been out of the mill for a month, having spent all she had on board and doctor's bills. "The doctor says go home . . . because I have the quick consumption." James Dow wrote his father in Greensboro 16 January 1853 that he had moved to Londonderry, working at shoes, after being sick most of the time in Danvers, Massachusetts. "I peg twenty pair of women spring heels in a day and I get ten dollars a month for two month and then I shall have more if nothing splits."[15]

At the other extreme from the large, extended family in one dwelling, conforming to the main moral standards of the times as Clarina Nichols did, is the situation of Charles Paine and his mistress. A professor at Norwich University advised the Woodstock Democratic editor on tactics for the 1841 gubernatorial campaign: "You have touched once or twice upon one of Col. Paine's weak points (his licentiousness). . . . let it ring in the ears of every good old matron in the land; that he gives it as a reason why he does not get married, that he has an unlimited intercourse with their daughters . . . in his factory—that he already has several illegitimate children by them—& boasts of his conquests, at his midnight revels."

The untitled memoirs of the governor's nephew shed a different light:[16]

> He never married; he left a son and a daughter under other names, the children of Lorinda Stevens, who was always proud of having been his mistress. He built for her a comfortable brick house [in full view of the villagers at 41 South Main Street] in Northfield; she was *fine-drawer* in the factory for many years, a very beautiful woman but not of sufficient culture to be possible as his wife. . . . I talked with her about him after his death, and her *gratitude* towards the one who had really wronged her, separating her children from her, was very touching. . . . My uncle did everything for her and for her family which popular prejudice would permit; her brothers and other relatives were always in his employ.

Vermonters put up with Clarina Nichols because she only edged out of "woman's place" and with Miss L. A. Stevens because Paine had his way with the town as with her, but John Humphrey Noyes went too far. Like Paine the scion of a substantial family, educated at Dartmouth and under

---

[15]Dow Family Letters in St. Michaels College Library in 1941.

[16]Charles Paine (b. 1830), *Memoirs*, 8-9.

Nathaniel Taylor at Yale, with a sister married to Larkin G. Mead, Noyes had become a communist. In 1847, when his Putney neighbors learned that he was practicing "free love," he fled and founded the Oneida Community. Had he stayed he would have been tried for adultery (rarely brought to court except as ground for divorce), imprisoned, and his church run out of town anyway. In his Perfectionist publications he asserted that the Kingdom had come in his tiny commune. Complex marriage and stirpiculture (Noyes's name for eugenics combined with birth control) he avowed and defended as Bible-based and Christian. Vermont, however, would not tolerate this deliberate destruction of monogamy.[17]

Not that Vermonters were sexual saints. Records of church discipline show the normal sexual sins. An evangelical minister in 1867 claimed police records proved "over a hundred" brothels in Burlington, and the most liberal discounting of clerical enthusiasm still leaves the likelihood that the business flourished before the war, too. The premarital sex of the subsistence period, testing the fertility of the future farmer's wife where children were valuable labor, presumably continued in the backwoods. A *Rutland Herald* advertisement of 6 January 1854 announced a lecture "for ladies only" explaining the physiology of sex. The Rutland Free Convention of July 1858 discussed a resolution that a woman has a sacred right to determine "how often, and under what circumstances" she shall have children, with many voices in favor.[18] The *Rutland Courier* of 17 February 1860 advertised "a useful invention for married people," perhaps a condom, recently improved and cheapened as a result of the discoveries in processing East Indian rubber. How many wives' protracted visits to relatives or to a water cure were to delay unwanted pregnancies or escape marital rape, or to protest their husbands' infidelity when divorce was not respectable? Without public registration of divorce required until 1866, the 1867-70 ratio of one divorce per eighteen marriages was apparently the result of a gradual trend toward greater frequency.[19]

---

[17] George Wallingford Noyes, *John Humphrey Noyes: The Putney Community* (Oneida, New York: G. W. Noyes, 1931), 271-353.

[18] *Proceedings of the Free Convention held at Rutland, Vt., July 25th, 26th, and 27th, 1858* (Boston: J. B. Yerrinton, 1858). They did not vote on but only discussed the resolutions presented by the organizing committee, consisting of two Rutland spiritualists, the publisher, and one other.

[19] Susan Harry, "Divorce in Vermont in the 1800's: A Study of Chittenden County Court Divorce Records," a term paper in History 283, Women's History, at the University of Vermont, May 1984, gives no totals for all causes. She is concerned with the choice of plea, the predominance of the plea of desertion because society wants the deserted to remarry. She finds alimony rare and unenforced, and a series of laws, 1855-60, suggesting the growing independence of women.

Dislocation was the watchword of the day: more marriages dislocated, more people dislocated by internal migration. Business was dislocated by frequent bankruptcies, often caused by technological change: rail over stage, photograph over painting or silhouette, mowing machine over scythe. Political parties fragmented because normal coalition politics failed among reformers who put their own cause ahead of compromise. The world at midcentury was fractured by tensions between the dying and the dawning. Politicians, as ever, found the instability intolerable and worked steadily to regain the normality of winning elections by coalition and compromise.

7. The Press and Politics

Out of the turbulence of mid-century politics came the flat calm of Republican hegemony, not to be disrupted for over a century. What were the habits and customs of the Vermont political animal, in a state that delivered two to one Republican majorities for so long? Before 1854 the parties were in fragments. Thereafter, although the Democrats reflected their national schism in 1860, no Vermont third party made much of a dent until the Progressives of 1912. To explain Republican durability is the theme of Samuel B. Hand and D. Gregory Sanford in *The Star That Never Set: The Vermont Republican Party, 1854-1958*.[1] They point to the skills of Republican party managers, both in taking advantage of such fixed customs and constitutional restraints as the Mountain Rule, rotation in office, and one-year terms, and in settling conflicts within the party as they arose. My theme is to describe the behavior of Vermont political parties, fixed in the second quarter of the century, and the process by which the multi-party conflicts of the decade before 1854 were resolved.[2]

In the two decades after the Anti-Masonic Party died, Vermont politicians learned two lessons: a party focused on one issue can win, and when it destroys its enemy, nothing fails like that success. In the fever crisis of 1849-54, both major parties pursued the first goal on the free soil issue, and the Democrats lost because they were anchored to a proslavery-dominated national party. They were anchored because of their equally strong desires for Union and federal patronage. They also lost for local reasons: they could not take more than temporary advantage of Vermonters' feelings for personal liberty and against prohibition; they could not woo the nativists because of their many Irish Catholic supporters. The same political style had been common to both parties since the Whig hullabaloo of 1840 had proved that Jacksonian tactics won big.

---

[1] Professor Hand has kindly let me read a draft of this work in progress.

[2] Except for documenting quotations, I have omitted the footnotes that appear in my "Vermont Politics and the Press in the 1840's," *Vermont History* 47 (Summer 1979): 196-213, and in my treatment of the 1850s in my dissertation, "Urban Penetration of Rural Vermont," Harvard University, 1952, 2 vols.

This political style depended on village lawyers and the village press as principal agents. Lawyers and editors were valuable because they traveled among the voters and their leaders. Lawyers followed the courts to the many county seats and probate districts and discussed politics and policies in the taprooms and lobbies after sessions. Newspapers circulated within their counties, and their editors circulated on political and business errands. Businessmen traveled too, but except for providing "the needful" (money for campaigning), and lending their prestige by gracing the heads of tickets, they stayed in the background. The newspaper was not only in league with the politicians; it stayed in business because it made money, because it was the most widespread form of popular education and propaganda, and held the mirror up to village society.

Editors were fond of saying they had printer's ink in their blood. They told the census takers they were printers, but they were really politicians, building a base in community acceptance. They prided themselves on boosting local interests. Regardless of party allegiance, they defended the farmer and wool grower and promoted railroads, manufacturing, and trade. The *Montpelier Watchman* was practically the official organ of the Vermont Central Railroad for the decade after 1842. The *Rutland Herald* and the *Burlington Free Press* countered most strongly in defense of the Rutland Railroad, while the *St. Johnsbury Caledonian* was the chief Vermont promoter of the Connecticut and Passumpsic. Businessmen repaid the press with advertising, jobbing, and much of its circulation. Consequently, newspapers and printing offices flourished on main-traveled roads, where mills turned out and merchants turned over, and carriers moved the most goods. The larger the town, the better it supported continuous publication.

At county seats the press of the party locally in power could expect a comfortable backlog of legal advertising and a good source of political news and views among the lawyers and litigants assembled. Parties supported only one weekly per county, where newspapers circulated postage-free. These papers followed the rule that "the longer a journal has been established the greater is its chance of holding its own."[3]

Before the Civil War, fourteen leading Vermont villages supported twenty-five long-lived papers. Except for four denominational weeklies and two reform papers turned Republican,

---

[3] S. N. D. North, *History and Present Condition of the Newspaper and Periodical Press of the United States; Tenth Census of the United States* (Washington: Government Printing Office, 1884), 8; summarizes postal laws applying to newspapers, 1845-80, 149-162. In 1846-47 newspapers were postage-free within thirty miles of the publishing office; then for four years there was no subsidy.

nineteen started as major party organs. Scarcely any new journal between 1846 and the Civil War lasted over five years.

Principal Vermont Weekly Newspapers, 1840-61

Title	Place	Dates	Affil.
Vermont Journal	Windsor	1783-1835,44-	W,R
Vermont Gazette	Bennington	1783-1853	D*
Herald	Rutland	1794+	W,R
Sentinel (cont'd as	Burlington	1801-67	D
Democrat)	"	1871-74	D
Vermont Watchman & State Journal	Montpelier	1807-1911	W,R
North Star	Danville	1807-91	D
Universalist Watchman & Christian Repository	Montpelier	1820-77	U
Vermont Patriot (Argus & Patriot, 1863-)	Montpelier	1820+	D
Vermont Chronicle**	Windsor, etc.	1826-99?	C
Free Press	Burlington	1827+	W,R
Vt. Telegraph (cont'd	Brandon	1828-42	
as Vt. Observer)	"	1842-46	B
Register	Middlebury	1834+	W,R
Vermont Phoenix#	Brattleboro	1836-96+	W,R
Windham County Democrat	Brattleboro	1836-53	D
Vermont Mercury	Woodstock	1837-55	W
Caledonian	St. Johnsbury	1837+	W,R
Vermonter	Vergennes	1838+	W,R
Messenger	St. Albans	1838+	W,R
Gazette (cont'd as Times, 1856-)	Bellows Falls	1838-96+	W,R
Voice of Freedom (cont'd as	Montpelier	1839-44	L
Green Mountain Freeman)	"	1844-85	L,FS,R
Spirit of the Age	Woodstock	1840-1913	D
Banner	Bennington	1841+	
Vermont Temperance Standard	Woodstock	1845-49, 53-90	T,W,R
Christian Messenger%	Montpelier	1847-68	ME
Argus (merged with Vt. Patriot, Montpelier)	Bellows Falls	1853-63	D

Titles vary. B=Baptist, C=Congregationalist, D=Democratic, FS=Free Soil, L=Liberty, ME=Methodist, R=Republican, T=Temperance, U=Universalist, W=Whig. * Briefly FS; ** Bellows Falls, 1826-28; Montpelier, 1873-, then St. Johnsbury; # Merged with Eagle as Republican, 1855, then Phoenix; % 1847 at Newbury.

In the 1860s village growth added a new group of papers in Hyde Park, Manchester, Newport, Barton and Lyndon, with a few others of brief duration. All but three of the newspapers had started during the strife of Jefferson's and John Quincy Adams's administrations, or in the decade after the party realignment of 1834-36. After the Baptist *Vermont Observer* stopped in 1846, only the Congregationalist, Universalist, and Methodist organs continued. The *Vermont Temperance Standard* and the abolitionist *Green Mountain Freeman* survived as Republican standard-bearers.

The political press of the capital and the denominational organs had wider than county circulation. The *Freeman* reported a circulation of 2,600 in 1850, two hundred more than the Methodist *Christian Messenger* and four hundred more than the next largest political organ, the *Brattleboro Eagle*. Both the *Watchman* and the *Patriot* published dailies during General Assembly sessions and reflected the importance of their editors in statewide party councils. The governing bodies of the Vermont Methodists, Congregationalists, and for a few years, Baptists, designated one journal, conducted by an approved minister, as their vehicle of communication. The feeble circulation and short life of all but the Congregational organ reflected the relative strength of the denominations.

Circulation methods had not varied since the beginnings of the Vermont press. When starting a weekly, and periodically thereafter, the publisher sent out a canvasser. The subscription price did not change until the Civil War. With "prompt payment" a weekly copy could be had at the paper's office or by mail for $1.50 a year. Reform papers cut rates and promotional drives sometimes lowered the price; so did subscriptions by "clubs" of ten to twenty delivered to one address. Publishers accepted payment in kind: E. B. Whiting of the *St. Albans Messenger* would take fifteen pounds of butter for one subscription. Rags could always be passed on for credit at the papermill. After calling in their columns for delinquents to pay up, on the theory that those who did not pay would not read, they absorbed the losses. Delivery within the village was already available by carrier at a higher price. In the country the stage either left copies at the post office or the post rider delivered them to the door.

The capital required to start a printing shop, with or without a newspaper, lay within the reach of the ordinary journeyman. The editors of the defunct *Castleton Vermont Statesman* valued their whole establishment at $200. The *Woodstock Vermont Temperance Standard* had an initial capitalization of $500 in 1853. Even the *Montpelier Vermont Patriot* was sold in 1839 for only $2,200, considered at the time a high price. Someone in the party could usually manage to lend the $500 to $1,000 needed to cover the first, modest expense.[4]

The editor could start with a secondhand, Washington-type press and secondhand type, take on a part-time partner and a boy, and charge his first order of paper stock. If business proved poor, and the press was his and worth moving, the printer tried another town. Otherwise he left his press, type, and debts behind and worked as a journeyman again elsewhere. The reputation of printers for itinerancy and intemperance arose from the uncertain fortunes of the country paper or job printing shop. "Journeymen printers won't work unless they have something besides *promises*," wrote Lyman J. McIndoe of Newbury, importuning Orange Scott for a draft to cover a textbook job for the Wesleyan Methodists.[5]

Job printing of books, public documents, and ephemera made the big difference whether printing was for love or money. Shops in nine large villages produced eighty-five percent of the Vermont imprints to 1897, as tabulated in the summary of Gilman's *Bibliography*. Local government before the Civil War needed little public printing, but the state patronage was lucrative to those in power. The state had no official printer, but E. P. Walton and Son, Chauncey Goodrich of Burlington, and Haskell and Palmer of the *Woodstock Mercury* printed four-fifths of the state documents in the 1840s. According to the rival *Vermont Patriot*, the Waltons had averaged almost $2,000 a year after the Whigs came to power in 1837, or over half the total bill for state printing and stationery. The Democratic "share" of this patronage amounted to about $5,500 out of more than $43,000, including the gravy that all papers shared in printing the public acts of the legislature.[6]

The Democratic press would have amounted to little without revenues from federal advertising, federal office, and party subsidies. Partners of Democratic editors were sometimes on the customs house payroll and frequently postmasters, as the law forbade postmasters from formally running a paper. John C. Haswell of the *Bennington Vermont Gazette*, successful at soliciting federal printing, asserted that there was "not a dem[ocratic] paper in this state that in my opinion can be

---

[4]L. R. H. Robinson and Southmayd to C. G. Eastman, 10 February 1843, in Eastman Papers, Vermont Historical Society; M. D. Gilman, *The Bibliography of Vermont; or, A List of Books and Pamphlets Relating in Any Way to the State. With Biographical and Other Notes* (Burlington: Free Press Association, 1897), 215. In 1840 the average capital invested in twenty-five Vermont printing offices was $2,000, excluding the four in Windham County totaling $144,000 because that total included the large, bankrupt Brattleboro Typographic Company.

[5]12 February 1847, in 1954 in the stampless cover collection of Roscoe C. Burleigh of St. Johnsbury.

[6]*Montpelier Vermont Patriot*, 16 August 1849; M. D. Gilman, *Bibliography of Vermont*, 294-305.

lucrative, and a tax upon each one in the County is dry business." D. C. Goodale of the *Middlebury Argus* put his situation in its best light in order to sell out and practice medicine. He figured his subscriptions at seven hundred dollars and his job work at "about 200 or 300 dollars—which together with the government patronage makes this office a respectable investment of capital." The *Castleton Statesman* complained of "very little job work—that being mostly in the hands of the Whigs."[7]

The "Whig times" of President Harrison ended with Tyler, and the four leading Democratic papers had over five hundred dollars worth of patronage annually until the election of Zachary Taylor in 1848. When Jeremiah T. Marston left Montpelier for the West in 1846 he had accumulated over fifteen thousand dollars during his eight years' ownership of the *Vermont Patriot*.

Commercial advertising provided maybe a quarter of newspaper income and filled a quarter of the weekly's space. The price of a square (as long as the column was wide) ran to about $1.50 for three insertions, with lower rates for the cards of local businessmen. Lottery and patent medicine advertisements, even at the lowest rates, were better than nothing, for they ran a long time. Advertisers sometimes paid extra to have their circulars slipped into mailed copies.

When politics quieted down between November and June, the weeklies clipped stories from their numerous postage-free exchanges and hospitably printed material supporting any cause. Therefore, most special purpose papers, for temperance, abolition, Canadian liberty, perfectionism, or nativism, or devoted to agriculture, education, literature, medicine, music, or military science, were short-lived. The political press, cutting and pasting from out-of-state papers, even printed state and local news, more state than local because village gossip still ran taller and faster than the press. But their meat and potatoes, in season and out, was politics.

Politicians, always called statesmen by their supporters, had little party work to do before and after campaigns except to repeat the American creed, quote "scripture" from the Declaration of Independence or the Constitution, pay homage to the "Founding Saints" of the Revolution, and intone the night watchman's "All's well" whether it was or not. Beyond a local concern for a ban on taking horned pout in Ticklenaked Pond or a more convenient location for the post office, immediate issues erupted only when competitors could not settle "out of Assembly." They roared to a boil when someone thought conflict would win votes.

---

[7]Robinson & Southmayd to C. G. Eastman, 4 February 1843; Goodale to Eastman, 6 May 1839; Haswell to Eastman, 11 September 1839, in Eastman Papers, Vermont Historical Society. In 1841, postmasters in Bellows Falls, Burlington, Middlebury, Montpelier, and Woodstock were connected with Democratic papers.

The 1847 proposal to make Fisk's marble quarry on Isle La Motte the site for a new state prison is one of many examples of conflicting economic and party interests. On the water's edge, the quarry had been worked since the eighteenth century. Recently, the rough building stone for border fortifications at Isle aux Noix, St. Jean, and Rouses Point, locks and bridges for the Chambly canal and the St. Lawrence and Atlantic Railroad had come from Isle La Motte. Its hearthstones, sawed at Swanton Falls, reached New York, Philadelphia, and Boston, and Swanton mills had cut Isle La Motte marble for grave markers since 1812.

In the 1847 session, Democratic Grand Isle County senator Giles Harrington of Alburg introduced a bill to move the state prison from Windsor to Isle La Motte. After a month's investigation and a close fight on the floor, the Whig majority defeated the bill. Only four Whigs, all from Harrington's county, voted for the transfer, although in the early stages of the debate all the senators from the northern eight counties along with the Democratic delegation from Orange County had supported it. Since 1842 prison labor at Windsor had worked on carriages and shoes, unprofitably, according to Harrington. Democrats could safely attack the business of "blue-light"[8] Windsor, a Federalist-Whig stronghold, in the hope of attracting votes in the northwest, where they had strength. The Fisk quarry was a declining business, which sought a government crutch as a last resort. The Isle La Motte forces had to agree to a year's investigation, which killed the project.

The economic side of politics saw chronic lobbying for and against railroad, bank, and other business franchises. Otherwise the business of politics was winning and holding office. That was what opponents did; "our side" responded to urgent calls for public service, for the rhetoric of discourse was semi- hypocritical. The great paradox of early American politics was that while most people assumed that the way their governments behaved made more difference than anything else, political behavior made very little difference indeed. Federal government had little contact with the average citizen. Its corps in Vermont consisted of part-time postmasters, customs inspectors from Windmill Point in Alburg to Canaan, an occasional recruiting officer, and four officers of federal justice. When the Canadian rebels tried to collect arms and recruits in 1837-38, no mobilized constabulary opposed them. Federal money did not flow into Vermont except for lake improvements and for printing U. S. laws and departmental advertisements. Little revenue was extracted except at the border and through postage. Yet Vermonters had strong patriotic attachments and

---

[8] Epithet perpetuating Stephen Decatur's charge that Federalist traitors signaled the British with blue lights in New London harbor in 1813.

were proud of the revolutionary tradition and aware of current national events reported in their weeklies.

No state establishment existed on a year-around basis at Montpelier. The building of a new statehouse in 1836-38 confirmed the decision of 1805 to have one state capital at Montpelier, and the architecture changed to fit the new bicameral legislature. The building was practically never used except during the four-week fall session (six weeks in the 1850s). Its dome stored archives, but mainly served as a Roman republican symbol of state rights and sovereignty, of local control of local affairs. The sergeant-at-arms was year-around janitor, and his grounds were in grass, cut with scythe or sickle once or twice a summer, just like any other hayfield. In 1862 G. B. Dodge was accused of selling four tons of hay off state property for private gain, although he claimed it cost him the seven to eight dollars a ton price of the hay to cut and remove it.[9]

State officers did little, even away from the capital, where their offices were in their homes. The governor occasionally uttered ceremonial syllables during the ritual observances of patriotic religion: Fourth of July, Muster Day (June training), and fair day. Even in 1902 Governor John G. McCullough could deprecate in his annual address that his duties were neither arduous nor extensive. The other officers had even less to do. The treasurer kept his petty accounts and signed orders to pay. The adjutant and quartermaster generals tried to keep track of ancient arms and equipment and rosters of local militia units. The state librarian shelved in the statehouse whatever federal, foreign, or other state documents he was on the mailing list for. The state geologist did not at first have a cabinet, although several colleges and academies had stone collections.

While legal matters focused on the county seat, or the "half-shire" towns of Vergennes, Manchester, and Newfane, where judges of probate sat as well as at the county seats, most government occurred in the town. Even there, authority was divided among the school or fire district committees, selectmen, pound keepers (controlling strays), fence viewers (settlers of boundary disputes to avoid litigation), and the rest. Before the efficient barbed wire fence, fence viewers were significant mediators where stock trespassed because of poor fencing. Town government was basically nonpartisan, except for the September election of town representatives, who could be town clerks or selectmen at the same time.

---

[9]*House Journal* (1862), 487-488. He was also charged with making small profits on wood fuel and furniture. In 1856 the Committee on Claims charged the Sergeant-at-Arms with ordering too much stationery at too high prices (and from a Democratic printer), and wrongly using it, as many other state officers did, for personal business. It also complained that he hired too many maintenance men about the statehouse and grounds during the session (*House Journal* (1856), 741-742).

Town officers devoted nearly all their attention to real estate. The town clerk was the town archivist, usually re-elected as long as he (not yet she) would serve, and recorded deeds, vital statistics, and town meeting business. Selectmen authorized, listers set, constables collected, treasurers handled, and auditors checked taxes, primarily on real estate. The three selectmen, chief executive officers, were sound, widely respected, and usually second-flight businessmen, because the village aristocracy had more important business. The selectmen with the surveyor or road commissioner were responsible for laying out, maintaining, and improving roads, and restraining livestock from running at large. The selectmen with the overseer of the poor, after relatives had been forced to do all they could, had the power to warn off non-residents, provide relief in the home, or send the needy to the poor farm. Fires were major hazards to property, but private, volunteer fire companies, not town officers, attempted to put them out. The law exempted a specified number of their members from militia duty.[10]

Village corporations had larger powers in case of fire, and over stray animals, but better fire protection awaited more than a steam pump for the water, bought by larger villages in the 1850s.[11] Village bylaws governed streets, sidewalks, plantings, and parks. A main reason for the separation of Montpelier from East Montpelier in 1848 was a village grievance over highway taxes. The division occurred in spite of rural protest against losing so much taxable property in Montpelier. The difference between towns and villages was not one of size, for a place could be an incorporated village if it had over thirty houses. The General Assembly chartered villages in most of the largest towns before 1860, but town historians have testified to the insignificance of village charters by usually not even mentioning them. The difference between the city of Vergennes, incorporated in 1788 under a delusion of future grandeur, and a town or village was formal: Vergennes had a mayor instead of selectmen, and a city court.

The part-time officials at every level tended other affairs, including politics. People consulted the governor and the Congressional delegation especially on personal matters such as getting a military pension or a job in Washington. I cannot think of a nineteenth-century politician who was called the "head" or sole leader of his party, not even those who came close: Cornelius Van Ness, David Smalley, Justin Morrill and Redfield Proctor. No one felt that a head was necessary. The

---

[10]Andrew Nuquist, *Town Government in Vermont; or, "Making Democracy 'Democ'"* (Burlington: Government Research Center, University of Vermont, 1964), describes the history and contemporary functions of each office and its relation to town meeting.

[11]See pp. 83-84, 201-202.

low rural density, about thirty people per square mile and more evenly spread over the land than at any other time before or since, produced little congestion, less friction, and, consequently, the need for very little government. Parties were people organized to promote their best understanding of the best interests of the whole country, and led by statesmen representing the interests they understood. It was immoral to promote your own selfish interests. Only the politicians of the other side did that.

Whereas most people had many needs, the successful politicians concentrated on one issue claimed to be fundamental to all the rest. In the 1780s it was how the adoption of the federal constitution would affect a frontier republic and state trying to steer a safe course through international complications. Until 1815 it was our proper relation to Great Britain, especially with British Canada. For a long time after, economic nationalism through tariff and transportation aid and the management of money and land were issues that divided the parties. Politicians estimated how many voters wanted the very limited services of government and supported a collection of those interests that most likely would maintain them or their partisans in power.

Two generations of politics before 1840 had crystallized methods. As a settled, rural, border state Vermont received a continuing education in diplomacy, and its politicians, watching the state's national influence drain to the growing West and the more industrialized states, did what they could to check their state's fading importance. Vermont had six members of the United States House of Representatives in the 1810s, five beginning in 1822, four from 1842 to 1851, three through 1880, and until the implementation of the 1930 census, two. Although today's political methods differ vastly where technology and a changing population affects them, the basic ways of choosing candidates and getting out the vote have varied little since the 1840s. Then, as now, those powerful in central places achieved their aims in spite of a constitution geared to insure rural dominance.

Vermont had enjoyed universal manhood suffrage since its first constitution of 1777. Voters chose annually, on the first Tuesday in September, state and county officials and congressmen. After one reelection, rotation was the norm for all parties and most offices. Which men to elect depended on their occupation, residence, wealth, age, experience in other offices, and, of course, their party. Voter turnout varied with the weather and the excitement of contests. State elections the first week in September drew more votes than the vote for presidential electors in November, regardless of the weather and the busyness of the season. Even in 1840 six thousand more voted for the incumbent Governor Silas Jenison than for William Henry Harrison for president two months later.

Until 1853 a man had to be a Whig to hold most statewide offices, although third parties frequently prevented the Whig candidate from receiving a majority and required his election by the General Assembly. Still open to worthy Democrats were Supreme Court judgeships; federal patronage under Tyler, Polk, Pierce, and Buchanan; offices in the few (mostly northern) Democratic counties.

One could not call Vermont a one-party state in an era when the Whigs' share of the vote for governor never reached fifty-two percent after their 1840 landslide, and when they won a bare majority only five times in the next dozen years.

Nearly twenty percent of the population (56,452) voted in 1840, a total not exceeded until 1868, the percentage declining to fifteen percent in 1860. The three-party situation also meant that many posts that required a majority to elect went unfilled. From 1843 through 1853, from twenty to forty-three towns had no representatives in the lower house because no candidate could win a majority.

Where candidates came from made a big difference, except for gubernatorial candidates, who consistently failed to win strong majorities in their hometowns. Although the phrase itself was not in common use before 1880, Vermonters steadily observed the "Mountain Rule" that each side of the Green Mountains should share important offices equally. From the start they chose one United States senator from each side, except in 1853-55. The rule became customary for the governorship in the 1840s and for Congressmen when Vermont was reduced to two districts after 1880. For these major offices Lamoille County was considered west side and Washington and Orleans counties east side.

Geographical distribution was carried much farther. A rough north-south alternation often appeared, representing the older and newer sections of the state. Alternation also occurred between counties in congressional districts, between probate districts in the six southern counties, and among all the towns of a county in the case of state senators and other minor officials. Those who could not agree to take turns usually lost out to those who could.

Lawyers formed the largest group of officials. Editors were occasionally elected for special reasons but they were usually too busy promoting candidates to run for office themselves. No United States senators, no governors, and only three congressmen (William Slade, Eliakim P. Walton, and Charles W. Willard) in the half century after 1830 had been newspapermen. Other professionals were even less common in top offices, the exceptions being the Reverend Congressmen James Meacham and Alvah Sabin, and Governor Horace Eaton, M. D. The dirt farmer tied to his farm

Vermont Vote for Governor, 1836-60

(Total in thousands. Percentage of vote by parties: 1) Whig or Republican; 2) Democratic; 3) Other (Liberty Party, 1840-47; Free Soil, 1848; Free Democratic, 1849-53; American, 1855; a few temperance and abolitionist votes, 1850-55; a few Whig, 1854-55)

Year	Total	1	2	3
1836	37	56	44	—
1837	40	56	44	—
1838	44	56	44	—
1839	47	52.5	47	—
1840	56	59	40	-1
1841	48	49	44	6
1842	53	51	45	4
1843	51	49	43.5	7.5
1844	55	51.5	38	10
1845	50	47	37	13.5
1846	49	48.5	37	15
1847	48	47	39	14
1848	51	44	27	29
1849	53	50	6	44
1850	49	51	9	40
1851	45	51	15	34
1852	46	49	31	20
1853	47	44	38	18
1854	45	63	34	3
1855	43	59	29	12
1856	46	74	25	1
1857	40	67	32	1
1858	43	69	31	—
1859	45	68	32	—
1860	48	71	25	4

work was a rare bird in any office except as a town representative, and his weight was less than his numbers in the legislature.

The average citizen gained more honor than profit from office holding, for most offices brought low salaries and part-time employment. Only Rhode Island paid its governor less than Vermont's $750 (1801 until 1857, then $1,000). The per diem of the legislator provided good pay for a farmer who had help or had his harvest in. For the non-farming majority in office, the fringe benefits of statewide contacts often made the four- to six-week session in Montpelier well worthwhile. Some had axes to grind (to shepherd a private claim or corporate charter), wanted a start in politics, or used state office as a symbol of local prominence.

Although aspirants held minor offices before major ones, and each candidate had to win a reputation somewhere, there was no recognized political ladder. The young lawyer usually served two years as state's attorney for his county and, to acquire the parliamentary experience, sought a position in the tiny secretariat serving the governor or the legislature. To reach those upper levels he needed wide endorsement through party and legislative committee work or perhaps experience on the Supreme Court or as Speaker of the House. From Silas Jenison to Paul Dillingham only four were soon elevated from lieutenant governor to governor, with special considerations in each case more important than mere promotion. Julius Converse thought he deserved it in 1854 but had to wait until 1872. Two longer series of such progressions occurred in the late nineteenth and mid-twentieth centuries.

Business managers ran for governor for special reasons; for example, Charles Paine and Erastus Fairbanks to promote their railroads and allied factories. Otherwise being governor, wielding little power except in wartime, was an honor and a privilege. Businessmen left places in the congressional delegation mostly to lawyers, except for George Hodges, Justin Morrill, Portus Baxter, and Worthington C. Smith.

Vermont's formal political structure, highly decentralized, focused at the state level on the lower house where representatives of small towns held an overwhelming numerical preponderance. Yet residents of large villages monopolized more than two-thirds of all major offices.[12]

Some of the positions, especially those with long tenure, required the incumbent to be near the repositories of records at capitol or courthouse. The state treasurer lived in or near Montpelier

---

[12]See my table, "Residence and Tenure of Principal Vermont Officials, 1840-80," in *Vermont History* 47 (Summer 1979): 203.

for all but six years between 1838 and 1890. Burlington, port of entry for the customs District of Vermont, was the logical residence of the collector, and a Burlington man held the office for all but six years of the four decades after 1840. Court business required five Supreme Court judges appointed from smaller towns to move to central villages during most of their terms: Isaac F. Redfield of Derby to Montpelier, Luke P. Poland of Morrisville and Benjamin H. Steele of Derby to St. Johnsbury, Loyal C. Kellogg of Benson to Rutland, and William C. Wilson of Bakersfield to St. Albans. On the other hand, Montpelier was the residence of the secretary of state less than a third of the time, of the auditor of accounts only six years, and of the secretary of civil and military affairs only one year in the same period.

Why did two-thirds or more of the governors, auditors, Speakers, congressional delegations come from leading villages? Even one of every four state senators and half the state committee of the Whig Party lived in large towns. An answer to these questions, and to others on the influence of central villages in politics, is found in the way a party was organized, the way a party chose its leaders, wrote its platform, conducted campaigns, and got out the vote. Men of influence and wealth in business and of importance in the bar held the steering positions unobtrusively. Their advice carried the weight of command. They contributed to campaign funds. They served as delegates to national conventions partly because they could afford the trips. They solicited offices in Washington—the best way to secure them—for themselves and their friends. They stayed in the background except to speak occasionally at the most important meetings and to run for top elective offices.

The rank and file sometimes displayed resentment at this dominance. "We Democrats," wrote a Swanton henchman to C. G. Eastman, 21 October 1839, "do not belong to the aristocracy." He listed eleven well-to-do, patronage-receiving Democrats, mostly from leading villages, who supported Jackson throughout the Anti-Masonic fever, from whom, he said, the real Democrats did not take orders. "Our friends are," he continued, naming eight, mostly from small towns, sympathetic to economic and social reform, "because they, we believe, are friends of the people." In the backwoods of Barnard, a Democrat reporting to Eastman on 17 July 1839 that the new Methodist church had improved the party's fortunes, remarked on how to distinguish his friends from Whigs. "But say the Whig we [Democrats] is too much slang bang rag tag and bobtail."

"The friends of the people" gained a bit of ground under the banner of "Smilie and Bank Reform" in the depths of the depression. Nathan Smilie, a farmer from "spunky Lamoille" County, won a higher percentage of the vote for governor than any other Democrat running for governor in the nineteenth century. But when offices were to be had under Democratic presidents Tyler and Polk, they went to the Old Guard "Hunkers." Cornelius P. Van Ness, the elder statesman and founder of the Vermont Jacksonian party, left Burlington when appointed collector of customs for New York City, where he hoped to promote John C. Calhoun's presidential candidacy. David A. Smalley, another Burlington lawyer, gradually succeeded to the leadership of the Democratic Party with the aid of his *Burlington Sentinel*. The editors and the young lawyers who traveled a good deal on their own business played the more active and public roles, with the assistance of forgotten corporals and lieutenants in each town. Editors printed campaign papers hotter than their usual editions, both of which carried "the record" of individuals and parties in General Assembly or Congress. They reported their own partisans' speeches fully, with editorial exegesis, and omitted, cut, attacked, or distorted their opponents'. They made much of independents and bolters from the other side. For their own party they preached support of regular nominations and castigated the lukewarm and the bolters. On the eve of the election they printed ballots with the names they had been carrying on the masthead, to be used by the faithful.

Editors repeated slogans and epithets. The Whig Party, calling itself the "Star That Never Sets," consisted, according to Democrats, of Tories, Federalists, blue-lights, cidercrats and coons (from the 1840 campaign featuring hard cider and backwoodsmen's coonskins). The Whigs called the Democrats Tories, Patriots (favoring the Canadian Rebellion of 1837-38), Locofocos (referring to matches used by bolting antislavery Democrats at a New York convention), Barnburners (antislavery Democrats who would burn down the barn to get rid of the rats), Hunkers (the other Democratic faction), Doughfaces (proslavery Northern Democrats), and slavocrats. All these labels came into Vermont from party battles elsewhere. The response of John Moseley Weeks of Salisbury, declining his appointment to the town committee of the Free Soil-Democratic coalition of 1849, demonstrated the party confusion of tongues:

> I am a Democrat of 1798, a Democratic Whig of the revolution . . . all the way down to 1849; and a Whig Abolitionist, which I consider the only true abolitionists of our country. I am a Free Soil Democratic Whig, and shall act with them as long as they are governed by pure Democratic principles. I entertain . . . friendly feeling towards

any individuals of any political party, but I am jealous that the *loaves* and *fishes* have too much influence.[13]

Officeholders' influence was to be felt but not seen. The most convenient offices for campaigning were those under the collector of customs and, especially that of secret customs agent, who could cover the northern half of the state on legitimate business. All appointed officers except district judges expected to pay for their jobs by working for the party. Even lesser postmasters, often chosen because they kept the most convenient store, interfered with or even unsealed their enemies' mail. The congressional delegation often lent dignity to functions or offered petty patronage (Washington clerkships, minor consulates, military or naval academy appointments). They also stayed at the capital with the time-honored excuse that their "attention to official duties forbids the pleasure of meeting" the state convention or voters.

Vermont politics was pretty much a home game. The importation of outsiders to draw crowds was expensive, and Vermont electoral votes were never in doubt. Henry Clay came looking for delegates in 1839, and Daniel Webster sought a cabinet seat in 1840. Horace Greeley, who grew up in West Haven and Poultney, returned several times to Vermont. He combined politics with visiting old friends and boosting the circulation of his *New York Tribune*. It paid off: between 1854 and 1860 Vermont averaged the highest ratio of *Tribune* circulation to voters; close to twenty percent of Vermont voters subscribed from 1856 to the Civil War.[14]

A sure sign of spring was the reduction of "readin' matter" in the newspapers to make room for straight political articles on time-tried themes. Party committees issued calls to nominating conventions, especially the state convention appointed by the state committee chosen during the fall session of the legislature. Leaders had actively corresponded, so that by the time the delegates had gathered, if the party was united, the nominations were already settled. What could not be decided by mail the leaders concluded by advanced conferring. Preconvention decisions by a few "choice spirits" were easier for Democrats who had fewer to consult.

They carefully selected the time and place for meeting. It was no use gathering before the completion of spring work, even though farmers did not have a strong voice in the conventions. At times it seemed better tactics to come out first; at others, to wait and see what the other party would

---

[13] Quoted from the *Middlebury Galaxy* in the *Montpelier Watchman*, 16 August 1849.

[14] Jeter A. Isely, *Horace Greeley and the Republican Party, 1853-1861: A Study of the New York Tribune* (Princeton: Princeton University Press, 1947), Appendix A.

do. The place had to be accessible, but it would vary to provide the maximum hotel or hall accommodations, to change the strength of delegations, to reward towns strong for the party, or to stage a first rally in a doubtful region.

Campaigners, who studied the election returns, knew that the Whigs profited by "hot politics" to lure lukewarm voters to the polls, and the Democrats by "fighting dark." In the odd years, without congressional or presidential contests, the Democrats worked quietly so as not to "alarm the coons," and these tactics consistently increased their percentage of the vote. One version of "hot politics" was to create a lively, local contest by naming two candidates for town representative from the same party, provided it did not cause bitterness. Whichever the tactic, both sides prepared more or less complete registers of voters classified as safe, indifferent and undisposed, absent or doubtful, by towns or school districts. They assigned workers to deal with all but the safe and absent and see that they voted right. Stores sold campaign buttons. In 1840 Pangborn & Brinsmaid's Burlington variety store offered "A few log cabin Bosom Pins, with a barrel of Hard Cider, 'mighty handy', and 'the string never pulled in'."[15]

Most party propaganda matched like two sides of a coin, whether barking the tariff up or down, swishing the sword, or whispering malicious gossip. Truman B. Ransom, Acting President of Norwich University, wrote to C. G. Eastman 21 December 1843, favoring Richard M. Johnson of Kentucky for president in 1844, "Yes, Sir, that old mutilated [sic] hand held up to the gaze of the people, will win more votes than all the editorial flourishes & finely formed syllogisms of the Whig orators." The *Woodstock Spirit of the Age* on 22 February 1844 printed a list of Captain E. A. Kimball's eighty-four-man company in the 9th Regiment, U. S. Infantry, with the comment that Whig Private Chaplin "battles the rest of the company, who are mostly democrats with arguments upon political questions as earnestly as he does the greasers with powder and ball."

Vermont politics was generally "clean," without brawls, but Vermont politicians did employ tricks. For example, C. P. Van Ness, the "pirate fresh from the defiles of Spain," (ex-Minister to Madrid) caused a boatload of Whigs to miss most of a Plattsburgh rally on September 11, 1840, by refusing to tow their chartered boat in rough weather.[16] Middlebury Whig authorities broke up a Liberty Party convention by renting the hall to traveling theatrical dancers. Because each party gave its own ballot or "ticket" to the voters at the polling place, watchers could tell whether the votes they

---

[15]*Burlington Free Press*, 6 June 1840.

[16]*Burlington Free Press*, 18 September, 20 October 1840.

bought were delivered. Charges were common that employers used threats and that money, rum, and promises of patronage were exchanged for votes. Another trick was to print "bastard tickets." For example, the Democrats printed ballots substituting the name of a sure-to-be-elected Whig for that of the weaker Democrat. This attracted Whig votes for the stronger Democrat.

Both sides stooped to *ad hominem* arguments with charges of sexual license, intemperance, gambling, and financial turpitude. Whispering campaigns charging Charles Paine's promiscuity with his woolen mill women did not prevent his election as governor in 1841, nor the suggestion of John Mattocks's adultery his winning in 1843.[17] Governor Slade threw mud when he contested Senator Samuel S. Phelps's re-election in 1844. Slade charged that his rival had neglected his duties and jeopardized the Whig tariff because of drunkenness and stubborn independence of party whips. Phelps won for services rendered for Clay, Justin Morrill wrote in 1850. Morrill, who later won six elections for congressman and then six for U. S. senator, was supporting Solomon Foot against Phelps, now a Cotton Whig. He claimed, ironically in view of his long service in office later, that two terms were enough for Phelps.

Cold-blooded analysis of ways and means, of names called and offices sought, of campaign strategy and tactics and of the fun of whooping it up, seems to imply a cynical conclusion that politicians were hypocrites. If hypocrisy is saying one thing and doing another, they were, like most other people. But they were so profoundly dedicated to their principles that they failed to see their essential unity on the issue that came more and more to divide them, the slavery question.

"All or nearly all" Vermonters opposed slavery,[18] but the issue proved most damaging to the Democrats. For party harmony and national union Democrats accepted the evil of slavery as a constitutional right of slaveholders. They counter-attacked, as politics required, against sectionalism, extremism, and the unwillingness of Whig or Republican tycoons to touch their own vested interests.

Only a few Vermonters took direct action by violating the law and helping escaped slaves to freedom. Not fearing pursuers, conductors of the Underground Railroad took main routes via the Connecticut or Hudson valleys to Middlebury, Ferrisburgh, Burlington, and St. Albans, or Bellows Falls, Randolph, and Montpelier. They probably did not take the fugitives all the way to Canada.

---

[17]Truman B. Ransom, Norwich, to C. G. Eastman, Woodstock, 27 August 1841; George W. Nichols, Brattleboro, to C. G. Eastman, 8 September 1843; Eastman Papers in the Vermont Historical Society. See pp. 100-101 on Charles Paine's liaison.

[18]Erastus Fairbanks to A. G. Whittemore, 26 October 1843, Fairbanks Papers in the Vermont Historical Society.

Secretary of State Chauncey L. Knapp in 1838 settled one boy in Montpelier. Among the correspondence of Rowland T. Robinson at Rokeby, Robinson's Ferrisburgh home, are two letters from a North Carolina slaveholder declining the slave's offer, through Robinson, to buy his freedom for $150, which he has earned working at Rokeby.[19] Vermont's personal liberty law made fugitives feel safe. There was no ex-slave colony in the Eastern Townships of Quebec as there was in the Province of Ontario.

"A large and promising business" was reported for fall, 1847, and in 1854 the *Burlington Tribune* flaunted notices of arrivals and departures; but few cases have been documented. Rowland E. Robinson of Ferrisburgh, whose family was abolitionist, recalled that "activity must have declined in the forties" when he was young. The Reverend N. R. Johnson of Topsham's Covenanter Presbyterian church confided in 1856 to the black abolitionist William Still, "You are probably not aware . . . that fugitives are never seen here. Indeed the one half of the people have never seen more than a half-dozen of colored people."[20]

The abolitionists claimed that they had more support in the hill country. Alanson St. Clair, editor of the *Norwich Vermont Freeman*, wrote that he collected more money for the Liberty Party in smaller places, except Randolph. His successor, the Reverend John Gleed, reported collecting "more as experience has taught me which towns to avoid. Let me into your districts among the honest and industrious farmers. . . . [who] feel for the oppressed and . . . will save their country from slavery. Our villages are the abodes of slaveholders—not owners, but *holders*. . . . and they will not hear us."[21] The Liberty Party also won more votes in the farming districts, but the villages contributed leadership, management, convention sites, and the press.

By the mid-1840s antislavery crusaders had won Vermonters' personal support, but it took another decade to break the national ties that bound the major parties to compromise. While

---

[19]Ephraim Elliott, Perquimans County, N.C., to Rowland T. Robinson, 19 April 1837, with a copy of Robinson's reply of 3 May verso, and 17 June 1837, Rokeby Museum, Ferrisburgh, Vt., on loan to Special Collections, Bailey/Howe Library, University of Vermont.

[20]Larry Gara, *Liberty Line: The Legend of the Underground Railway* (Lexington, Ky.: University of Kentucky Press, 1961), 8-9, quoting R. E. Robinson to W. H. Siebert, 19 August 1896; 89-90 quoting N. R. Johnson to William Still, 18 December 1856, and 145; C. L. Knapp to Anthony Morse in Editor's note, "Antislavery Acting in 1838: A Letter from Vermont's Secretary of State," *Vermont History* 14 (Winter 1973): 7-8; *Montpelier Green Mountain Freeman* (9 March 1848). The treasurer's record of the Vermont Antislavery Society, in the Special Collections of the Bailey/Howe Library of the University of Vermont, has one entry of a dollar given to a fugitive in 1843.

[21]*Montpelier Green Mountain Freeman*, 20 April, 14 June 1844.

continuing their evangelical propaganda the abolitionists shifted their emphasis to coercing the recalcitrant. Except for the few who would deny slaveholders constitutional protection, the new antislavery gambit was to win elections until slavery could be limited and then destroyed by law. In the decade before 1854, overwhelmingly antislavery Vermont shifted from a three-quarters majority for subordinating the slavery issue to other matters, to a three-quarters majority for subordinating other issues to containment of slavery.

The Vermont Democrats were the first to be wounded by schism. Supporters of the Wilmot Proviso (against slavery in the Mexican cession) bolted to the Free Soil Party at their 1848 state convention. George W. Nichols of the *Brattleboro Windham County Democrat* expressed the party's dilemma to C. G. Eastman on 3 July 1848. He would join a party that could both preserve the Union and contain slavery, but the bolters could not guarantee both, he wrote.

In 1849, the Democratic organization thought it could win by merging with the Free Soilers, but some held back because offices were at stake. That, and the possibility that the Whigs pulled more votes out of the pool of indifferent voters, prevented victory for the fusion. The alliance gradually became strained, chiefly from lack of patronage and Democratic hope for federal offices after 1852.

Antislavery rhetoric dominated this period, but other moral issues roused emotions. The temperance movement, after the successes of "moral suasion" by the end of the 1830s, called successfully on the voters and the government to stop those who could not be persuaded, as related in Chapter 5 (see p. 79). The strong-arm methods of some Sons of Temperance and the strong support of the Maine law by Whig gubernatorial candidate Erastus Fairbanks produced a reaction in favor of "personal liberty," which gave Fairbanks only a forty-four percent plurality in the three-cornered contest. In the name of personal liberty Vermont had in 1843 and 1850 virtually nullified the enforcement of the fugitive slave acts within its boundaries by making it difficult for slave catchers to prove ownership.

With only 95 Whigs in the 1853 House and not even a Whig majority in the Senate, the Democrats had to persuade less than half the Free Soilers to vote for their candidate. A temporary team of Democrats and Free Soilers elected Free Soiler Horatio Needham Speaker after thirty-one ballots, and Democrat John S. Robinson governor on the twentieth ballot, along with Democrat Jefferson P. Kidder of Randolph lieutenant governor and Democrat John A. Page, Montpelier banker, state treasurer. When the Free Soilers, feeling they had delivered their votes for state officers, wanted the Democrats to vote for their Lawrence Brainerd or Oscar L. Shafter for U. S.

senator the coalition broke down. The joint assembly gave up after thirty-nine ballots, when Democrat Daniel Kellogg of Rockingham was still a dozen votes from a majority. Vermont was represented only by Senator Solomon Foot until Jacob Collamer took his seat in 1855, because the Senate would not seat Samuel S. Phelps, Governor Fairbanks's appointee, once the legislature had the opportunity to elect a senator. Here was more evidence that a U. S. senator held a position of power while state offices were mainly honorific. Where sessions had lasted about a month from the second week in October, increasing from 1847 because of the three-party situation, the fifty-six-day marathon of 1853 was unequalled again until 1862, but it became the norm for the thirty years from 1870.

Historians have accepted the Whig view of Vermont politics that the Democrats, thirsting for office, tried through "truck and dicker" to build a winning combination. When they achieved it in 1853, by corrupt bargains, they were properly chastised for being immoral and unprincipled. But when the Whig party managers did the same thing much more successfully the next year, they had restored morality to politics.

Vermont-born Senator Stephen A. Douglas, introducing the Nebraska bill in January 1854, was mainly concerned with paving the way for a transcontinental railroad from Chicago and with his own presidential aspirations. But the bill, justified on the principle of popular sovereignty, raised the tension over the slavery issue notches higher. Vermont Whigs had no more intention of abandoning their party organization than the Democrats of 1848-53; but they and Free Soilers of every stripe across the North saw an issue that could put an unbeatable coalition together, and a victory under any other party label would smell as sweet. The popular sovereignty doctrine renounced congressional power over slavery in the territories. As the Republicans reiterated, it repealed the limits expressed in the Northwest Ordinance of 1787, the Missouri Compromise of 1820, and the part of the Compromise of 1850 admitting California as a free state.

By framing a platform on the Kansas issue, soft-pedalling all the issues that divided them, and distributing offices to each element of the coalition of Whigs, Free Soilers, temperance men and nativists, Eliakim P. Walton, editor of the *Montpelier Vermont Watchman*, George W. Benedict, editor of the *Burlington Free Press*, Thomas Hale of the *Windsor Vermont Journal*, Enoch B. Whiting of the *St. Albans Messenger*, Broughton D. Harris of the *Brattleboro Eagle*, and a few other "choice spirits" organized the Vermont Republican Party.[22] The unanswered question is why the Republican Party in other states with similar rural, Protestant, antislavery, and other reform strengths did not follow this pattern.

I assume that territory owned in common should be ruled by the common government, yet policy was on the side of those agreeing with Webster and Douglas, who would leave the slavery issue to be settled by each territory's voters. They believed that climate, soil, immigration, and other non-political forces would bring slavery so near extinction in the United States that a slight nudge would finish it, without the need of Congress to prohibit it while still lusty. Alexander II emancipated Russian serfs in 1861; Spain abolished slavery in Cuba in 1886, and the Emperor of Brazil ended his country's slavery in 1888, all with minimal violence. One cannot make or write history without unprovable assumptions such as Webster's about what might have happened from alternate actions. Indeed, to call the Civil War inevitable or irrepressible makes such an assumption.

The Whigs inched gingerly forward to the rendezvous of a fusion ticket. Their editors wrote of a "new party," an "anti-Nebraska" movement, while confidently expecting the "Star That Never Sets" to re-establish Whig hegemony in 1854. They met at Rutland June 7 and nominated Stephen Royce of Berkshire for governor, Oscar L. Shafter of Wilmington lieutenant governor, and Henry M. Bates, Irasburg bank cashier, treasurer. Someone persuaded ex-governor Fairbanks not to press for the second term he was "entitled" to, and he pleaded pressing business responsibilities. It was debatable (although not debated in the press) whether the East Side should have the choice of successor. Frederick Holbrook, founder and president of the Vermont State Agricultural Society, 1851-58, had run for the Whig nomination against Fairbanks in 1852, and was waiting in the wings. Those opposed to Holbrook could have argued that Fairbanks, running in 1853, used up the East Side's "turn." Royce, promoted as above politics, had had a normal legal-political career. Retiring to his farm in 1852 as chief judge of the state supreme court after over twenty years on that bench, an elective office, he avoided the hard feelings of the 1853 session. He was known as a temperance, antislavery Whig.

Shafter (1812-73), successively a Democrat, Liberty Party abolitionist, Free Soil candidate for governor in 1848 and a Free Democratic candidate for U. S. senator in 1853, had name recognition across a wide spectrum of voters. Insiders also knew that he had made arrangements

---

[22]George W. Benedict, Burlington, to Frederick E. Woodbridge, Vergennes, 17 July 1854, and John Porter, Quechee Village, chair of the Whig state committee, to Woodbridge, 19 July 1854, both in the Sheldon Museum.

to move to California in the fall. Arriving there in November, he joined the law firm including Vermonters Frederick Billings and Trenor W. Park, made a fortune, and served on the state supreme court. Bates (1808-65) had held local offices in Orleans County through the 1840s and became cashier of the Northfield Bank months after his election.

The radical reformers had too often too bitterly attacked the Whigs to accept overtures to join them, at least without a share of the nominations, so they proceeded to make separate slates. The Vermont Temperance Society met in Montpelier July 12 and nominated Lawrence Brainerd (1794-1870), wealthy St. Albans farmer and railroad man; "Old Garden-seeds," the Vermont and Canada railroad engineers called him, who as a perennial candidate for state offices had a clear antislavery and temperance record.[23] A mass anti-Nebraska convention met the next day, with a different set of ringleaders but including Walton, on the anniversary of the Northwest Ordinance, and chose his father, Ezekiel P. Walton, the senior editor of the *Montpelier Watchman*, a pro-Holbrook man, to show that this convention was not a tool of the Whigs. He was not a serious candidate and declined on July 21, stating that he stood on the same platform with Royce. Shafter having already declined, the mass convention nominated for lieutenant governor Ryland Fletcher (1799-1885) of Cavendish, like Brainerd an antislavery and temperance radical, and also a nativist. After this union convention adjourned, many of its members reconvened as the Free Democratic Party and nominated the same slate. Brainerd, who had chaired the union convention, declined the Temperance nomination, perhaps with the assurance that he would have coalition support for election to the last year of deceased Senator Upham's term. He asked Royce to fill the union vacancy for governor, and Royce accepted August 1, saying that the two platforms were "substantially the same." All conventions had named Bates for treasurer.

It took two months to fuse a ticket of Royce, Fletcher, and Bates, and one month of campaigning, wild as the forest fires that swept through the Adirondacks and southern Vermont that year of drought. Free Soil Republicans won by an overwhelming sixty-three percent majority. Left out of the nominations were Democrats turned Free Soilers since 1848; first they had to prove their divorce from the Democrats. Also Daniel Pierce Thompson, editor of the Free Soiler *Montpelier Green Mountain Freeman*, and Dr. Thomas E. Powers, editor of the *Woodstock Vermont Temperance Standard*, each intransigent for their parties, were pointedly ignored, and sulked. This sulking was

---

[23]Charles Paine (b. 1830), "Memoirs," 107; Walter H. Crockett, *Vermont: The Green Mountain State* (New York: Century History, 1921; 5v.), 3:432-433, the standard sketch he gives for all state and federal officers.

reflected in a total for governor of three thousand less than usual, with over six hundred votes for Brainerd, almost three hundred for Powers's candidate, Judge W. C. Kittredge (declined), as well as a few for another judge, proposed by a Webster Whig editor.

The coalition needed two more victories to crystallize the new party. Many third party voters recognized, as Powers and Thompson insisted, that they had sold out to the Whigs. Beyond emphasis on national exclusion of slavery from national property, the platforms quietly asserted the old Whig planks of protective tariff, internal improvements, and free land. They also mentioned prohibition, cheap postage and no franking, and attacked the post office patronage. Late in 1854 non-Democrats began moving in droves to the nativist American Party, a way station for unhappy, unpromoted radicals until it bolted, as so many Vermont Democrats did, over proslavery dominance in their national party. One attempt of the village leadership of the unruly Americans was to reapportion the House of Representatives to reflect population and thereby, it would seem, let the large towns control their foreigners better. The 1855 Council of Censors, largely Know Nothing village merchants and lawyers, proposed such amendments, which the 1856 General Assembly condemned and the 1857 constitutional convention quickly rejected.

The *Rutland Herald*, cool toward fusion in '54, advised Republicans on 27 June, 1855, to "do their quarreling privately and not before the people." With nowhere to go, the Know Nothings won the governorship for the head of their delegation, Ryland Fletcher, and fell in line. By 1856, wrote retiring Congressman Andrew Tracy, the Republican "*scabby state ticket* has the hearty support of the Know Nothings, the Main[e] Law men & the Abolition portion of the Republicans and the acquiescence of the bal[an]c[e] of the Republicans, except here and there one, who, like myself, do not deem it necessary to swallow a nauseous draught."[24]

No sooner had the motley Republican phalanxes marched in November 1856 for "Freedom and Fremont" than a local issue vital to villages threatened Republican harmony. On Tuesday evening, January 6, 1857, the statehouse burned. A cold wave followed by a driving northwest hailstorm made the janitor force the furnaces to reach even fifty degrees in the chambers to prepare for the constitutional convention the next day. Floor timbers ignited over one furnace and flames spread over the wooden interior, sending embers over the village, saved by snow on the roofs. Within three hours of the alarm only a granite shell was left. Within a day, E. P. Walton had wired

---

[24]Tracy to Morrill, 22 July 1856, in the Morrill Papers, Manuscripts Division, Library of Congress, 2:299-299A.

Ammi B. Young in Washington to come and estimate the cost of repairs for the building he had designed twenty-five years before.

The flying embers of village rivalry, blowing up a fire-storm that winter, brought no profit to the Democrats because the fight for the state capital, re-enacting two previous contests in Vermont and in some form almost universally a part of American state history, was kept nonpartisan, and the coalition was united on its Free Soil platform. After Montpelier was selected in 1805 the defeated villages, especially Burlington, did not give up. In 1826 and 1831-32, Burlington bids were narrowly defeated. Burlington is "fast becoming a City," wrote editor D. W. C. Clarke in the *Burlington Free Press* 4 April 1849; "some of these pleasant summer mornings she proposes to move the State House hither." The Assembly turned down Burlington proposals of 1852 and 1854. Her persistence explains Walton's haste in calling for repairs.

On the rational level, Montpelier claimed it had the state's commitment to be the permanent capital, and that it was central. It offered to pay for the repairs, although after it won the offer was forgotten. On the other side, Burlington and Middlebury offered $100,000 toward the cost, Northfield $75,000, and Rutland through quarryman W. F. Barnes, the site and the marble. Junctions like White River, Bellows Falls, and Rutland were more accessible than villages on spur tracks like Montpelier, and with respect to the Central, Burlington.

On the political level, Burlington had to win solidly in the third Congressional district of northwestern Vermont, and then persuade enough representatives from the corner counties. Portus Baxter of Derby, looking to succeed Congressman Homer Royce of St. Albans, and with an influential brother Carlos in Burlington, supported Burlington. Both sides importuned Congressman Morrill. Thomas Powers of Woodstock, still strong among temperance men, first hoped to take state government out of that "rum-hole," but visited Montpelier and changed his mind. He became superintendent of reconstruction. "[Thomas H.] Canfield, a Burlington agent came . . . some two weeks since with Gold and fine promises," wrote Charles K. Field of Newfane to George W. Grandey of Vergennes, "& . . . the 4 papers in this county are all out for Burlington. . . . they have been bought." Lesser and rival towns reacted like Grandey: Burlington, he wrote Field, wants the state capital. It is time the superiority of "That great JEWrusalem . . . the 'Queen City of Lake Champlain,' fulgarly [*sic*] called Burlington by the rustics and barbarians. . . were acknowledged by the dwellers in the *rural districts*."[25]

---

[25]Grandey to Field, 6 February, Field to Grandey, 9 February, 1857, in the Sheldon Museum, Middlebury.

Although the issue was probably decided in the six weeks between the fire and the opening of the ten-day special session February 18, there was plenty of "engineering" at Montpelier between the "third house" and the solons. Walton bestirred himself to offer an enlarged and improved daily *Journal*, for one criticism of Montpelier had been the poor coverage and tardy distribution of session news. Towns sent their weightiest orators to lobby: former congressman Paul Dillingham for Montpelier, former lieutenant governor and circuit court judge Robert Pierpoint for Rutland, and George F. Edmunds, the next Speaker, for Burlington. As long as the favorite town principle operated among a dozen prospective capitals, Burlington held the edge in the Senate and ran a close second in the House. In the end, mileage and rural antagonism to the largest village and its methods triumphed for the incumbent. Burlington was not enough larger than her rivals to steamroller or cajole the votes, and the backfires raised by others in favor of removal to their towns canceled out much of Burlington's strength.

Fletcher was the last reformer-governor for more than a generation. The regular politicians had always stood for "principles, not men," and as soon as they could they ignored the radicals except to shout their shibboleths. The Republican managers, like magicians, focussed the rural voters on distant Kansas and the South, and used the antislavery majorities to "do their quarreling privately" and divide the offices among themselves.

8. Villages Go to War for Freedom and Unity

"If the lightning should announce to the Legislature of Vermont that the Union was dissolved, what would they do?" asked Congressman Meacham of Middlebury. "Would they resolve themselves into a military community and expend their money for arms and ammunition? No, not one dollar.... They do not talk of fighting; and for the plain reason that, if they must fight, Green Mountain Boys can do that extempore, as they did at Ticonderoga, and Bennington, and Saratoga, and Plattsburg."[1] Speaking on the floor of the House during the sectional crisis of 1850, Meacham pointed to peaceable Vermont, where agricultural fairs had replaced militia musters. South Carolina drilled for war, but leading Vermonters held a peace convention. Meacham's speech seemed to support the view that the North would not coerce secessionists.

For twenty years, most ministers in the leading villages, some of the village businessmen and their Whig press, and of course the few Garrisonians, Covenanter Presbyterians and Quakers who had peace or non-resistance principles, had spoken out for the international peace movement. It attracted antislavery reformers like Lawrence Brainerd of St. Albans and educational reformers like Thomas H. Palmer of Pittsford, corresponding secretary of the Vermont Peace Society in the early 1850s. Four governors, four congressmen, and such businessmen as Ferrand F. Merrill of Montpelier and Joseph P. Fairbanks of St. Johnsbury signed an anti-war circular.[2] Episcopal deacon Zadock Thompson of Burlington was Vermont delegate to the London Peace Congress in 1851. Universalist John Gregory and Methodist Royal Gage published anti-war sermons. The venerable Thomas A. Merrill, Middlebury Congregational minister, awarded a five-hundred-dollar prize for a peace essay, and the Congregational state convention kept adopting peace resolutions. Some Southerners sensed the sword behind the back in these left-handed pronouncements for peace, but many saw the irrepressible conflict *within* the North. John Cain, editor of the *Rutland Courier*,

---

[1]Speech printed in *Montpelier Watchman*, 30 May 1850, and praised by editor E. P. Walton.

[2]For a sampling of such sentiments, see the *Montpelier Watchman*, 21 March, 26 September 1850, 24 March 1853; *Middlebury Register*, 16 February, 16 March, 15 June, 6 July, 31 August 1853, 20 February 1856; *Boston Liberator*, 4 April 1856.

repeated the refrain of Democrats elsewhere, that before a brothers' war and "massacre of our own race" should come, Democrats would rise and attack abolitionist "disturbers of the peace on our own soil."[3]

James Meacham's peroration was a true prediction about "fighting extempore." "June trainin'" had degenerated into a farce with an alcoholic aroma, exaggerated in the oft-repeated joke attributed to Lieutenant Governor Robert Pierpoint of Rutland, that "in the troops, there were but three words of command—Mount! Drink! Fall off!" The Vermont militia, however, were foot soldiers with nothing to mount. The same paper thought it news in 1836 that "very few got corned—about the same number put under guard." Julius E. Higgins of Salisbury closed a letter of 6 June 1843 with "You will pardon my hurry, for today is trainin here and I've got lots to do, selling the boys lemons, crackers & candy."[4] From 1844 to 1856 the militia was enrolled and on call, but without training responsibilities. University of Vermont students burlesqued "the burial of June training" (sometimes merged with "the burial of calculus") with an annual costume parade to the Burlington Female Seminary and Court House Square, where crowds flocked to hear the college boys' satires.

Vermont's martial spirit revived in the late fifties with the organization of volunteer militia companies. Brandon, a banner antislavery town, was the first to organize one on 8 March 1855. Its company, the Allen Greys, paraded and lobbied in Montpelier until under radical Governor Ryland Fletcher, the state offered three dollars a year to each man who would drill properly accoutred. In 1857 the legislature renewed poll tax exemption for militia duty. Respectable men of the best families joined the new companies and received a flood of publicity, but not a word was said about the obvious reason for this revival: suspicion of the South. Dress uniforms brightened the winter social season of sleigh rides, soirees, levees, balls, anniversaries and banquets, and in the summer, with parades, excursions, and target shoots, all events flooded with speeches, but apparently not with liquor. At the governor's first muster of nine companies, held 1-2 September 1858, the crowds were pleased in spite of the confused behavior of green men and the injury of three from the "premature discharge of a cannon." Subsequent musters in 1859 at Rutland and 1860 at Montpelier improved in numbers and ability to keep in step, but not much more. Vermont's First Regiment, mustered

---

[3] *Rutland Courier*, 9 December 1959.

[4] *Montpelier Vermont Patriot*, 27 July 1848, also 13 June 1836; Higgins to C. G. Eastman, Woodstock, in the Eastman Papers, Vermont Historical Society. Anthony Marro, "Vermont's Local Militia Units, 1815-1860," *Vermont History* 40 (Winter 1972): 28-42 is the most recent summary.

into federal service 2 May 1861, was drawn from ten of the seventeen companies active by the end of 1860.

Governor Erastus Fairbanks shared Meacham's bifocal vision: willingness to make concessions for the sake of peace but not to sacrifice the free soil principle. In 1857 he had supported compensated emancipation. During the secession crisis, when Vermont's congressional delegation refused to participate in the last minute compromise effort, the peace conference of February 1861, Fairbanks appointed five leading Republicans from the villages of Burlington, Rutland, Bennington, and Brattleboro to represent Vermont. "I think there would be a willingness to repeal the personal liberty laws, should our friends in Washington see occasion to advise it"; but we should never permit the extension of slavery.[5]

Responding immediately to Lincoln's first call for troops, Governor Fairbanks convened a special session of the General Assembly in April and after six days signed an unprecedented million-dollar war appropriation bill. The regular fall session was preoccupied with mobilization. The governor, relying on his experience as the chief executive of a scale factory, had for six months made the decisions necessary to launch five regiments and a company of sharpshooters. "The duties and responsibilities of the Executive are no longer merely nominal," noted the *Rutland Herald* on 31 October 1861, "They are fearfully great." For the first time, individualistic Vermonters were cooperating in a huge, public, collective enterprise, which proved its merit by helping win a great war. The immensity of the resources focused to this end, the complicated, extensive, and large-scale logistics and the size of the labor force, dwarfed all previous Vermont private enterprise, even the building and operation of the railroads.

Although the Civil War was far from total war, the state and local authorities spent "not one dollar" but eight or nine million dollars for Vermont's share of war costs, not to mention uncounted private contributions. As Arthur Wallace Peach has written, the Civil War was one of the "great dramas where Vermonters spoke only a few lines," but spoke them well.

The most important facts in the conscious lives of Vermonters during the war years were the heroic fighting of their volunteers in the South and their willing sacrifices at home. So important were the battles in which Vermonters engaged that they appropriated town money to erect

---

[5]Fairbanks to J. S. Morrill, 29 December 1860, in the Morrill Papers of Special Collections, Bailey/Howe Library, University of Vermont. The participation of Lieutenant Governor Levi Underwood, Lucius E. Chittenden, H. H. Baxter, Hiland Hall, and Broughton D. Harris is recorded in L. E. Chittenden, ed., *A Report of the Debates and Proceedings in the Secret Sessions of the Conference Convention, for Proposing Amendments to the Constitution of the United States* (New York: D. Appleton, 1864).

monuments in their parks and state money to have a detailed history prepared while many participants survived. George Grenville Benedict, who had reported his experiences to his father's *Burlington Free Press* during service with the Twelfth Vermont Regiment (nine months, no battles), molded the myth of Vermont's major service in nine retellings, culminating in his two-volume publication.[6] Newspapers devoted major space to war news. Their editorials shifted focus from the slavery issue to union. Agreed on opposing slavery and secession, with few Copperhead exceptions they differed only on how to win the war.

The federal government and the 1861 legislature made the one-horse executive responsible for six thousand volunteers under arms. From October 1862 to the end of the war the number of Vermont soldiers on active duty fluctuated between twelve and eighteen thousand. The adjutant general reported, for example, 12,127 in service as of 1 October 1864. For every man in service, paper work continued for another resigned, discharged, disabled, deceased, deserted, captured, or unaccounted for. State treasurer's reports show close to $3,900,000 spent for all kinds of state pay for soldiers resident in Vermont when they went to war. This amounts roughly to ten thousand constantly in the services and subject to a peculiar kind of "urban influence" for the duration of a fifty-month war, or upwards of thirty-five thousand who had some brush with the military. Enlistment varied from three months for the First Regiment to nine months for the Twelfth through Sixteenth, and three years for the rest of the Seventeen, the cavalry, and the light artillery. Bounty jumpers, men who enlisted for the bounty, deserted at the first opportunity and repeated the process at a safe distance, "serving" only a few days. On the other hand, some in the First Regiment re-enlisted and served over four years.

The troops, technically employed by Uncle Sam, were constantly reminded by Vermont leaders that they were *Vermont* volunteers. They owed part of their pay, the care of their families, their commissions and promotions, and even their little comforts to the home-state administration. Friends and relations tended morale; Governors Fairbanks and Holbrook and their quartermaster generals tended to supplies, and as federal agents gradually took over, Governor J. Gregory Smith and state treasurer John B. Page of Rutland kept after Washington for reimbursement.

---

[6]G. G. Benedict, *Army Life in Virginia; Letters from the Twelfth Regiment Vermont Volunteers, and Personal Experiences of Volunteer Service in the War for the Union, 1862-3* (Burlington: Free Press, 1895), reprinted from the *Free Press; Vermont in the Civil War: A History of the Part Taken by the Vermont Soldiers and Sailors in the War for the Union, 1861-5* (Burlington: Free Press, 1886-1888, 2 vol.).

In the long run, every town filled its enlistment quota, supposed to be proportioned to population. However, James Harmon found only eighty-nine of the four hundred listing St. Albans as "residence" in the adjutant general's *Revised Roster of Vermont Volunteers* to have been enumerated in the 1860 census for St. Albans. This supports many complaints in the contemporary press that the large towns got credit for recruits who should have been accredited to their home towns.[7]

The leading villages played a key role in assembling and supporting the great military labor force. They had contributed the leaders of the local peace movement, of the militia revival, and of the compromise movement of the winter of 1861. They secured the major recruiting stations, furnished their officers, and held the biggest rallies. They raised the most money for bounties, and served as induction centers and army hospital sites.

Adjutant General H. H. Baxter of Rutland countermanded a federal order that the First Regiment assemble in Burlington, and they rendezvoused in his hometown. The militia companies, including Burlington's, were quartered for two nights in hotels, showing that Rutland hostelries could house a regiment of transients, until the tents arrived. For a week on the fairgrounds they attracted large crowds of family and friends, the curious and the commercial, to spy upon their naked inexperience and enthusiasm, and tend their wants for love or money.

The economic benefits of hosting a rendezvous forced the distribution of induction center patronage among eight principal villages during the first year of mobilization, as shown in the table on the following page. Beginning in January 1862, Brattleboro, the home of Governor Frederick Holbrook, became the induction center for all Vermont troops.

---

[7] James E. Harmon, "St. Albans Volunteers in the Civil War," (term paper for Vermont History, 14 December 1974, in Special Collections, Bailey/Howe Library, University of Vermont), 1. In subsequent conversation with the author, Harmon said he was able to supplement the original list of sixty-four found in the 1860 census. See the Adjutant and Inspector General's *Reports*, 1862-66, and Theodore S. Peck, ed., *Revised Roster of the Vermont Volunteers, and Lists of Vermonters Who Served in the Army and Navy of the United States, 1861-66* (Montpelier: Watchman Publishing, 1892).

Vermont Civil War Camps, 1861-1862

Unit	#	Location	Name of Camp	Weeks in Camp	Period
1st	781	Rutland	Fairbanks	1.0	May
2nd	866	Burlington	Underwood	2.5	Je-Jy
3rd	881	St. Johnsbury	Baxter	7.0	Je-Jy
4th	1,048	Brattleboro	Holbrook	1.5	Sept.
F	116	W. Randolph	—	2 days	Sept.
5th	986	St. Albans	Holbrook	2.0	Sep-Oct
6th	966	Montpelier	Smith	2.5	Oct-Nov
E	91	W. Randolph	—	2.0	Oct-Nov
Cav	1,174	Burlington	Ethan Allen	9.0	Oct-Nov
2Bat	111	Brandon	—	1.0	Oct-Nov
H	100	Brattleboro	—	1.0	Dec
7th	943	Rutland	Phelps	5.5	Ja-Mr
8th	1,016	Brattleboro	Holbrook	9.0	Ja-Mr
1Bat	156	Brattleboro	Holbrook	7.0	Ja-Mr

F. First U.S. Sharpshooters, Company F
E. Second U. S. Sharpshooters, Company E, in leaky horse shed
Cav. First Cavalry in fair bldgs., then Sibley tents
2Bat. Second Battery, Light Artillery
H. Second U. S. Sharpshooters, Company H
1Bat. First Battery, Light Artillery, in portable wooden barracks

The camps had mild epidemics of measles and mumps, a sign that the farm boys had not traveled very far from home before. Insubordination, intoxication, and AWOLs resulted from camp conditions, delays, disappointments over equipment and arms, dislike of officers, and civilian habits. Discipline was better maintained, after experience with the Second and Third Regiments, when officers were promptly commissioned and stayed on the job. Punishment at first consisted, for the repentant or recaptured, of drumming the guilty out of camp or five dollar fines and the guardhouse. The long delay in preparing the Third Regiment at St. Johnsbury resulted in such games as raiding the sutlers' shanties and running the guards, until one ringleader was killed and another wounded while attacking a "refreshment saloon." Filling the county jail in such a situation did not solve the problem. One answer was to keep each company near home until arrangements were completed at the rendezvous. Brattleboro's Company C, Second Vermont, while awaiting the call to Burlington, was removed to Newfane "both for the economy of boarding and as a 'means of grace' in the avoidance of the temptations incident to a large village."[8]

---

[8] *Rutland Herald*, 31 May 1861.

Below: Camp Holbrook at Brattleboro, 1862-65, with Sibley tents in foreground and prefabricated barracks in background. *Above:* Brattleboro military hospital, 1863-65, using the same barracks, shown from a different angle. From the photograph collection of the Vermont Historical Society.

The general atmosphere, however, was one of festivity and adventure. Railroads offered excursion rates to the camps; ladies brought sweets; bands blared; chaplains exhorted at compulsory Sabbath worship to "trust God and keep your powder dry." New buddies and new scenes counteracted homesickness. The eager, earnest boys, brought up on romantic notions of Napoleon and of the American Revolution, felt they were entering the peak experience of their lives. War was still a picnic in the early Vermont camps.

Top-down military discipline did not stop politicking for officer appointments. The elections to be carried were now for company officers and the appointments to be pulled were regimental. The game went on as long as bullets, bayonets, and bacilli found their marks. The players used every kind of pressure. They spoke to the governor or his staff, presented petitions, enlisted their congressmen, family, and friends, argued for geographical distribution, recalled past favors, and pointed to military experience and seniority.

The winners were most often from influential families in the large centers. Fifteen out of eighteen colonels came from large towns, eighteen out of twenty-nine chaplains, and sixty-two percent of the quartermasters. Since Governor Fairbanks complied in five out of six of his appointments with the War Department recommendation that regulars command volunteers (the sixth was a son of the president of Dartmouth, a captain in the Seventh Indiana), early politicking was mostly at the company level. Here a firm custom called for officers who represented their fellow townsmen, yet men from the ten largest towns won nearly a fifth of the commissions. St. Albans and Burlington each had thirty-seven. Late in 1861, when recruiting failed to secure enough from any one town to form a company, hopefuls from different towns competed in company elections. Pressure from the ranks and from home could nullify village influence, as in the cases of Col. Edwin H. Stoughton, age twenty-three, of Bellows Falls, and Major John G. Tyler, age nineteen, of Brattleboro. Tyler resigned. Stoughton, promoted to brigadier general, "was one of the many untried soldiers whose civil influence . . . had gained them high commissions. . . . [He] galloped about on his fine horse, occupied a handsome house, and . . . . gave splendid dinner . . . parties at his quarters in Fairfax Court House."[9] One night after the guests had left, a dozen of Mosby's cavalry entered his bedroom and abducted him. He was exchanged and, although officially cleared, retired to the family law firm.

---

[9] William H. Jackson, *Time Exposure: The Autobiography of William Henry Jackson* (New York: G. P. Putnam's Sons, 1940), 61.

Conflicts in forming the Sixth Regiment erupted onto the floor of the House and Adjutant General Baxter was unseated in favor of Peter T. Washburn of Woodstock. When Col. Henry Whiting of the Second Regiment tried to improve discipline by transferring company officers, Washburn defended the militia's elective principle, and Governor Holbrook objected to applying army rules to "men of property, education and standing." Popular Major Charles H. Joyce, an ambitious young Northfield lawyer, violated regulations by criticizing Whiting, with no harm to his career.

Governor Holbrook, in office two years from October 1861, controlled the initial patronage for all the remaining Vermont units, except the Seventeenth and the Third Battery. Two-thirds of the original field staff of the Second Brigade (the five nine-months regiments called in October 1862) came from large towns, especially St. Johnsbury, Montpelier, and Rutland. They were largely "substantial citizens who had not felt able to leave their business or professions for three years" and did not often re-enlist.[10]

Redfield Proctor of Rutland and Wheelock G. Veazey of Springfield laid the foundations of their political careers in the Second Brigade. Proctor, who had resigned from the Fifth in July 1862 on a plea of ill health, bartered the colonelcies of the Fifteenth for himself and the Sixteenth for Veazey on the promise to appoint Holbrook's choices for staff. This despite his protesting against "military engineering" and "the new order" to appoint from districts that were sending companies. Six weeks later, arguing against a field officer petition for their senior colonel, he pushed Veazey for brigadier general, "the best officer in the Brigade ... my superior an admission I will make for no other officers here."[11]

There was good fishing in 1861, even with very little bait on the bent pin except the appeal to patriotism. Stephen Thomas could even harangue his Eighth on the news of Grant's capture of Fort Donelson that if they didn't hurry up the war would be over and they would get no glory.

Citizens held rallies to raise hundreds of dollars, then thousands, by private subscription, until forced to resort to taxation and bonds. What business-cycle historians call the secession depression was over, and "times" were good in the countinghouse, mill, and hayfield. Many, wrote one irate patriot to the *Montpelier Watchman* of 29 July 1862, have seasonal hands who want to enlist, but these hay-season patriots require "*damages for quitting*, and weigh an acre of grass against our

---

[10]G. G. Benedict, *Army Life in Virginia*, 1.

[11]Proctor to Holbrook, 24 September, 4 November 1862, Proctor Papers in the Vermont Historical Society.

common country." Industrial employers, such as the Vermont & Canada and Vermont Central railroads, and Charles Clement & Son, marble dealers, promised the same or equal jobs after the war to their enlisting employees. If the recruits died, Clement would let their families have their tenements rent-free until the war was over. "All we ask in return is," that when you get South, "you make a market for all the gravestones possible."[12]

When recruiting was renewed in June 1862, the casualties of George B. McClellan's Peninsular campaign and the accumulated complaints from a year since the battle of Bull Run dampened enthusiasm. Letters from the front detailed the usual grievances: more would-be officers disappointed than appointed; dishonest quartermasters; grasping sutlers; continued shortages of good (especially repeating) arms, equipment, and food; idleness; long sick lists and death by amputation; storms, dust, and mud; the strange, annoying ways of a neighboring German regiment; "niggers" (no doubt OK as fighting men, but "I would to God that we could ever say this Flag is a *white one*"[13]); and worry about how things were going with the home folks and bonny Eloise. They knew now that it would be a long war.

As sources for soldiers dried up, competition intensified between regular army recruiters, officers trying to fill their decimated ranks, and unauthorized (especially out-of-state) recruiters. War rallies continued night after night, like protracted meetings, until the town had topped its quota. A New York regiment had offices in Rutland, Burlington, and Montpelier, and rewarded its recruits with a sleigh ride. Vermont recruiters returned the compliment by going outside the state to fill their quotas. Some were not above crimping in Canada. Quartets, choruses, and bands enlivened the rallies, and peals of applause greeted each new recruit. Orators, including officers from the field and former "doughface" Democrats, appealed to the ladies, proclaimed a holy war, a people's war. By 1863, prisoners of war had been released to enlarge upon the horrors of Libby or Andersonville prisons. War correspondents, "contrabands," and Southern Unionists, like the out-of-state big guns in peacetime politics, stirred flagging zeal with atrocity stories and reported how enthusiastically other states were raising men.

Towns could not meet their quotas without ever-increasing bounties, raised by private subscription, then on the grand list; first payable on honorable discharge, then on enlistment. The large towns spent the most: toward the end of 1864, Rutland had paid $134,000 (its final total soared

---

[12] Ibid., 13 August 1862.

[13] H. G. Sanford to Daniel Sanford, 14 March 1863, in the Sheldon Museum.

to $217,000), Bennington $78,000, and Rockingham $70,000, in a state total of $3,876,000 for all kinds of payments to soldiers, $5,181,000 for the whole war. Only a quarter of a million went to nine hundred re-enlisting veterans, while another 350 got no bonus for the same sacrifice. Towns along the Canadian border and in the Champlain Valley apparently drew enough recruits from immigrant labor to spare the veterans. A bill to equalize bounties was kicked around by the General Assembly and never passed.

Almost from the start conscription shamed the reluctant and threatened the recalcitrant into enlisting. The draft, however, was never an important direct means of raising the army: 2,954, or under ten percent of the Vermont aggregate, served under the enrollment act of 1863. To avoid service another 1,971 paid commutation of three hundred dollars, supposed to equal a year's wages of a day laborer, and 816 furnished substitutes. It was a vicious system for finding soldiers in a rich man's war and a poor man's fight.

> Fall in, fall in, you common man,
> The Provost cries, as Pat he collars;
> Don't you wish you were a gentleman,
> That you could spare three hundred dollars?[14]

Such village businessmen as John McKeogh of the Rutland & Washington Railroad, M. C. Huling (Bennington), and Edwin Vallette (Middlebury) paid commutation. From the summer of 1863 a drafted man could pay only three hundred dollars and not have to serve, yet the substitute market, at much higher prices, continued to be brisk. Commutation did nothing to fill town quotas. If shame persuaded men to volunteer, those concerned for their local reputations could buy substitutes and help fulfil their town's obligations. C. A. Reed of Montpelier; Daniel Kellogg, Jr., Brattleboro postmaster; F. F. Holbrook of Brattleboro, the governor's son; Trenor W. Park, Bennington millionaire; ex-Governor Hiland Hall of Bennington; and Rockwood Barrett of Rutland furnished substitutes. At Burlington in later drafts the draft officer of the district, several merchants, a lawyer, a railroad man and LeGrand B. Cannon, president of the Champlain Transportation Company, paid their way out.

During the first draft, begun 10 July 1863, business practically stopped for days in Rutland, Northfield, Montpelier, Woodstock, and probably other centers, yet the papers said all was quiet.

---

[14]*Woodstock Spirit of the Age*, 2 May 1863.

It prompted Bishop Louis de Goesbriand to preach against draft resistance, racism, and strikes.[15] The West Rutland Irish quarriers had organized and armed a "home guard" to protect them from conscription and a "fracas" ensued, followed by the silent departure of the draftees. Three weeks later, when the provost marshal served draft notices at the quarries, he took guards and arrested Hugh Corey, the ringleader.[16]

There were many other ways to avoid conscription. Jay Gould, postwar railroad stock manipulator, then in Rutland managing the Rutland & Washington Railroad, was exempted as a nonresident. Newspaper lists of those exempted for physical disabilities included abnormally large numbers with injuries to extremities. One accused of cutting off two fingers of his right hand was found to be left-handed and sent to the field. Others were said to have pulled their front teeth. Some tried the insurance gamble. In Burlington, for instance, a mutual insurance company of fifteen members, each paying a hundred dollars, was organized the morning of draft day. Five were drafted and used up the fund in commutation pay-offs. Some skedaddled across the border or were prudently sent to schools in Canada East. Some got married.

Substitute brokers and their wares earned a bad reputation in Vermont as elsewhere, both for desertion and extortion. Individuals paid $1,688 each for thirty substitutes in Corinth. A St. Albans man was said to have offered a quarter section of Iowa farm land valued at $960 and on the rise, and $200 cash, a take of more than $2,000 counting pay and bounties. Vermont brokers had a market both in big cities and at home. That raised the price of substitutes and also made it harder for local recruiters to fill their quotas. Brokers swarmed around the draft offices until in Burlington a town meeting authorized a committee to remove them. Long after Vermont sources had been exhausted, Canada contained a pool of enticeable "volunteers." Deserters from the Royal Engineers, Montreal, appeared at the Burlington draft headquarters in 1863, while agents "bought up" parcels of *habitants* to inaugurate the organized immigration business from Canada East.

Draftees and recruits, shipped to Brattleboro barracks, wandered through the grounds without drill, the idle day punctuated by rations, bed on boards, jokes, swearing, and gambling at cards—according to the diaries of more sheltered lads. Since some substitutes escaped, guards paced with loaded muskets.

---

[15]James O'Toole, Archivist of the Archdiocese of Boston, provided the Burlington diocesan archives with a copy of the report in the *Boston Pilot* (19 July 1863) of de Goesbriand's sermon of the previous Sunday.

[16]*Rutland Herald*, 1 August 1863.

Adjutant General Washburn claimed that the ugly substitute business, more profitable and devious than horse trading, was stopped in the end by withholding all but twenty dollars of the recruit's cash, strengthening the guard, and stopping enlistments for everything but the infantry. Perhaps these measures helped, but in the last six months of the war the mercenary motive was supreme; only thirteen conscripts were shipped out. Last resorts for the recruiters, by the summer of 1864, were to enlist civil prisoners or blacks and poor whites behind the Union lines. Meanwhile a large proportion of the replacements were of questionable military caliber, and a third of the substitutes deserted before reaching the front.

Benedict's boast that Vermont sent more soldiers than any other state in proportion to its size is empty in the light of state quotas based on enrollment of draft-eligible men, which went into effect long before the end. Perhaps some day a computerized study will show that Vermont volunteers served more man-days and more fighting days. There may have been fewer non-resident mercenaries and more natives. The final surplus of 697 over all quotas may have been larger than other states', but at the time it was a source of loud complaint that towns had been fooled into spending more money than necessary to squeeze for more soldiers. The other common boast of local patriots, that their troops were bravest because they suffered most casualties ("Put the Vermonters up front"), can also be read to show they were not well trained to take cover or run to fight another day. The romantic cult of Napoleon had a strong hold on Johnny Reb and Billy Yank.

Regardless of comparisons, Vermonters survived an ordeal with less control over their lives than ever before. The legislature piled up new directives to towns and citizens. Governors assumed more power. Their secretaries, the lieutenant governors, and the military establishment no longer had sinecures but busy assistants. They moved their offices from homes to hotels. Governor Holbrook made his headquarters at the Brattleboro House after the 1861 legislature adjourned. John Gregory Smith wrote to Congressman Frederick Woodbridge, "I am as busy as I can possibly be trying to get time to *commence* my inaugural."[17] Add to this embryo state bureaucracy another crowd of federal assessors, collectors, pension agents, quartermasters and provost marshals, with new or reinvigorated duties, and the result was a decided gain in the power of impersonal forces over Vermonters. In executing this power, the same villages furnished the principal agents.

---

[17]John Gregory Smith to Frederick E. Woodbridge, Vergennes, 2 October 1863. Zebina C. Camp, Montpelier, wrote C. M. Fisher, Vergennes, 10 September 1863, that the governor had asked to reserve all the rooms he had available on the lower floor of his boardinghouse. Both letters are in the Sheldon Museum.

Besides the new swarms of officials, appointed and self-appointed agents looked after the soldiers' welfare and kept Copperheads and radicals from diverting energy from the main goal of saving the Union. Against persistent opponents of the war the minutemen proved more zealous for one hundred percent Unionism than for civil liberty. The majority released its resentment at war hardships upon slacker Democrats, yet they had enlisted as readily as Republicans. Partial returns of the vote by Vermont soldiers in the field had as high a percentage for George B. McClellan, the Democratic candidate for president in 1864, as the vote by civilians back home.

Nineteen Democrats served in the 1864 House, and Democratic editors in Rutland, Burlington, Montpelier, Danville, and Woodstock supported McClellan without serious violations of the freedom of the press. They might miss an issue or reduce content for lack of help or cash, or because "the staff" said he had been haying that week. One Republican businessman offered five hundred dollars to those who would sack the *Montpelier Argus and Patriot* office. The *Bangor* (Maine) *Democrat* was sacked, but the *Argus* was not; editor Hiram Atkins survived to show the brickbats that broke his windows.

Free speech, however, was at a discount. Lieutenant Governor Paul Dillingham, former Democratic Congressman, told a Montpelier rally the first thing "was to stop, as far as possible, free speech"—that is, fault-finding.[18] U.S. marshal C. C. P. Baldwin arrested three "for expressing secessionist sentiments," but a grand jury refused to indict and Baldwin was fined a hundred dollars for unlawfully suspending habeas corpus. Baldwin charged Lewis S. Partridge of Norwich with treason for cutting down an American flag and brandishing pistols when soldiers came to raise it again. Two years later Partridge was tried for draft obstruction and acquitted. In Rutland Provost Marshal C. R. Crane stopped such subversive influences as the singing of "Tenting Tonight" and "When This Cruel War Is Over." Hiram Walker, Burlington wholesaler and substitute broker roughed up by Crane and Rutland selectmen in 1864, eventually won heavy damages for assault and false imprisonment. John McKeogh, suspected of aiding the Montreal defense of the St. Albans raiders, spent six weeks in a Washington prison but the government dropped his case after the war ended. In spite of compulsory flag-raisings, rotten-eggings, store-burnings, and fist fights, civil liberties survived better in Vermont than in places where the opposition was stronger.

---

[18]Reported in *Montpelier Watchman*, 25 July 1862. The *Watchman* of 25 June 1863 called free speech "the curse of republics," but approved of the conscientious expression of moral judgments.

While patriots muffled the scapegoat Copperheads, a term not much used to describe Vermont Democrats, every home-bound citizen found some way to help win the war. Governors' agents looked into soldier welfare along the Potomac, town agents looked after soldiers' families, while lawyers and bankers served as middlemen on claims for bounties, back pay, and pensions. Governor Fairbanks appointed Joseph Poland of the *Montpelier Green Mountain Freeman* financial agent to handle the transfer of state pay from soldiers to their families. Although the Assembly remonstrated at Fairbanks's usurping its power and not using the state treasurer, Governor Frederick Holbrook followed the same course in appointing John Howe, Jr., Brandon scalemaker, to superintend family disbursements and explain the federal allotment system. Fairbanks appointed his New York scale agent to the position of deputy quartermaster general; his successor, Governor Holbrook, appointed John Howe's brother and partner Frank. Instead of overseers of the poor, special town agents investigated cases, but some used private channels, subject to embezzlement, to send money home.

The ladies enlisted for the duration, sending packages while the authorities were improvising. They sent old table linen, cotton sheets, and lint for bandages; favorite pills and tonics; clothing; red, white and blue sewing kits; soap; maple sugar, barrels of apples; prayer books; good luck charms—whatever the soldier might want but could not carry. Even the despised German Jewish peddler won esteem by donating his wares. In cash contributions to the U.S. Sanitary Commission, a centralized way to help the soldiers, the centers ultimately outstripped the back country. Merchants provided free storage, the papers gave free publicity, and the railroad carried the materials free. The express companies apparently charged.

Politics was bitter over the lucrative business of supplying the troops. Governor Fairbanks, a business executive of thirty years' national experience, expedited the outfitting of the first five thousand troops, and bypassed Quartermaster General George F. Davis of Cavendish and Adjutant General H. H. Baxter of Rutland wherever possible. The fight probably started with Fairbanks's defeat of Holbrook in the "primary" canvassing for governor in 1860, if not in 1852. Also involved were the clashing interests of northern and southern Vermont, and between conservative and radical Republicans. In September 1862 Fairbanks suspended Davis for insubordination and substituted Worthington C. Smith of the St. Albans Foundry, resolving to prevent Davis's re-election in joint assembly. Davis was a small-town trader and local politician, with the support of ex-Governor Ryland Fletcher of Cavendish, ex-Speaker Abram B. Gardner of Manchester, and Governor Holbrook's following. Cold fury animated the contestants, who snubbed each other in the halls of the capitol. Few questioned Davis's integrity, wrote one legislative correspondent, but some doubted his ability. Opponents taxed Fairbanks with overweening vanity, Davis with having back tracks to cover. The current business of forwarding another twenty-five hundred men kept both parties up to their ears in vouchers. In spite of a crowded calendar and the longest session since 1853, solons found time for a Burlington junket to watch a cavalry parade, visits to Camp Smith in Montpelier, a lavish dedication of Larkin G. Mead's statue of Ethan Allen, and endless palaver about retrenchment.

Fairbanks and his New York agent Hatch spent $67,000 for English Enfield rifles, hard to get and favorites with the men. Hatch sent tons of provisions to the First Regiment at Fortress Monroe, with Vermont purchases totaling half a million those first few months of the war. They were mainly from out-of-state because local manufacturers and dealers had small stocks.

Amid charges and countercharges of corruption and mismanagement, and for lack of sources, it is hard to tell who was right. Fairbanks collected 174 draft horses at about $110 each; a little later Sheriff William M. Field of Brandon bought cavalry mounts for $100. Rations for the first five regiments in Vermont camps came to $27,000, or half the subsistence bill, mostly to hotel keepers and wholesale grocers, or about thirty-three cents per man per day. Davis, after some war inflation, spent fifty cents per man per day and made at least $12,000 for the state on the liberal federal repayment.

Uniforms, the next necessity after food, could be made of Vermont woolens by Vermont tailors. Clothing contracts and deliveries were the crux of the debate. The *Woodstock Standard* accused the state of breaking its contract with Solomon Woodward, Woodstock woolen manufacturer, and accepting shoddy (only half wool, "heavily flocked") from Prosper Merrill of Felchville at a quarter above the normal price. This sixteen-thousand-dollar contract was defended as eighty percent wool, the rest cotton, a standard cloth among Vermont farmers. Rutland, Brattleboro, and other merchant tailors made uniforms with blue trim and gilt buttons out of this cloth and overcoat material bought for six thousand dollars from Fullertons & Company, Proctorsville. The House sent Davis to survey conditions at the front. He admitted that the gray uniforms were faded and ragged and the sewing had given out. Whether it was his fault or not, he was re-elected on other grounds than competence, and continued until the end of 1864, when Perley P. Pitkin of Montpelier replaced him. There was many a heated contest thereafter, over banks, railroads or whatnot, but people soon took petty war inefficiencies, inequities, and corruptions for granted.

Officer petitions and privates' letters home eloquently documented deprivations. Tents, overcoats, and blankets were lost in the pell-mell flight from Manasses—"We lacked underclothing after Bull Run," wrote one soldier.[19] Davis reported a shortage of 460 pairs of shoes, and the shortages continued throughout the war.

Brattleboro business boomed in 1862, when eight regiments encamped at Camp Holbrook. The fourteen hundred troops in September swelled to nearly five thousand men in October. Twelve dealers in lumber, stoves, iron, tinware, and dry goods grossed $4,600 from the state in 1862; some grocers and bakers received twice as much, and others, including Governor Holbrook, Levi K. Fuller, Estey & Green, and the Brattleboro House, supplied wood, straw, and incidentals. Lawrence Barnes of Burlington hastily fabricated portable houses in sections for the Eighth Regiment. Built like summer cottages, they admitted the sub-zero winds of January and were replaced by "permanent" barracks.

Rutland kept the Seventh in the winter of 1862 with corresponding profits, especially to Frederick Chaffee (overcoats), French & Kingsley (hardware), and Pond & Morse (drugs). Other winners were the Chester Boot Company ($2,720), Lamson, Goodnow & Yale of Windsor and Shelburne Falls, Massachusetts ($2,227 over two years, including hospital knives and forks), and stoves from the St. Albans Foundry for the Seventeenth in Burlington. Dorr, Proctor & Co. (Seneca Dorr and Redfield Proctor, later involved in the Sutherland Falls Marble Company; Proctor had just resigned with "well advanced consumption" from the Fifth Regiment) handled $333 worth of "subsistence."

State disbursements for equipment and subsistence declined and expenses for hospitals at Brattleboro, Burlington, and Montpelier increased:

	1861-62	1862-63	1863-64
Equipment	$71,000	$400	$2,600
Subsistence	3,000	100	2,800
Hospitals	8,000	12,000	30,000
Total	147,000	64,000	41,000

Judge David A. Smalley's white elephant of a Marine hospital at Burlington was turned over to the state during May and June 1862. Samuel W. Thayer of the University of Vermont Medical

---

[19]*Rutland Herald*, 6 November 1861.

Department, Fairbanks appointee as Chair of the State Board of Medical Examiners, took charge, and opened a small infirmary at Brattleboro that September.

The government disposed of its surplus camp property at bargain prices. Lumber, fixtures for bunks and partitions, and a hundred rods of lead water pipe at the St. Johnsbury fair building went for $61.50 after the Third Regiment left town. The hospitals, costing about $100,000 to fit and furnish, went at fractional prices. Quartermaster General Davis had used Lawrence Barnes's method of sectional construction at Montpelier, intending to sell the buildings later as private dwellings, but the trustees of the Methodist Vermont Conference Seminary and Female College persuaded his successor to sell at half-price in 1866. Burlington's Home for Destitute Children passed the hat and bid off the Marine hospital for seven thousand without competition. Congress had appropriated thirty-nine thousand federal dollars to build it in 1856-58.

State military expenses continued high as the militia expanded in response to the scare caused by the spectacular St. Albans bank robbery of 19 October 1864. A score of Confederates held up the three banks, set fires, and made off to Canada with $200,000 in notes and greenbacks. A militia bill, annually proposed and ignored, was again being considered at the moment the Rebels crossed the border. The crisis achieved what discussion could not, and the pattern of federal enlistment was embodied in a new law, with geographical districts and the draft to back it.

Soon hundreds of militia took arms, officered by such future political leaders as W. W. Grout, John L. Barstow, Redfield Proctor, Roswell Farnham, and G. Grenville Benedict, and were quartered in St. Albans barracks and along the border. Eventually a "division" guarded the frontier, staying until June 1865, when the war was over. People kept seeing Rebels instead of Champlain sea serpents. All over New England "raiders" were arrested on suspicion. The quartermaster general, still spending upwards of eighty thousand dollars in May 1865, sold off state installations in 1866. No more bodies went a-mouldering to the grave, but the militia kept marching on. Hostility to Canada for its dilatory procedures in trying the raiders helped kill Vermont support for Canadian-American commercial reciprocity, ended in 1867.[20]

The test of Vermont's wartime economy was not in its catering to the needs of a few thousand state volunteers and militia, but how it competed for federal war contracts. It furnished rifles, gunpowder, and woolens, but not much else in quantity. Fairbanks Scales partially converted

---

[20] Parts of this chapter were published as "For Freedom and Unity: Vermont's Civil War," *Vermont Life* 15 (Spring 1961): 36-37, 47-50, and are used with permission.

to making harness irons, and hired three hundred workers by the end of 1862, nearly four hundred in 1864. Howe's scale contract was too small to prevent its failure and reorganization within the next few years. Lamson, Goodnow & Yale, their Windsor armory idle for two years, contracted in June and July 1861 for 110,000 Sharps carbines totaling $2,800,000, and other ordnance throughout the war. Things were popping for the Bennington Powder Company, but the price was worth the hazard and the periodic shut-downs between explosions and between contracts. The big woolen mills, notably the Harding factory in Winooski and the Carpenter mill at North Pownal, filled orders in six digits.

Beyond war contracts, prosperity with skyrocketing prices followed established lines, woolen textiles leading the field. Lumbermen were coining money in the Bennington district and in the northeastern woods, with attendant stimulation of woodworking. Davey & Nichols's Fair Haven rolling mill rolled steadily on through the winters. The St. Albans car foundry and machine shops retooled in 1862-63, and in 1864 hired 450 to make ten locomotives and other castings. The Rutland & Burlington built a three-thousand-dollar car house at Rutland and acquired the Brandon car shops in 1864; all its freight cars had been made in Rutland since 1862.

Marble shipments from the Rutland quarries reached a low of $450,000 worth in 1862. In the fall of 1863 Baxter sold some of his quarries and granted a winter increase of $1.25 a day, but the Irish workers were still restive. The following spring they folded their arms against the Rutland Marble Company, demanding $1.75 for a ten-hour day. In spite of the company's winning a test case among sixty-nine suits of ejectment from company tenements, the strikers won, and the company still declared a five percent dividend in 1864.

Labor shortage and revived demand finally brought to birth the mechanical stonecutter. George J. Wardwell built the first workable steam channeler for the Sutherland Falls Marble Company in 1863. Essentially a locomotive pile driver on a temporary track, it pounded a set of chisels arranged like a stepped gable, moving along the groove half an inch per stroke to the end of the track and back. After two or three inches of cut they stopped the engine and adjusted the chisel clamps. It was still considered an experiment five years later. With the expansion of the marble business it caused no technological unemployment.

Other mining and quarrying was spotty. City demand for marbleized slate mantels, table tops and fireplace trim grew and Fair Haven's slate business began to overtake Castleton's. Orange County's copper and copperas, and Bennington's and Pittsford's ironworks prospered. Tyson Furnace in Plymouth blasted only a few months of 1864 and then closed down.

Neighborhood industry, trade and business services shared the war boom. Men worked longer and harder for better wages[21]; women and children perforce took on a larger share. People complained about speculation in firewood and the 1864 strike of Burlington journeyman tailors. Business school Bryant & Stratton foresaw enough patronage to open the Burlington Commercial College in 1863.

Building construction, most active in Rutland and Burlington after 1863, featured new streets, business blocks, and public buildings, especially churches. Burlington introduced gas streetlights in 1862, improved pavements, sidewalks and parks, added Congregational, Baptist, and Roman Catholic houses of worship, and in 1865 broke its record for lumber sales.

St. Albans joined the big three in banking—Rutland, Burlington, and Brattleboro—and the four towns handled about half the state's banking affairs. By mid-1865 sixteen national banks had been organized, all but four from eight leading towns. Circulation and discounting swelled while alarmists feared the decline of specie backing and the larger amounts sent to city banks where rates were higher. Few worried about the ultimate fate of greenbacks, although they repeated the riddle that they were like the Jews, issues of Abraham and knew not their Redeemer. Shinplasters, a term of derision for privately issued paper money, were a nuisance and many Rutland and Burlington merchants refused to accept them. Even postage stamps were made legal tender.

The daily newspaper, which can survive only in cities, got a toehold in Burlington in 1848, where the four factors necessary for its nineteenth-century success first came together in Vermont: the telegraph, fast power presses, an urban population, and train service. After a rocky start, the original entrepreneur sold out in 1853 to G. W. Benedict, who kept the daily with its supporting weekly on a firm business basis thereafter. Burlington was nearing a population of seven thousand when the *Burlington Free Press* started.[22]

Rutland reached the same population level in the late 1850s, but George A. Tuttle waited until the war broke out to launch his daily *Herald*, while the First Regiment camped at the fairground. The *Herald* pioneered in publishing the full telegraphic reports of the Associated Press. While it could not supplant city papers in county circulation, it had features that the metropolitan press could not duplicate: detailed accounts of actions involving Vermont troops, and abundant

---

[21]T. M. Adams's averages for day labor with board are $.82 in 1861, $1.29 in 1865; by the month with board, $13.28 to $24.88 (*Prices and Wages*, 70). Monthly pay did not reach $25 until 1910.

[22]This summary is based on my article, "The First Vermont Dailies: A Chapter in Newspaper History," *Vermont Quarterly* 14 (October 1946): 155-162.

correspondence from the Vermont camps. The price of the daily *Herald* rose from six dollars a year to ten in 1864 because of increased telegraphic rates, increased editorial staff, higher printers' wages, and the higher cost of paper.

Compared to the leisurely pace of personal journalism before the war, the process now seemed hectic. All the night wires and much of the local news and communications had to be hand set in type (the linotype machine was more than twenty years off), proofread, corrected, and sent to press between nine in the evening and three in the morning to catch the early trains. The staff had once consisted of a printer, his helpers, and an editor who had plenty of time to play politics and perhaps run another small business. Now there were twelve to twenty printers, an editor-in-chief and one or two associates, a local editor, a legislative correspondent, and town correspondents. Headlines and extras appeared at every war crisis, on the front page, not buried inside as before.

Rutland typesetters, perhaps realizing their slim chances of becoming editor-publishers and feeling the bite of Civil War inflation, organized a genuine typographers' union in 1862. At first a mutual benefit society of ten *Herald* employees, it reorganized in December 1863 as a full-fledged business union with wage and closed shop demands. The *Herald* foreman was president; the foreman of the rival *Courier* was treasurer. Promptly after reorganization the union struck, "took possession" of the *Herald* shop according to the employer's story, printed circulars warning scabs away, picketed the depot, and threatened personal violence to incoming printers. The publisher complained that he was a practical printer excluded from the union; sporadic "press unions" of the fifties had been editor-dominated newspaper associations. The *Herald* missed four issues and announced six weeks later that the cost of typesetting had risen fifty percent since 1862. Was the publisher concealing his concession to the union as merely war inflation? No other Vermont printers struck before 1879.

Two papers in Montpelier tried daily publication during the war, as well as another in Burlington and one each in St. Johnsbury and St. Albans. The *Burlington Times* sold out to the *Free Press* in 1868, and only the *St. Albans Messenger* survived, as its town reached the urban threshold of 7,000 in 1870.

Vermont Payers of Poll Taxes, 1860-64

County	1860	1864	Gain	% Gain
Windsor	7,064	8,437	1,373	19.4
Chittenden	4,157	4,823	666	16.0
Windham	5,250	6,068	818	15.6
Rutland	6,285	6,990	705	11.2
Franklin	3,900	4,301	401	10.3
Grand Isle	618	781	63	10.2
Addison	3,869	4,256	387	10.0
#VERMONT	56,524	61,743	5,219	9.2
Bennington	3,289	3,551	262	7.9
Orange	5,023	5,378	355	7.1
Orleans	3,717	3,839	122	3.3
Lamoille	2,458	2,520	62	2.5
Caledonia	4,142	4,167	25	.6
Washington	5,548	5,551	3	.1
Essex	1,204	1,181	-23	-1.9

Selected Towns

Town	1860	1864	Gain	% Gain
St. Albans (railroad, foundry)	475	752	277	58.3
Fair Haven* (iron,woolens,slate)	460	662	202	43.9
Windsor* (rifles)	291	413	122	41.9
Orwell* (sheep)	212	281	69	32.5
Cavendish* (woolens)	596	762	166	27.9
Springfield (machines, woolens)	564	721	157	27.8
Pittsford* (iron, foundry)	590	740	150	27.1
Highgate (small mills, trade)	281	353	72	25.6
Pownal* (woolens)	200	250	50	25.0
Shaftsbury* (iron, tools)	259	321	62	23.9
Randolph (trade)	470	575	105	22.4
Corinth* (copper)	320	390	70	21.9
Colchester (woolens, foundry)	487	592	105	21.6
Brattleboro (machines, woolens)	703	842	139	19.8
Woodstock (machines, woolens)	604	713	109	18.0
Rutland (RR, foundry, marble)	1,230	1,434	204	16.6
Middlebury (small mills, trade)	383	441	58	15.2
Burlington (trade, woodworking)	980	1,116	136	13.3
Swanton (small mills)	349	389	40	11.5
#Rockingham (RR, woolens)	563	622	59	10.5
Montpelier (capital, small mills)	520	556	36	6.9
St. Johnsbury (scales)	769	807	38	4.9
Brandon (iron, scales)	378	395	17	4.5
Castleton (slate, marble mills)	538	559	21	3.9
Bennington (powder,textiles,iron)	648	650	2	.3
Newbury	509	501	-8	-1.6
Derby*	391	382	-9	-2.3
Vergennes* (small mills)	177	166	-11	-6.2
Danville	470	413	-57	-12.1
Dorset* (marble)	410	320	-90	-22.0
Northfield (RR shops closed)	849	654	-95	-23.6

*Population under 2500 in 1860. Bennington gained in 1864-65. #Counties and towns above these two lines grew more than overall state percentage.

Those who forwarded and financed the farmers' produce benefited from the general prosperity. Lacking a mid-decade state census like New York's, we can guess population trends reflecting that prosperity from published poll tax figures. The available breadwinners, that is, all men between twenty-one and sixty, not exempt for extreme infirmity, military or fire duty, were subject to the two-dollar tax. The returns for 1864 showed a ten percent gain over 1860, shared to some extent by all but seventy-four towns, but most pronounced in the Champlain Valley, the southern industrial centers and adjacent farming communities, and some of the lumbering areas. Sales of cattle and swine for army rations and to Boston, a brisk city market for matched carriage horses, and peak prices for hay, wool, pedigreed merinos, and Morgan cavalry mounts rewarded the farmers.

Vermont farmers had begun to use mowing machines in the middle fifties, but the rough terrain and the crudity of the first models had prevented their widespread adoption. As girls replaced their soldier brothers in the hayfield, mowers became a must. Sales rose, especially during the frequent competitive trials during haying season. The St. Albans Foundry Company set itself a quota of seven hundred Buckeye mowers for 1865. By that year the more affluent farmers were using not only grass cutters but hay presses, turnip cutters, sowers, and threshers.

Railroad, express, and telegraph companies did well. On the Passumpsic, Lyndonville (with new car shops), Barton, and Newport grew, but Northfield, which lost its Vermont Central car shops to St. Albans, slipped badly, not regaining its 1860 level of population until 1950. In the spots that missed the upswing, people prospected for copper and gold, or thought a railroad spur would bring a boom. The first of these postwar projects, the Woodstock Railroad, was chartered during the war. Two Lake Memphramagog steamers, the *Mountain Maid* and the *Ironside*, carried freight between Magog and the Passumpsic Railroad terminus at Newport, but as on Lake Champlain, the new focus was on tourists. For the same class of passenger the Central added "smoking and euchre" cars in 1863 and parlor cars the next year.

Inns by mountain, spring, and lake, such as at Manchester, Clarendon Springs, and Mount Mansfield, shared the wealth with village hotels doubling in tradesmen. Congressman E. P. Walton wrote in his paper:[23]

---

[23]*Montpelier Watchman*, 13 August 1863.

> We have tried mountain and sea-shore, and learned that the only place where one can find plenty of room and comfort is at home. . . . The mountain houses are full; the sea-side houses are full; the way-side houses are full; the railroad trains are full . . . of gasping humans and grasping inhumans. . . . eager in the search of health and pleasure. War seems only a moderate excitement to keep people contented for an hour or two after the arrival of the morning and evening newspapers.

Gasping and grasping were keynotes of wartime when people felt keenly for those suffering for the cause of Union, and forgot about the endemic ills: schools and churches poorly attended and limping along while their teachers and preachers were in the army; higher education, except military academies and female seminaries, stripped of students. Men made gifts and functionaries went through the motions, but social progress on the home front was suspended.

While the pious outdid themselves in offices of tenderness to suffering soldiers, and paid meet adoration to their household gods, the revivals of the late fifties died out. Camp meetings became unnecessary as social functions while emotions were released at parades, rallies, and victory celebrations. Businessmen were too busy for prayer meetings. The recognized value of fighting men of any faith suppressed anti-Catholicism, yet when the legislature urged the appointment of Fr. Zephyrin Druon of Montpelier as Roman Catholic chaplain for Vermont troops, he was not appointed. Druon did travel to Washington for Governor Holbrook in November 1861 and spoke at recruiting rallies.

In the superabundance of wartime recreation, "blue lights" detected an insidious note of city corruption. While they blessed patriotic celebrations, target shoots, oyster suppers for soldiers' benefits, and receptions for returning veterans, they felt there was altogether too much betting on horse races and football in the streets. They raised no serious objections to the further spread of the baseball fad and tolerated commercial roller skating rinks, magicians, circuses, and exhibitors of war panoramas. The strait-laced objected to raffles, grab bags and lotteries at local fairs, raising money for bandages and other soldier needs. Altogether too many females taught penmanship, read sketches, or declaimed in public. In St. Johnsbury, stricter than any other large Vermont village except possibly Windsor or Woodstock, young America patronized a dancing school, which wound up with a ball at the St. Johnsbury House. The North and South Congregational churches got even through the aqueduct company, which closed the St. Johnsbury House the morning after by shutting off its water.

Worst of all was the resurgence, with Mars, of the rest of the unholy trinity, Venus and Bacchus. Two Vermont soldiers, in Poughkeepsie a few days, were married on the spot. Bennington justices of the peace got up a petition that secured the repeal of the required publication of the banns—that is, a decent interval between intention and consummation of marriage. Rivals across the state line were getting all the business. Other phenomena were of the sort not recorded, although, as usual, there was a bawdyhouse keeper in Windsor prison.

Temperance was a war casualty. One irate citizen wrote to the *St. Johnsbury Caledonian* that vulgarity and profanity prevailed in one railroad car on the Passumpsic from St. Johnsbury to Newport. He deplored "smoking, drinking and card playing . . . whisky openly retailed in the car at 'fifteen cents a drink.' . . . the almost universal increase of intemperance, especially among our young men and boys."[24] Prohibitionists renewed their efforts, fines from tavernkeepers increased, spellbinder John Gough drew capacity audiences, S. W. Hewlett gave his celebrated "Rum and Rebellion" lecture, and drys swept elections for county liquor commissioners. Yet consumption increased as quality deteriorated with advance in price. Many soldiers who had taken the temperance pledge when they left home came back demoralized. "Our streets are almost daily disgraced by some soldier or citizen in a state of beastly intoxication," lamented a letter of 17 January 1865 to the *Montpelier Freeman*.

The war could not fail to transform mores and institutions, but social changes come slowly. While submerged in the fog of battle, Vermonters dreamed only in terms of conditions they knew before. They could see that times were fast and good, that cash came easy, but prices were high and money had wings. When this cruel war was over, the lasting would emerge from the chaff of passing fashion and temporary luck.

---

[24] Quoted in the *Rutland Herald*, 19 July 1864.

9. Postwar Village Industry

Victory was uppermost in Vermonters' minds during the spring of 1865. Bells ringing after Appomattox, then tolling for the death of President Lincoln, symbolized the feelings of relief and hope, hatred and sorrow, uncertainty and optimism that churned in men's minds. The earliest returning regiments were feted; most of the others drifted back during the summer without getting much attention. The last soldiers, 348 of the Seventh Regiment out of an aggregate of 1,571 on its roster at some time during its four years' service, mustered out at Brownsville, Texas, in March 1866. Many of the young skilled or unskilled laborers who were discharged in the South declined the free fare home and chose to try their fortunes where opportunity seemed brighter. Some checked in at home, looked around, and left. Those who had a property stake or professional promise were more likely to come back and stay.

The return of the privates was bittersweet. Everyone who had gone to war, or had supported those who did, knew someone dead or damaged by the ordeal. Everyone who survived was determined to move ahead. Yet for most of them the good times of the first postwar years were the last times that fortune would smile broadly on that generation in Vermont. In the valley villages and in three dozen recently developed lumbering towns, prospects were good, but abandonment was the main theme for the large majority in the hill towns. Hal Seth Barron's case study of Chelsea has shown the differentials between those who stayed home or nearby and those who found nothing worth keeping them there. The long-held notion that the hill towns were generally hard-pressed to make ends meet is borne out by the gross figures. Revisionists are also right that an ingroup of comfortable, homogeneous farm managers, merchants and professionals, with limited horizons, were satisfied to stay in rural communities like Chelsea, bound by the familiar and the familial to their basically static but not stagnant ways. For example, forward-looking farmers, advised by the agricultural press, were using mowing machines and horse rakes instead of scythes with cradles, steel instead of cast-iron plows, and mechanical cornplanters, but felt they were farming in the ways of their fathers. The silo would arrive by the 1880s, and the manure spreader not long after.[1]

Two-thirds of the land was "improved," the census word for cleared, and lumbermen were rapidly harvesting the mountainsides. Few came to settle in the country. Self-exiled Vermonters came back for visits, institutionalized from the 1890s as Old Home Week. Some Irishmen and French Canadians, whose fathers had been farmers, left railroad, quarry, or mill for a run-down farm they could afford in places like Underhill or Barnard. But as Harold F. Wilson has pointed out, rural decline did not imply the general collapse of agriculture: "Abandonment . . . was a sign more of economic readjustment than of decadence."[2]

By 1870 the value of farms had increased to a peak of $139,368,000, much of which, however, represented Civil War inflation. The number of farms increased to 35,522 in 1880, although the peak probably came earlier, as the census included farms that were unoccupied or unworked. The average size of a farm, 1850-80, stayed just under 140 acres, because the number of larger farms kept increasing, but the median size, well below a hundred acres, declined. This reflected abandonment by sale to more prosperous neighbors and to the few immigrants beginning small.

Production of all grains had peaked before the Civil War, except oats, raised to feed horses, twice as numerous as oxen in 1870. Vermont began to have more cattle (never more cows) than people during the 1870s, while there were only a third as many sheep in 1870 as thirty years before. Now that railroad refrigerator cars kept summer butter fresh, by 1880 Vermont ranked tenth nationally in total butter production. This was a shift from cheese production, in which Vermont was third in 1850.

Some of the increased appraisals and increased production related to the new wave of railroad building. If the railroad tonic had made the valley villages healthy, why not more railroads for those still deprived? Railroad conjurers reappeared in forgotten valleys, repeating the old arguments and exciting the old hopes. Between 1865 and 1900, 458 miles of single track were added to the existing 544, nearly three-quarters of it in the 1870s. The hype still talked of through routes west, but except for the Portland & Ogdensburg (from 1880 the St. Johnsbury and Lake Champlain), they were only spurs, forced to close by the 1930s by automotive and air competition.

---

[1] Hal Seth Barron, *Those Who Stayed Behind: Rural Society in Nineteenth Century New England* (New York: Cambridge University Press, 1984) outlines the rural conservatism of this period.

[2] Harold F. Wilson, *The Hill Country of Northern New England: Its Social and Economic History, 1790-1930* (New York: Columbia University Press, 1936) 97-138, quotation on 155.

The short lines benefited shippers and their terminals, but not their stockholders. When funds ran out during construction, town bonding was the panacea. The legendary Vermonter is a pay-as-you-go person, but farm mortgages were numerous and towns had bonded for five million dollars in bounty obligations. Why not borrow to bring the benefits of the rails to more people? The legislature granted each separate petition for town subscriptions to railroads until 1872, when it allowed any town, with the approval of a majority of taxpayers, to assume railroad liabilities up to eight times its grand list.

The Portland & Ogdensburgh had the seaport's power, out to win western traffic from Boston, and Governor Horace Fairbanks to push it 120 miles from Lunenburg to Maquam Bay on Lake Champlain, as a club to beat down the Central's freight charges. "Finished" to the lake in 1877, it had a "tap," the Burlington & Lamoille, completed the same year from Burlington to Cambridge Junction. After the Central leased the B. & L. in 1889, it operated only from Essex Junction to Cambridge Junction, using C. V. tracks into Burlington.[3]

Southwestern Vermont was thrown into an uproar in 1867-68 by the contest between H. Burden & Sons' Troy & Boston Railroad and the Rutland & Bennington, led by its president, Trenor W. Park. He wanted a connection south to New York via his Lebanon Springs line, free from control by the Troy interests. The Burdens, having lost the lease of the Rutland & Bennington, wanted at least a road they could control to their iron mines and limestone quarry in Bennington, if not the traffic of Bennington and Rutland counties. Governor John B. Page, who controlled the Rutland and with John Gregory Smith had leased the Rutland & Bennington, attached the Troy & Boston's rolling stock, stopped traffic, and called a special session of the legislature. High-powered lobbyists debated, and Page and Park won. Edward C. Kirkland has shown how the larger rivalries between Troy, Albany, New York, Boston, Portland, and Montreal affected their Vermont feeders.[4] This episode shows how villages fought for advantages within that larger framework.

The gap between dreams and realities was perhaps greatest along the Ottauquechee. Promoters in the forties talked of a White River to Whitehall line following the present heavily traveled Route 4, except that no one ever explained how a train could hurdle the ridge in Sherburne

---

[3]Robert C. Jones, *The Central Vermont Railway: A Yankee Tradition*, vol. 1, *The Early Years, 1830-1886* (Silverton, Colo.: Sundance Publications, 1981), 94, 114.

[4]E. C. Kirkland, *Men, Cities and Transportation*, 1:228-231 discusses Troy and Albany rivalry for northern business; "The Failure of a Route," 1:433-465, summarizes Boston's efforts to consolidate and overcome the difficulties posed by five jurisdictions, 1870-1887.

or Chittenden. Chartered in 1847 and again during the Civil War, the Woodstock Railroad broke ground in 1868. The first laborers netted only $4.60 a week and soon walked off. Probable accessions from Rutland quarry strikers and transient French Canadians enabled the work to straggle on. The supply teamster left owing $600. Ralph Jones & Company, contractors from Port Hope, Ontario, got two months behind on the payrolls and were attached. In April 1870 people were buying wage claims in St. Johnsbury at a quarter on the dollar. A debt of a quarter-million stopped construction in 1870, but legislation and town bonding brought completion of the fourteen miles to the county seat by the fall of 1875. Woodstock continued to lose population, but was able to develop an early resort business from being a minor railhead.

Lumber and charcoal interests built the ten-mile Bennington & Glastenbury in 1872, with a life of twenty-six years. The Missisquoi Valley twisted back and forth across the old stage road to Richford in 1872-73, and in 1874 connected with Newport via the Missisquoi & Clyde, partly in Canada. The Barre & Chelsea, more valuable than all the other spurs combined, unlocked the Barre granite deposits in 1875. In 1888 it proved to the ghost of Charles Paine, who had rejected the route in 1846, that a railroad could negotiate Williamstown Gulf. The Montpelier and Wells River, a dream of 1850, opened in 1873, missed the copper towns, and went bankrupt in 1877. The narrow gauge Brattleboro & Whitehall worked its way up the West River as far as South Londonderry by 1880, and went no farther.

Extravagant railroad lobbying persuaded some politicians to call for throwing the railroad rascals out and abolishing the "third house." But the *Montpelier Watchman* of 20 July 1868 declared that Governor John B. Page, actively promoting the Portland, the Rutland, and the Bennington lines, had a perfect right to discharge "all the duties that devolve upon him as a citizen, or which legitimately pertain to his business engagements." Managers of corporations were free of nearly all state controls, with no conflicts of interest.

Criticism focused on the Vermont Central, which in 1870 by its lease of the Rutland, became one of the seven largest rail networks in the nation. Only the stable Passumpsic, most of the new spurs for a short while, and the western entry into Rutland, taken over by Cornelius Vanderbilt's Delaware & Hudson, remained outside the Central's control. Freight rates, passenger service, labor conditions, almost every aspect of Vermont Central under the Smith dynasty, was open to attack. Governor Dillingham had noted discriminatory freight rates in 1866, but a long-short haul bill failed in 1867. As everywhere else for twenty years, interstate business opposed both state and interstate regulation. A bill to regulate the inhumane transportation of livestock through the state failed for the same reasons. An elaborate investigation of the Central's management, with respect to its car purchases and rentals, free passes, spying, and dealings with other lines, reached damaging conclusions based on substantial evidence, with zero results.[5]

Collusion between railroads, shippers, and customs officials led to the firing of the Grand Trunk agent at Island Pond. Washington removed William Clapp of St. Albans, Collector of Customs, for padding deputy lists, leaving too much up to railroad officials whom he was supposed to be policing, and being careless about the locks on bonded goods entering duty-free.

General George J. Stannard, Vermont's most popular war hero, a partner in the St. Albans Foundry Company run by Congressman Worthington C. Smith, ex-Governor Smith's brother, replaced Clapp. "We were glad," recalled G. Grenville Benedict in the weekly *Burlington Free Press* of 19 April 1872, that Stannard "was placed in the best Federal office in our State." Vermont further honored the thrice-wounded hero in 1869 by the incorporation of Goshen Gore as the town of Stannard. Controlling a twenty-two thousand dollar payroll for fifty-five men, Stannard (like Clapp) appointed Central men. But after six years he had spent not wisely but too much on his cronies, could not account for thirty-six thousand dollars, and resigned, to be replaced by General William W. Wells, Burlington drug company official. The generous general went bankrupt with scarce a ripple on the smooth surface of Vermont Grantism, and was taken care of with a job as doorkeeper in Congress until his death in 1886.[6]

Was railroad labor contented? The consolidated Central controlled over two thousand employees, more than any other postwar enterprise in Vermont, yet it never had a strike. Even the universal wage reductions of 1877, which set off strikes and violence in many states, caused no interruption of service in Vermont. The unions threatened to strike if their old wages were not restored, but J. G. Smith merely presented figures showing reduced earnings and promised to help his employees get jobs elsewhere *if* they could do better. They did not walk out. Railroad

---

[5]*Report of the Joint Special Committee to Investigate the Vt. Central Railroad Management. Ordered by Joint Resolution Adopted at the Biennial Session, 1872* (St. Albans: Messenger Printing, 1873); Albert Clarke, *The Free Pass Abuse; the Constitutional Power of the State to Regulate Railroads. Speech of Hon. Albert Clark, of St. Albans, Delivered in the Vermont Senate, Friday, November 13th, 1874* (St. Albans: Messenger Steam Printing, 1874).

[6]See "General George J. Stannard, One of Our Self-Made Vermonters," *Expansion*, 3 (February 1905): 20; Ezra T. Warner, "George Jerrison Stannard," in his *Generals in Blue* (Baton Rouge: Louisiana State University Press, 1964), 471-472. The Democratic *Woodstock Spirit of the Age* of 21 April 1866, asserted that U.S. Senator L. P. "Poland and ex-Gov. Smith wanted a man of their own" to appoint border inspectors who would rally support for Poland's bid for the Senate.

Commissioner Myron W. Bailey of St. Albans recommended, however, if there ever *were* a strike, that it be "a crime for [an] . . . engineer, brakeman, or conductor, to leave his train [before] . . . it arrives at its destination."[7] Although passenger connections improved under the Central, one has only to recall the 1865 jingle of E. J. Phelps ending "I hope in hell his soul may dwell / Who first invented Essex Junction," to know that the Vermont system was not streamlined for the busy traveler.[8]

Railroad commissioners recommended proceeding cautiously as a way to prevent accidents, although gradually and belatedly laws were adopted regulating the height of cars (1872) and engineer-controlled air brakes (1880). The provisions of the 1872 railroad safety law for grade crossings of two trains were to stop within five hundred feet, toot, and cross slowly. Commissioners universally favored inspection and publicity instead of regulation, which the Patrons of Husbandry (Grange) in the west were clamoring for to check railroad corruption. The Patrons of Husbandry organized its first local Grange in St. Johnsbury in 1871 and completed its state organization the next year. Seneca M. Dorr, Rutland marble dealer, published a strong Granger argument for "Equal taxation for all property; pure men for legislators, and no railroad men for State officers."[9] Such arguments attracted only a minority, yet the commissioners could not get all the information they needed to publicize railroad abuses. The Vermont Grange tried cooperative buying of seed and fertilizer, and after indifferent success, turned to social and educational activity.

Grange reform failed for many reasons. The Masons, although forced to close, revived in ten years. The temperance movement failed to stop the "rummies," who seemed to have nine lives. And the slavocrats were far away. Most important, small businessmen were trying to expand their own railroads and reluctant to attack the instrument that they believed was their economic salvation. Vermont railroads were poor and managed by local men with good war records, friends in both parties, in the courts and the legislature. Most governors from the Civil War past 1880 were either railroad lawyers or railroad officials. The Smiths of St. Albans easily ducked the charge of being subject to "foreign" interests, although they were dependent on Portland, Boston, and New York decisions and had a foreign interest in the Northern Pacific. Unlike most antebellum reformers,

---

[7]*Report* (1877-78), 3-4.

[8]Francis Parsons, *Six Men of Yale* (New Haven: Yale University Press, 1939), 95-96.

[9]In *The Farmer's War—Equal Taxation—Granges—Patrons of Husbandry; A Series of Letters Published in the Rutland Daily Globe* (Rutland: Rutland Grange of the Patrons of Husbandry, 1873), 4.

Grangers attacked the focal interest of American business. When communitarian John Orvis made similar charges, he won few followers.[10]

Rural Vermont was poor and had been for years. What energy had gone into reforms now went more and more into little out-of-state investments, directly, through emigrant children, or via the local storekeeper or shire bank. Many a threadbare widow or shabby-looking villager had a trickle of returns on money invested in the west. Creditors, even of modest means, do not attack the sanctity of contract, whether applied to wages, prices, currency, rail rates, or mortgages. Whether Democratic or Republican, they supported their Congressmen's views on resumption of specie payments, "an honest currency," and against the eight-hour day.[11]

In a dozen issues affecting the relations of business and government, all attacks upon business, except the repeal in 1882 of the extraordinary tax exemption of the Central Vermont, were slapped down. New factories were tax-exempt for five years, or ten by town vote. The office of bank commissioner was abolished in 1867 with the closing of state banks while commercial and savings banks went unregulated until 1874. The inspector of finance opposed bank taxes and favored limiting the amount of loans to one firm. He noted the rapid increase in western loans. The National Life Insurance Company, in 1880 one of the fifty-eight largest in the country, had half its $225,000,000 of assets in real estate, especially in the West. In Burlington, lake interests, able to compete only feebly with the rails, made yet another effort for a ship canal in 1870. In this heyday of free enterprise and faith in competition, public opinion acquiesced in monopoly.

Did manufacturing and quarrying show a similar tendency toward monopoly? Before telling the story of how Redfield Proctor achieved predominance in marble, a brief round-up of Vermont industry will show the ebb and flow of village fortunes, linked in people's minds more to manufacturing than to farming or trading.

Annual changes in number of poll taxes assessed, although only a rough measure, correspond with other indicators of prosperity or depression. Western and northeastern Vermont gained the most; most of Franklin, Caledonia, and Bennington county growth and all of Windsor County's large losses occurred before 1873, while the recovery of Orange, the acceleration of Rutland, and the leaps

---

[10]See above p. 49.

[11]Senator Justin S. Morrill's speech reported in the *Burlington Free Press*, 5 January 1870; Edward J. Phelps to Morrill, 17 September 1875, in the Morrill Papers, Special Collections, Bailey/Howe Library, University of Vermont; Charles H. Joyce, *Early Resumption of Specie Payments* (Washington: Government Printing Office, 1876).

of Chittenden and Orleans took place despite the depression after 1873. If polls relate to employment, the depression meant general slackening, but every year from 1865 to 1880 was the worst year for work in some town. Besides, the worst years for the principal centers were only relatively bad. Two-thirds of them exceeded their county's rate of growth, often by phenomenal percentages.

St. Albans was the creature of the Smiths' railroad enterprises. Without the St. Albans Foundry and the car and machine shops of the Central Vermont, together hiring 445 hands at $236,000 a year to make locomotives, cars, Buckeye mowers and railroad repairs, St. Albans would have been a market town for a dairy county, but no embryo city of seven thousand in 1870. A patent infringement suit of 1868-69 forced the foundry to discontinue the profitable hundred dollar Buckeyes and substitute horsepower threshers. When toward 1880 the Smiths pulled in their horns in all departments, St. Albans tightened its belt. In central Vermont, the loser to St. Albans in railroad business, a few strong woolen mills, Northfield slate, and many small ironworkers expanded before 1873, and held on. Montpelier grew more as a capital and commercial center than as a fabricator.

The new railroads gave the necessary push to start granite moving. Because of new machinery for working it as much as transportation, granite became competitive in the monument trade after the Civil War. Soldiers' monuments in Peacham, St. Johnsbury, Derby, Rochester, and other Vermont towns—even the base of Senator Solomon Foot's memorial in marbleized Rutland's Evergreen Cemetery—were of Barre or Ryegate granite. Until reached by rails, Barre, Woodbury, and Ryegate either wagoned their blocks to railheads for local monument shops or shipped them by water west from Burlington. Nine of the twelve quarries reporting in 1880 had started within the decade. Barre cut a third of the $233,600 worked in ten of the seventeen Vermont granite sheds. The granite industry from 1870 to 1890 reproduced the marble trends of 1840-60.

Northeastern Vermont was somewhat tributary to St. Johnsbury, with its Fairbanks railroads and scales. From this prim town came over half the national production of balances, sent to world markets. After landing a quick order for three thousand U. S. postal scales in 1874, Fairbanks won a similar contract from Japan. At the Philadelphia Centennial Exposition they showed their scales used in twenty-three foreign countries. Forty-two of their patents were still in force in 1879.

North of St. Johnsbury the region was in the economic stage of the rest of the state in the 1850s. Lyndonville, with a village charter in 1880, owed its growth to the Passumpsic railroad shops, built in 1866 after those in St. Johnsbury burned. Nearer the border, Barton and Newport contested Derby's former supremacy through growth in trade, woodworking, pulp, and lumber.

In the Windsor region woolen mills were still widespread, but other mills had closed. Those that survived were larger, with more expensive plants and more male operatives. Except for Hartford, Windsor, and Bellows Falls, two of them having the benefits of being railroad junction villages, woolen and other manufacturing did not sustain long-term growth. Cavendish, with three mills in two villages producing $375,000 worth of woolens in 1870, reached its all-time population peak that year. The Franco-Prussian war pulled woolens out of the doldrums. One agent bought Thomas Greenbanks' entire year's production at Stockbridge for forty thousand dollars.[12]

Solomon Woodward's Woodstock mill, in addition to typical difficulties of freshet, fire, competition, obsolescence of equipment, and expensive improvements, faced the only other women's strike I know of before 1900. A hated boss kept eighteen girls overtime one fall evening in 1866, and when they got "home" the boardinghouse keeper would not feed them supper. Already fed up with bad rations, with no light or fire in their cubicles, they stayed out three or four weeks. Those not fired returned to a fourteen-hour day, but the overseer left immediately. Woodward would not let the paper boy into the factory because his Democratic paper supported the strikers.[13]

The Lamson industries of Windsor sold their gun equipment after the war but suffered from overdiversification. In 1865 they advertised double circular saws, stone channelers, iron planers, engine lathes, punch presses, diamond-pointed drills, screw millers, three-spindle drill presses, hat-trimming presses, screw and gripping wrenches, index millers, small trip hammers, as well as their cutlery, scythe snathes, and leftover rifles. Windsor hurt when Lamson and Goodnow's cutlery works closed in 1869, but soon big orders for machinery and machine tools attracted a large force of workmen. The same year Lamson brought in Hiram Harlow, former superintendent of the state prison, and Russell L. Jones, a Colerain, Massachusetts, cotton manufacturer who had just lost his dam in a flood, and added cotton manufacture in the old armory, heated by steam and lighted by gas. The Jones & Lamson Machine Company, separated from the cotton enterprise in 1876, made large profits by concentrating on a turret lathe designed by Henry D. Stone, who had been in the Windsor region since 1836. The failure of the textile firm and the death of Harlow, a major

---

[12]*Woodstock Spirit of the Age*, 19 September, 3, 11, 18, 25 October 1866; 2 January, 9 April, 3 December 1868, 14 October 1869, 10 March, 11, 18 August 1870.

[13]*Woodstock Spirit of the Age*, 19 September, 4, 11, 18, 15 October 1866 (strike); 2 January, 4 April, 5 December 1868, 14 October 1869, 10 March, 11 August 1870 (other difficulties).

stockholder on the machine tool side, led to the company's moving seventeen miles to Springfield in 1888, where it found better waterpower, more capital, tax exemption, and a pool of equally skilled mechanics, but worse transportation.[14]

Bellows Falls gained by the advent of pulp paper, an invention made practicable by the high Civil War prices of rag newsprint. William J. Russell, a native of Wells River and a paper manufacturer since 1848, organized the first Bellows Falls pulp paper company in 1870, and by 1882 five pulp papermills were using most of the power of the falls. The most important of the other users was the Vermont Farm Machinery Company, whose churns, horse rakes, maple syrup evaporators, and patented portable creamers and cans represented industrial response to the shift in northeastern agriculture.

Down river the Brattleboro Melodeon Company expanded rapidly after its second big fire in January 1864, and again when it built a new steam-powered plant after the 1869 flood. Levi K. Fuller, Jacob Estey's son-in-law, who came to Brattleboro in 1860 to manufacture cylinder planers, became a partner in 1866, supervised manufacturing, and patented many improvements. Toward 1880, competitor Riley Burdett, who had made musical instruments in Brattleboro since 1850, won $150,000 damages for the Esteys' patent infringement. The patent was for a "harmonic celeste" or "vox jubilante," which produced a popular vibrato that added twenty-five dollars to the organ's price. In 1880 the company's four hundred employees made some six thousand hundred-dollar cottage organs, or eleven percent by value of the reported national output of musical instruments, organs, and materials.[15]

Brattleboro had greater variety and volume of manufacturing than in the 1850s: machinery, paper, printing and binding, silk spinning and sewing machines. N. B. Williston & Co. shipped its carriages to a national market. The E. A. Stearns ruler business continued as a branch of the Stanley Rule Company of New Britain.

Bennington almost duplicated the organ town's economic complex, except that its strengths were in cotton prints and wadding, knit goods, footwear, and ochre. Bennington County cotton textiles, mostly made at the county seat, amounted to half the state's expanding production after the

---

[14] Guy Hubbard, "Development of Machine Tools in New England," *American Machinist*, 60 (26 June 1924): 451-454; *Woodstock Age*, 25 March, 13 May, 3 June, 29 July 1869, 16 February 1871; *Burlington Free Press*, 17 December 1869; Wayne G. Broehl, Jr., *Precision Valley: The Machine Tool Companies of Springfield, Vermont* (Englewood Cliffs, N.J.: Prentice-Hall, 1959), 6-10.

[15] This paragraph is revised from my article in the *New England Quarterly* 19 (March 1946): 32-49.

war.[16] Bennington's wavering economy in the 1870s was checked partly by two large failures: Seth B. Hunt's half-million dollar shawl factory, 1868-74, and the North Bennington Boot & Shoe Company, whose mechanized, steam-heated and steam-powered plant produced a quarter of the state's total footwear in 1870, but was abandoned before 1880.

Otter Valley gains were by existing factories. Outstanding was the Howe Scale Company, bought by new Brandon, Rutland, Boston and New York capital, consolidated with a New York firm in 1870, and moved to Rutland after 1876. Smaller than Fairbanks, Howe thrived on army, navy, custom house, and foreign business. The Batchelder & Sons' Wallingford factory passed $100,000 in hay fork production, and even isolated Middletown Springs boasted of A. W. Gray's horsepower threshers. New products—kerosene storage tanks at Fair Haven, milk strainers and new quarrying and mining machinery at Rutland—were made on a small scale.

Slate quarrying, mainly for roofing and flagging, dominated by Welshmen, mostly by small firms, moved southwest, away from Lake Bomoseen and Castleton, after the war. All but three of the twenty-eight quarries reporting in 1880 had been opened after 1863. Few used more than gunpowder, a steam pump, derricks, and dressing machines. Much was shipped rough; the rest was marbleized (enameled) and milled into mantels, lamp bases, billiard beds, table tops and tiles. Production apparently peaked around 1870, although census figures are very erratic.

Population and poll trends faithfully reflected the vitality of each Vermont village. Many could maintain three to seven thousand people with county trade and a complex of small industries with limited markets. Rutland and Burlington, by exploiting the blessings of site, transportation, power, raw materials, skills and labor, crossed the urban threshold in this period. Marble in Rutland, textiles and wood products in Burlington, pushed their cities ahead. Probably Rutland had the larger non-transient working population until after 1893. Burlington had two advantages. As a junction for water and rail routes it attracted Canadian lumber and other commerce. Satellite

---

[16] The Vermont cotton industry, concentrated in Bennington, Springfield, Middlebury, and Burlington, grew, according to the census, as follows:

	#	Cap.	m.	f.	c.	Hands	Cost of Materials	Annual Wages	Value
1840	5	118	—	—	—	261	—	—	113
1850	9	203	94	147	—	241	114	39	280
1860	10	321	142	225	—	367	133	78	357
1870	8	670	125	242	84	451	292	125	547
1880	8	956	219	354	181	754	555	173	916

Children not recorded separately until 1870; capital, materials, wages, and value in thousands of dollars.

Slate Quarries
(Capital and value of product in thousands of dollars)

	Number		Capital		Labor		Value	
	'70	'80	'70	'80	'70	'80	'70	'80
Castleton	12	6	362	111	226	97	124	38
Fair Haven	7	3	81	16	114	38	85	24
Poultney	13	8	79	72	98	140	84	106
Guilford	3	—	12	—	39	—	29	—
Northfield	6	1	166	*100	106	38	60	12
Pawlet	—	9	—	128	—	*252	—	91
Wells	—	1	—	—	—	4	—	0.5
Total	41	28	700	427	581	565	382	271.5

Milled and Marbleized Slate

Castleton	4	4	*300	55.5	143	32	197	61
Fair Haven	3	3	115	112.5	120	104	139	120
Poultney	1	—	100	—	70	—	59	—
Total	8	7	513	168	333	136	395	181

*Questionably large.

Winooski, just beyond its political border, had an up-to-date woolen mill with managers of proven skills and output of significant volume and quality, using Winooski Falls, the second best waterpower in Vermont.

The Winooski mill of the Burlington Woolen Company had pioneered in burr-picking machinery, which made cheap and dirty foreign wool usable. In 1866 its skilled spinners, William and Oliver Brothers, designed an automatic mule (for drawing and twisting wool into thread), which further mechanized the industry. This adaptation, almost simultaneously worked out in Worcester and Providence, substantially increased production, decreased costs, reduced waste, and maintained greater uniformity. The only remaining hand processes at Winooski were wool sorting, tying breaks in the thread or yarn being spun, moving materials in the mill (the wool came from the storehouse by rail), embroidering the finished article with silk, and repairing machinery. Up-to-date Leffel turbines powered the machinery in the steam-heated mill. The company made its own machinery, soap, gas, and packing cases, and marketed its bales through agents in Boston (where its financial affairs were managed), New York, and Chicago, and produced roughly a fifth of Vermont woolens.[17]

The Burlington lumber business resulted from site advantages. At the junction of rail routes to industrial New England and New York with a water route from Canada, with the wide bay protected from northwest storms by a breakwater, with ample yard space made by fill at the waterfront, Burlington could receive by water lumber cut and sawed near Ottawa, and cheaply sort and dress it for particular markets. Albany, at the junction of three waterways and rails from all directions, tapped not only the Canadian but also the Adirondack and western New York supply. But it was more convenient to ship Canadian lumber to Boston via Burlington, and out of Boston to the world.

Up to 1837 the rafting of logs to Quebec had started at Winooski Falls. Then the timber region moved to northern Maine, Canada, and the West, and the flow of lumber reversed during the 1840s. By the 1850s Ottawa sawmills were operating Burlington yards, reducing freight costs an eighth by planing and dressing at the water's edge. While this business was developing slowly, Burlington suffered from the loss of marketing advantage to the railroads in northern Vermont and sought to compensate. Its businessmen invested in the Pioneer Mechanics Shop Company, incorporated in 1852, and erected a large building with steam engines on the waterfront, to rent to woodworkers, machinists, and ironworkers. It burned in 1858, and lumberman Lawrence Barnes rebuilt it in brick. The lumber business was the foundation upon which these shops prospered. Imports of Canadian lumber spurted forward after March 1855, when the duty-free provisions of the Canadian reciprocity treaty went into effect, and again during the Civil War, and yet again in the late 1860s. Lawrence Barnes, the largest operator, showed these gains (in board feet processed):[18]

1860	8,000,000	1866	51,127,612
1862	20,030,424	1867	48,590,497
1863	45,738,469	1868	57,868,790
1864	36,620,936	1869	74,172,536
1865	46,593,396		

---

[17]*Burlington Weekly Free Press*, 24 May 1872, describes the woolen mill, its supervisors and operations, as part of its 1871-72 series on Burlington industries.

[18]Lucius E. Chittenden, Commonplace book, account no. 45,689, in Special Collections, Bailey/Howe Library, University of Vermont. The *Burlington Free Press*, however, quoted the collector of customs that only sixty-three million board feet had been brought in from Canada in the 1879 season, a gain of eleven million over 1878. Chittenden's totals for Barnes must have included domestic lumber, for the *Free Press* added that "immense amounts of Michigan lumber" also came in.

The lakefront had not yet been planned for piling lumber. In the summer of 1860 his yards were so crowded, Barnes asked the collector of customs to let him put lumber on the breakwater.[19]

In 1868 Barnes disposed of his interest in the Pioneer shops and merged with his chief competitor, Otis Shepard, Davis & Co. No monopoly emerged in lumber, however. Shepard & Morse, the successor firm, planed thirty-nine percent of the Vermont total by value in 1880.

The prosperity of the marble industry, although less concentrated in one urban center than Burlington's diverse operations, enabled Rutland to cross the urban threshold. Typical of the times, its main story is the creation of the Vermont Marble Company monopoly by Redfield Proctor (1831-1908). He had every advantage for the successful consolidation of a multi-million-dollar business: inherited money and prestige, the freshness of an outside approach unhampered by the habits of a generation of marble operation, aggressive energy, thin-lipped determination, unequalled political skill coupled with a winning personality, and the finesse of a shrewd gambler. His father, Jabez (1780-1839), was not only the son of Proctorsville's founder, but also influential in conservative political circles and a solid businessman. His mother's mother was a Redfield, connected with weighty Democratic politicians and officeholders. Jabez Proctor tried to develop a verde antique deposit in Cavendish, but existing technology could not surmount the production and distribution problems.

As a young man Redfield burnt his fingers in Minnesota speculation and came back to manage the family finances. Although he was not cut out for a lawyer, with a taste for neither rhetoric nor research, his experience at Albany Law School and in his cousin's Boston office was invaluable. Isaac F. Redfield, a veteran of the Vermont bench and railroad authority, must have taught him much about Vermont transportation in their year's association. To Proctor the call to arms was a boon, for it gave him a war record to erase the memories of his previous Democratic associations and a chance to exercise his talents for management and command. Dartmouth College had been for contacts and legal study for contracts, as he ever preferred the action of the stage to the passion of the study. He excelled in making decisions and assuming responsibility and rewards, building on the spade work of others.

Starting as lieutenant and quartermaster of the Third Regiment, detailed to the staff of Brig. Gen. W. F. Smith, within three months he was appointed Major of the Fifth. On the eve of the

---

[19]L[ouis] Follett for Lawrence Barnes & Co. to Charles Linsley, Rutland, 23 August 1860, in the Sheldon Museum.

Peninsular Campaign, assured by the army doctor that he had advanced consumption and might not live a month, he secured sick leave. Vermont air restored him, first to mild activity supplying troops with Seneca Dorr, and that fall to the colonelcy of a nine months' regiment. In 1864 he took the lead with his Rutland law partner W. G. Veazey in organizing the Reunion Society of Vermont Officers, more powerful locally than the Grand Army of the Republic.

Two conflicts finished Proctor's education: *Rutland Marble Company v. Ripley*[20] demonstrated that a marble mill can control the marble quarries dependent on it, as Rockefeller was proving in Cleveland that oil refineries have power over the owners of oil wells. In 1868, during Proctor's second term in the Vermont House, he managed the bill to let Trenor W. Park's and Governor John B. Page's railroad build a spur to the West Rutland quarries, breaking the Troy monopoly of marble freight. During the debate the railroad committee revealed that the Troy line issued unfair rebates (the Rockefeller story of winning favorable rates through rebates). Proctor learned how easily resident enterprisers win over "foreign monopoly," and the importance of railroad alliances.

The history of the marble deposit at Sutherland Falls from its opening in 1836 is written in failure until technology provided adequate tools to work the potential treasure. The seamless stone, with high silica content, was hard to work. Its mottled gray "dove" shades were unpopular in the 1850s, but sales promotion, also emphasizing durability, changed taste in the 1860s. Every other condition was favorable. The Rutland Railroad ran right by the mill, where the Otter Creek dropped 121 feet, with an ample sandbank nearby for sawing abrasive.

The Sutherland Falls Marble Company grew to be the third most valuable marble property in the 1860s as shown by the annual appraisals of Rutland marble properties (in thousands of dollars):[21]

---

[20] 10 Wallace 339-363; also 904-page printed *Transcript of Records and Briefs*, and a summary in the *Rutland Herald*, 8, 10 October 1868.

[21] Appraisals then approximated nearer one-tenth than one-third of market value. Other real property, which for these three owners amounted to almost $40,000 in 1865 and $125,000 in 1870, is excluded. According to the U.S. Manufacturing Census of 1860, the Sutherland Falls Marble Company employed thirty-five quarriers to raise fourteen thousand cubic feet of blocks for ten gangs of saws to make into thirty thousand dollars worth of slabs. The 1870 census listed only one quarry (the Manhattan) and one mill (the Ripleys' at Center Rutland).

	Total Marble Properties	Rutland Marble Company	Sheldons & Slason	Sutherland Falls Marble Co.
1854	92	ᵃ10	36	ᵇ0.5
1857	209	62	46	11
1861	262	66	53	15
1865	ᶜ280	75	51	22
1866	336	94	63	47
1867	328	94	ᵈ53	49
1868	372	106	78	55
1869	419	111	80	ᶠ58
1870	467	116	80	ᶠ68

ᵃW. F. Barnes. ᵇNorth River Mining Co. ᶜThe 1864 total dropped to $247,000. ᵈAdjustment for fire loss. ᶠNot including Dorr & Myers' new mill.

The company opened a new quarry whose stone had no joints, used labor-saving machinery as soon as available, and found new markets by aggressive salesmanship. In the fall of 1865 two sons-in-law of William Y. Ripley, the marble miller at Center Rutland, leased the Sutherland Falls mill. John J. Myers, recently moved to Rutland, was one of the largest marble dealers in northern Ohio, with a steam finishing shop in Cleveland, 1857-79. Attorney Seneca M. Dorr had come from Columbia County, New York, in 1857. The pair got orders requiring a new eight-gang mill with several improvements, including tracks and cars for moving marble. The quarry shifted, with others in the region, from hoisting by oxen on sweeps to steam-powered derricks, with wire instead of hemp cables. It already had four Wardwell steam channelers in 1865. While getting out a large order in 1869 for the Portland, Maine, post office and custom house, it installed a diamond-bitted gadder.[22] All this expansion left the Sutherland Falls complex financially vulnerable, and Dorr & Myers went bankrupt.

Late in 1869 U.S. District Judge D. A. Smalley granted Myers's petition to dissolve his milling partnership with Dorr, appoint Redfield Proctor receiver, and force the Sutherland Falls Marble Company, which worked the quarry, to fulfil its $100,000 a year contract with the mill.

---

[22] A steam-driven single spindle, invented by the Sullivan Machine Company of Claremont, New Hampshire. Its water-cooled diamond bit bored holes in the base of the channeled block. Gads, or wedges, were then driven into the holes, splitting the block from its bed.

Proctor's cousin, Isaac F. Redfield of Boston, represented the stockholders opposing Myers's petition, saying in effect that the existing management could pull itself out of trouble. Edward J. Phelps of Burlington argued for Myers, and John Prout of Rutland, just retired from the Vermont Supreme Court, for Proctor. Obviously all sides recognized that the control of this marble complex was worth much money, for this was most expensive legal counsel. The winners proceeded to bring Proctor in, uniting mill and quarry in a new 1870 corporation, the Sutherland Falls Marble Company, and including J. R. Reynolds, the quarry manager, and stockholder and ex-governor John B. Page of the Rutland Railroad.

The Proctor group, with all the advantages, prospered in the 1870s. The three leading companies were each producing about half a million feet (measured as if all of it was in slabs) a year, over half the marble raised in the Rutland area, when the total production of twenty Vermont quarries, according to the estimate of the state geological survey some fifteen years earlier, was only half a million feet. The top three were using over a hundred gangs of saws, mostly the Merriman improvement made by the Lincoln Iron Works of Rutland, and paying over half the thousand quarry workers. After a bad fire in 1867, Sheldons & Slason won an $864,000 contract for a quarter-million headstones for national soldiers' cemeteries. On this 1875-76 job they used the Tilghman process of making bas-relief inscriptions with chilled iron shields and sandblasting the rest of the slab face.

Other battles raged in the late 1860s over production of steam channelers and other stone-cutting machines. George Wardwell, J. B. Page, and G. E. Royce of Rutland patented the first Wardwell channeler in 1863. They secured New York capital and organized the Steam Stone Cutter Company in 1865. Negotiations failed with E. G. Lamson of Windsor, who was using Arnold Ball's patent and had the skilled machinists and machine tools for efficient production. Both firms made channelers until Wardwell won some $300,000 in damages in a patent infringement suit. Ball and disgruntled Roger Love, who lost a big suit to Windsor Manufacturing over sale of stock, left Windsor for Claremont, New Hampshire, around 1870 and formed the Sullivan Machine Company, whose diamond drills competed successfully with Wardwell's. Wardwell had only five men making twenty thousand dollars' worth of quarrying machinery in 1880, two-thirds of its 1870 business; rentals and repairs helped keep them in business.

The Rutland Marble Company, the largest marble producer in the United States, remained the principal obstacle to Proctor's move toward monopoly. This million-dollar corporation had a milling capacity of some 800,000 feet a year after it built a steam mill at its quarries in the late 1860s. H. H. Baxter sold the company to New York bankers in 1863 and left Rutland for a spectacular career on Wall Street. The absentee owners tolerated the highest accident rate in the Rutland area and seemed interested only in dividends (8.5 percent in 1867). They were not going to let the Irish quarriers follow up their partially victorious strike of 1864, won under exceptional war conditions and because management was divided.

Quarrying was harder work than ever. The new Roman Catholic church bell rang morning, noon, and night to tell a thousand operatives when to start or stop work. The smoke of steam engines polluted the air and their din reverberated off the quarry walls. "Red City" on Pleasant Street, near the West Rutland quarries and mills, held 150 families in its crowded tenements, paying thirty to thirty-six dollars a quarter, automatically deducted from wages, as were debts at the company stores. (The quarriers did not have to trade at company stores, but they gave credit, even if they charged a third more to cover bad debts.) In 1867 the bosses had ringleader Patrick McGettrick locked up for threatening to strike. A year later, faced with another month-long strike for higher wages, the company imported French Canadian and "German" (i.e., Scandinavian) strike breakers. On the next quarry holiday liquor flowed and soon the blood of Canadians and Irishmen. The violence of this "big turn-out" was exaggerated over the years, partly because of the nature of story-telling, but also because there was no strike like it until 1935-36.

Proctor's was the Fairbanks way. After 1870 he moved his family to the edge of his marble yard, subscribed to churches and other public institutions, built a Pullman-type village, and did little kindnesses for his little men. At his death the funeral way was lined with his workmen, bareheaded in the blizzard, mourning their beloved feudal baron.

How did Proctor become king on the marble mountain? Since marble was an unusually political commodity, its best buyers bureaucrats, Proctor proceeded to scale the political ladder in the fewest leaps, from selectman in 1866 to governor in 1878. From 1880 on, with the Vermont senators Justin S. Morrill and George F. Edmunds, he wielded more influence in the state Republican Party than any other individual. No evidence has been uncovered, but it would be surprising if his firm did not win contracts and rebates through Washington and local railroad contacts, especially after he served as President Harrison's secretary of war, and later as U.S. senator.

One spring day in 1880 Proctor called on President Riggs of the Rutland Marble Company. They struck a deal advantageous to both sides but especially to Proctor, who took charge of the two companies. On returning from that visit, there was a smile on the face of the tiger. Later, when Proctor was in the U.S. Senate, George F. Hoar of Massachusetts remarked that no Vermonter was allowed to vote until he had bested a "foreigner" in a horse trade. Proctor interjected, "And we all vote."[23] The appraisal of the properties combined in the fall of 1880 as the Vermont Marble Company, a New York corporation, amounted to $450,000 in West Rutland, $450,000 at Sutherland Falls, $100,000 at Center Rutland, and $50,000 for mill improvements, etc. While the monopoly was not yet in hand, it was in sight, for the Proctor interests controlled almost two-thirds of the Rutland facilities, and Rutland marble set the pace, not only in Vermont, but also for the nation.

Rutland Marble Quarries and Mills, 1880, from the MS. Census*

	1.	2.	3.	4.	5.	Total
Quarry Opened	1845	1836	1844	1867	1845	
M cu.yds,'79/80	550	50	345	28	115	1,222
M cu.yds since opening	9,048	—	4,000	1,000	1,350	17,898
Capital	1,000	1,000	500	150	200	3,300
Value of Products	331	—	200	115	85	911
Ave. No. Men Working	462	295	355	110	80	1,457
Ave. No. Children	—	5	5	3	5	30
Disabled[a]	13	1	1	—	1	17
Annual Payroll	133	120	85	52	25	481
Steam Drills	16	[b]18	5	1	2	46
Steam Cranes	15	[c]6	6	2	3	36
Total Horsepower	[d]912	[e]642	250	100	80	1,584
Gangs of Saws	52	40	48	9	9	166
Marble Lathes	7	30	12	15	—	72
Rubbing Beds	1	3	1	1	—	7
Tons of Coal	2,850	200	2,500	800	600	7,550
Cords of Wood	460	—	650	75	25	1,275

*Total of all marble operations in Rutland. Capital, value of products, and annual payroll in thousands of dollars. 1. Rutland Marble Company. 2. Sutherland Falls Marble Company. 3. Sheldons & Slason. 4. Columbian Marble Company. 5. Gilson & Woodfin. [a]Rutland Marble Co. reported one permanently disabled; the rest all temporarily. [b]Including waterpowered and compressed air drills. [c]Including waterpowered cranes. [d]Four double-boilered steam engines and five turbines. [e]Three large turbines and a small auxiliary engine. Compare with *Tenth Census. Manufacturing* (1880), 15:844-845, 850, 852.

---

[23]Frank C. Partridge, "Redfield Proctor; His Public Life and Services," Vermont Historical Society *Proceedings* (1915): 69-70, 92.

For the state as a whole, and the large villages in particular, manufacturing barely held its own in the postwar years, as shown in this summary:[24]

Total Manufactures, Vermont, 1840-80

	1840	1850	1860	1870	1880
No. establishments	2,352	1,849	1,883	3,270	2,874
Capital	4,326	5,001	9,499	20,330	23,265
Average no. hands	7,883	8,445	10,497	18,686	17,540
Men	—	6,894	8,563	16,301	14,438
Women	—	1,551	1,934	1,872	2,271
Children	—	—	—	513	831
Annual wages	—	2,202	3,005	6,265	5,164
Value of materials	—	4,173	7,609	17,008	18,331
Value of products	5,586	8,571	14,638	32,185	31,354

The towns pushed ahead, especially Burlington and Rutland, all suffering the strains of growth. Competition was fierce, even among those firms protected by patents, combinations, or parent companies elsewhere. Railroads were essential but no panacea. The manufacturing tonic had proved less than a guaranteed ticket to the pearly gates of prosperity. Many felt called but few were chosen. The hope of glory was a forlorn hope except for the Smiths, the Fairbankses, the Esteys, the Proctors, and other specialists in management. The industrial effort was transforming and socially expensive. It remains to look at which villagers paid and what they paid for the social changes that accompanied industrialism.

---

[24]Compiled from the *Compendium of the Sixth Census* (1840), 114-114, 118-125, and the *Compendium of the Tenth Census* (1880), 928-931; capital, wages, materials, and products in thousands of dollars.

10. Village Society Reshaped, 1865-80

The State has received a foreign element, which poorly compensates for her loss [by emigration], an insidious and continuous invasion. [The first] few French Canadians were expert axemen, familiar with land-clearing, and as handy as Yankees with scythe and sickle; while their weather-browned wives and grown-up daughters could reap and bind as well as they, and did not hold themselves above any outdoor work.

After a while some built log-houses, that with eaves of notched shingles and whitewashed outer walls, with the pungent odor of onions and pitch-pine fires, looked and smelled as if they had been transplanted from Canada with their owners.

[Later] swarms of Canadian laborers came flocking over the border, baggy-breeched and moccasined habitants, in rude carts drawn by shaggy Canadian ponies. After a month or two of haymaking and harvesting, they jogged homeward with their earnings [and] some small pilferings, for their fingers were as light as their hearts. The place of habitants picturesque in garb, swinging their scythes in unison to some old [French] song, has been usurped by [the mowing machine]. The influx continued till they have become the most numerous of Vermont's foreign population.

What this leaven may finally work in the Protestant mass is a question that demands more attention than it has yet received. The character of these people [does not] inspire the highest hope for the future of Vermont, if they should become the most numerous of its population. The affiliation with Anglo-Americans must necessarily be slow, and may never be complete. Vermont has given of her best for the building of new commonwealths, [human] material whose place no alien drift from northward or over seas can ever fill.[1]

The coming of "Antwine Bassett," Rowland Robinson's stereotype of the "Canuck"[2] farm laborer, was quite different from the arrival of the "Patrick Kelleys," who had come in largest numbers in the fifteen years before the war. Both were part of a worldwide exodus from depressed

---

[1] Rowland E. Robinson, *Vermont: A Study of Independence* (Boston: Houghton Mifflin, 1892), 228-232, ellipsis dots omitted.

[2] This name, applied to French Canadians, had appeared in Vermont by 1852 (*St. Johnsbury Caledonian*, 14 February 1852), but it has also meant a Canadian horse or pony, or an English name for all Canadian troops in World War I. Whether it started as a French Canadian term for Irish immigrants (from Connaught) or was compounded out of Canada plus "uk," an Algonkian noun ending, is uncertain.

farms to industrial cities or to the wilderness. But the Irish, from Ireland, Canada, New York, or New England, had had a chance to accumulate a little property and rise a notch in the social scale. They spoke English, helped the dwindling stream of Irish newcomers, and knew how to vote.

From sixty thousand French-speaking *habitants* when New France fell in 1759, a more than tenfold increase in three generations made it harder and harder to sustain a living. Compared to tackling the cold forests and thin soils of the Laurentian Shield in northern Quebec and Ontario, or the hazards of the long trip to the Canadian or American plains, the best opportunities for French Canadians were in the mill towns of New England. They were kept out of the Eastern Townships between the Chaudière and the Richelieu by a forbidding land policy and bad roads. The flow to New England, stimulated by recruiting during the Civil War, swelled to 100,000 Canadians, a third to a half francophone, during the eight years before the crash of 1873. The Province of Quebec severely felt the loss of 400,000 emigrants to all the states and tried to win them back. Failing that in most cases, it tried to stem the tide by providing better opportunities at home.

After the Civil War some twelve thousand Quebecois stopped in Vermont on their way south and found work on the farms, in the brick and lumber yards, quarries, mills, construction crews, railroad gangs, and logging camps. On both sides of Lake Champlain they flowed in a thick fork past Plattsburgh and Burlington, and some followed the railroad lines out of the Champlain Valley until they could be found in nearly every Vermont town. Natives did not feel threatened by a few. Back in the hills of Franklin County Baptist and Adventist missionaries had captured small congregations in revivals, but they either emigrated from Berkshire, Enosburg, Richford, and Montgomery or fell back into their Catholic habits when priests arrived. Elsewhere in New England they comprised scarcely two percent of the total population and had little influence. In inland Vermont, where their substantial presence with the Irish in the industrial villages accounted for the net population gains of the decade, their influence was strong on its business and society. Perhaps every third Vermonter was of French Canadian birth or background by 1890.[3]

---

[3] My treatment of the French influence is derived principally from Ralph Dominic Vicero's unpublished "Immigration of French Canadians to New England, 1840-1900; A Geographical Analysis," Ph.D. diss., Univ. of Wisconsin, 1988; David J. Blow, "The Establishment and Erosion of French Canadian Culture in Winooski, Vermont, 1867-1900," *Vermont History* 43 (Winter 1975): 59-74; Mary Elizabeth Beatty, "Opportunity Across the Border: The Burlington Area Economy and the French Canadian Worker," *Vermont History* 55 (Summer 1987): 133-152; *History of Saint Joseph Parish, Burlington, Vermont, 1830-1987*, ed. Robert G. Keenan and Rev. Francis R. Privé (Burlington: History Committee of Saint Joseph Parish, 1988), 1-45; and thirty-eight titles in *Vermont: A Bibliography of Its History* (Boston: G. K. Hall, 1981), and its 1989 supplement.

Vermont Foreign-born, 1850-80

Nativity	1850 %	1850 #	1860 %	1860 #	1870 %	1870 #	1880 %	1880 #
Canada	42.9	14,470	48.2	15,776	60.5	28,539	60.1	24,611
Ireland	45.6	15,377	41.2	13,480	29.9	14,080	28.5	11,657
Other British	7.9	2,648	9.6	3,136	8.0	3,787	9.3	3,777
Other European	0.6	68	1.0	321	1.7	650	1.8	753
Other	3.0	918	—	15	—	21	—	55
Total	100.0	33,701	100.0	32,728	100.0	47,155	100.0	40,959

By 1865 the French Canadian immigrants were the best available mill operatives because they learned the necessary skills well, they were used to working hard, the father, mother, and older children all worked, and the low wages provided a better livelihood than their previous condition. Their language was a handicap but enough earlier arrivals could interpret for those who had no bilingual dealings in Quebec. They were Old Americans, thoroughly naturalized to the continent, the climate, and the constitution. They were near enough home to have come on foot or on carts, without the debilitating and uprooting hardships of the long Atlantic voyage, and with less social disorganization as they settled in Yankee culture. Dissatisfied, they could move on to Worcester, Lowell, Fall River, or Woonsocket, or return *chez ses anciens* in Quebec. They did not enjoy politics the way the Irish did. Sometimes they did not bother to vote, but when they did, because the Irish were Democrats, they usually voted Republican.

Beyond the Jim Crow stereotype pictured by Rowland Robinson (and although he limited his comments to farm and woods workers, he should be credited with being the first historian before the 1930s to give Franco-Americans more than a few sentences) folklore caricatured the Quebecois as illiterate, clannish, and docile. While an increasing volume of letters about jobs and conditions in the states proved a level of literacy, rural French Canadians had little need to read or write and began to improve these skills only after parochial schools appeared in the states. Of course they stuck together for mutual benefits of worship, gossip in a familiar language, and barter. Contrary to the condescending image of "docile" *habitants*, they were accustomed to run their church affairs and behaved with great "Yankee" stubborn individualism in their *survivance*, by clinging to church, language, and traditions. One sign of their independence: the census shows smaller new stateside families than back home. This was not because some of the children were put out for training and care in other places. The Franco-Americans sought and to a large extent achieved an accommodation, a pluralistic integration in their new homes.

More French Canadians came to Burlington than to any other place in Vermont. Nearly half of the almost five thousand in 1870 had left by 1880, but the residue was still five hundred more than in Colchester.

As the Burlington Woolen Company prospered, it hired upwards of five hundred for a wide range of wages averaging a dollar for an 11 1/2-hour day (eleven after 1875). When Montreal Oblates came on mission in January 1868, St. Joseph's on Fern Hill, Burlington, was so crowded that the already acknowledged need for a parish across the river stirred the bishop to action. He secured the Rev. Jean-Frédéric Audet, a twenty-six-year-old native of St. Césaire, who arrived in Burlington on 4 March. When he preached his first sermon on Passion Sunday, 29 March, with the bishop singing high Mass, he "saw contentment on all the faces" to have at last "a Canadian parish."[4] The new priest moved energetically; after three building seasons the parish had a convent for the Canadian teaching Sisters of Providence, a new wing on the bilingual parochial school of St. Louis, and a Church of St. Francis Xavier. Simply designed by a Montreal priest and set in the woods above the village, the building represented the cooperative efforts of bishop, *curé*, syndics (building committee), *marguilliers* (prudential committee), local contractors and workmen, and every concerned member of the parish. To this francophone community Fr. Audet was "married" until his death in 1917. English-speaking Catholics in Winooski went to St. Mary's in Burlington until the bishop established St. Stephens as a mission in 1871 and as a parish in 1882, with future bishop J. S. Michaud as its first resident pastor. Michaud's father, an Acadian (from Nova Scotia), reached Burlington in 1838 and married Irish Mary Rogan. Michaud personally represented the promise of peace between Irish and French Catholics.

The French majority in Winooski, many of them owning property, did not need Republican protection. In politics they worked with the Irish minority, first in electing John McGregor to the legislature in 1867, on the Workingmen's Union ticket, then Democrats Charles Lafountain (1874) and Francis LeClair (1880-82).

In other village centers of French Canadian immigration churches, schools, convents, and mutual benefit societies mushroomed around 1870. Some three dozen buildings were bought or

---

[4]J.-F. Audet, *Histoire de la congrégation canadienne de Winooski, au Vermont* (Montréal: Imprimerie de l'Institution des Sourds-Muets, 1906), 41.

St. Francis Xavier's church and rectory in 1876, built in 1868. From Jean-Frédéric Audet, *Histoire de la congrégation canadienne de Winooski* (1906), opp. 72.

erected by 1880, and Catholic church attendance probably exceeded that of any other denomination in the state. In Burlington, by actual count on 3 March 1867, it exceeded the combined Protestant attendance at eight houses of worship.[5]

Burlington's Cathedral of the Immaculate Conception was consecrated 8 December 1867, and St. Peter's on West Street Rutland was blessed in 1873. Patrick C. Keely of Brooklyn, New York, designed both of these $100,000 structures.

Seth B. Hunt, Bennington's millionaire shawl manufacturer, donated for the cathedral an expensive transept window made in Nantes, France, and other industrialists were cordial to Catholic building programs. Bishop de Goesbriand wrote in his diary for 10 June 1868 at West Castleton, "the Slate Company seem to be anxious to have a Church here, and offered lots for a Church, school house, &c." On 30 August 1868 he noted saying Mass in the former Masonic Hall in Woodstock for French Canadians who had been using "the railroad building." Again, his 22 June 1875 entry mentioned seven Irish landowners and many French Canadians near the Pownal cotton mill: "the Company has offered a lot . . . for a Church." Apparently for the first time on 6 October 1878 he was allowed to preach to thirty-five convicts at the Windsor state prison. Redfield Proctor gave the land and a hundred dollars for a church to serve seventy-nine families at Sutherland Falls in 1879, and, later, land for a cemetery.

In St. Albans, Rutland, West Rutland, and Fair Haven, the French Catholics felt strong enough to support ethnic parishes with francophone priests. The bishop recruited three Redemptorists in Quebec for an 1869 mission to West Rutland and collected almost four thousand dollars in France and Canada for "l'Oeuvre Canadien" of several more missionaries.

Nuns from Montreal supplied French parish schools, while religious orders in southern New England sent nuns to teach the Irish in Burlington, Rutland, St. Albans, and St. Johnsbury. The first six parochial schools had started between 1854 and 1858. From these strongholds came protests against the use of the Protestant Bible in the public schools and demands for tax support. In West Rutland, Fr. Picart of St. Bridget's secured the approval of the notables in School District 7, especially the Congregational minister, Aldace Walker, for a village school with Roman Catholic

---

[5]Edward Hungerford, *A Report on the Moral and Religious Condition of the Community, Being an Address Before a Union of Evangelical Churches, in the City of Burlington, Vt., Delivered in the White St. Cong. Church, March 10, 1867* (Burlington: Free Press Steam Print., 1867), based on "Religious Canvass of Burlington," MS. schedules copied from canvassers' notebooks, in Special Collections, Bailey/Howe Library, University of Vermont. Including Methodists, Congregationalists, and Catholics from Winooski and other neighboring towns, they found 52.65 percent of the churchgoers attended Mass at St. Joseph's or St. Mary's.

teachers and texts, supported jointly by the town and the patrons. Opened in 1865, it served Catholics all over town in its four rooms, crowded with pupils totalling 370 in 1867 and 400 in 1877, over an unusually long, forty-week year.[6] A "national convention" of Franco-American provident institutions at St. Albans in 1870 discussed the school question. Antoine Moussette, publisher of *L'Avenir National*, who had revived a Société de St. Jean Baptiste at St. Albans in 1866, continued to agitate the Bible issue in his weekly.

Except for such issues as schools, naturalization, repatriation, or Canadian annexation, French language weeklies avoided political issues. The longest-lived was Moussette's *Le Protecteur Canadien* (1868-71), edited by the Rev. Zephyrin Druon, pastor of St. Mary's, St. Albans, and continued under Frédéric Houde's editorship as *L'Avenir National* (1871-72).[7]

In the Rutland marble district as in so many other parts of Vermont, the new flavor was French, but the Irish still held most of the jobs, and better jobs than the French. In 1868, when the Rutland Marble Company faced its third strike in a decade, it supposedly imported two carloads of Quebecois, and, thereafter, Quebecois replaced the Irish as hewers and drawers of stone in the marble region. Actually, seventy French Canadian and a few Scandinavian scabs, the latter referred to as "Germans," were brought in to end the strike. By 1870, two-fifths of West Rutland's common laborers, but only one-sixth of its skilled marble workers, were French. They built the Church of the Sacred Heart of Jesus to check Irish-French antagonism, but by 1875, the bishop wrote, there were "but few Canadian families attached to this place,"[8] which was tended from Rutland until 1888.

Until the twentieth century it seemed as if the old French dream of conquering the continent, "Le conquête pacifique," would come true, as Rowland Robinson feared. Then the flow lessened, and Acadian Comeau became Gomo, Courtremanches became Shortsleeves, and Gauthier became Gokey. Even ethnic parishes began to stop using the French language, in spite of reinforcement by the Canadian French language media.

The growth of Roman Catholic numbers and institutions stimulated some revival of Protestant zeal. The Rev. Edward Hungerford had apparently organized the Burlington church

---

[6]Patrick T. Hannon, *Historical Sketches on West Rutland, Vermont, Celebrating Its Centennial, 1886-1986* ed. Victor A. and Ethel P. Sevigny (Rutland: Academy Books, 1986), 106-109.

[7]Malcolm D. Daggett, "Vermont's French Newspapers," *Vermont History* 27 (January 1959): 69-75, supplies details of other attempts in Burlington and Vergennes.

[8]In A. M. Hemenway, *Gazetteer*, 3:1050. My dissertation, "Urban Penetration of Rural Vermont, 1840-80," 586-588, analyzes the ethnic composition of West Rutland quarry labor.

canvass of 1867 with this aim. The revival mode continued in the hills and in the railroad towns in the style of Dwight L. Moody.[9] United evangelical Protestant efforts, foreshadowed by the fundraising for the United States Christian Commission and the United States Sanitary Commission during the Civil War, continued in Hungerford's 1867 canvass. Young Men's Christian Associations budded in 1855-59 in St. Johnsbury, Rutland, and Springfield, and blossomed in the late 1860s. Several town locals sent delegates to the 1867 international conference in Montreal and the Portland conference of 1869. With the Young Ladies they visited jails, held prayer meetings in the parks, sugar parties, and regular meetings in their rented rooms. St. Johnsbury had the first Y building in 1884.

This generation of Christian women led in starting and managing several private, Protestant welfare institutions: the Home for Destitute Children (1865), the Home for Aged Women (1868), a probably stillborn industrial school for girls "established" by the Burlington YWCA in 1868, the Howard Relief Society, incorporating an earlier poor relief organization (1884), the Burlington Cancer Relief Association (1886), the Adams Mission Home (1886), and the Home for Friendless Women (1890).[10] Just as the late twentieth century ecumenical movement was fueled by fear of secular materialism and new age sects, church union activities after the war were motivated by fear of the Roman Catholic church.

The Baptists benefited most from revivalism, and most denominations benefited fom war and postwar profits. The Baptists raised seventy thousand dollars to endow the Vermont Academy at Saxtons River, near Bellows Falls, opened in 1876, with Jacob Estey, Levi K. Fuller (Brattleboro organs), Lawrence Barnes, Mial Davis (Burlington lumber), and Alanson Allen (Fair Haven slate) among the incorporators. Barnes and Davis were principal donors to raise the proud Baptist spire on St. Paul Street, Burlington, in 1864, and in 1872 a mission chapel, at first near the waterfront, by 1877 at the north end of Elmwood Avenue. These and other signs of vitality brought Baptist membership statewide to 9,870 in 1881, its highest for the eighty years after 1840.

A steady home missionary spirit and the habit of church support preserved a defensive Protestantism. The urban Episcopalians rivaled the Baptists in gains under Bishop W. H. A. Bissell (1868-91), a moderate continuator without his predecessor John Henry Hopkins's fire as an

---

[9]My columns in the *Burlington Free Press*, 4, 11, 18 February 1979, describe Moody's October 1877 revival campaign in Burlington.

[10]See Marshall M. True, "Middle-class Women and Civic Improvement in Burlington, 1865-1890," *Vermont History* 56 (Spring 1988): 112-127.

originator. The Diocese of Vermont grew substantially without benefit of immigration like the Catholics' or revivalism like the Baptists'. In 1882 it had thirty-three priests, forty-eight active parishes, 3,488 communicants, and $476,000 worth of church buildings and rectories. St. Paul's Burlington had doubled and Christ Church Montpelier had tripled its adherents in thirty years. The Methodists continued comfortably in second place among Protestants, with strong new Montpelier Seminary on the Sloan military hospital site.

The first-place Congregationalists, seeming to tread water, were preoccupied with the issues of the relation between the theory of evolution, or the scholarly analysis of the Bible, and the fundamentals of the New England theology. The tendency toward modernism was most noticeable in the strong village churches. The College Street Congregational Church of Burlington, with many University of Vermont officers and faculty, was unable to accede to future Senator George F. Edmunds's 1862 proposal to join if the articles on Providence and predestination were excluded from the essential tests of membership. The church regretfully responded that it could not act independently of the Chittenden County Conference. Nevertheless, the church adopted a resolution framed by Matthew H. Buckham, Congregational minister's son and next president of the university, which recognized that human understanding of doctrine is inevitably imperfect, and therefore candidates need assent to the articles in substance and not in explicit detail. In 1872 the church adopted a new form of covenant not mentioning Providence or predestination, but asserting that it neither modified nor abandoned the old articles. The issue of religious liberalism or conservatism came to a head in 1879, when the College Street Church pastor, George B. Safford, and nine other liberal West Side ministers, protested the right of the Vermont Congregational Convention to excommunicate ministers, or to refuse to sanction their ordination or installation if they repudiated the evangelical doctrines enunciated at Boston in 1865 and later confirmed at Oberlin, Ohio. Although the issue seemed to be between Presbyterian and Congregational polity, the underlying issue was whether old guard evangelicals could exclude modernist clergy.[11]

Patterns of leisure activities were more secular and permissive in 1880 than a generation earlier. The ways of the summer resident, the tourist, the returned native, and the veteran combined with those of the Irish and French to loosen the corset of Madame Vermont.

---

[11]I have summarized the controversy in "The College Street Congregational Church, Burlington, and Its First Pastor, 1880-82," *Vermont History* 57 (Spring 1989): 116.

Creeping secularism found a bridge in the celebration of a new national holiday on 30 May 1868, "Commemoration Day." Vermonters would have picked a later date to be sure of abundant flowers for decorating soldiers' graves. Occurring at the start of the summer political season, Decoration Day enabled politicians to wave the bloody shirt and keep the Democrats in their place. It effectively replaced Fast Day, long indifferently observed in Vermont, and last proclaimed by Governor George W. Hendee in 1870. In 1868 at Woodstock, for example, a boxing match was scheduled on Fast Day between a black and a Franco-American.

Even during the war, families had visited their cemetery plots or had transferred soldiers' remains from battle graves; but in 1868, without publicity, small groups of veterans and their friends observed the day. The basic ritual was translated from the traditional Independence Day, but in a minor key. Participants quoted Lincoln's Gettysburg address annually. This simplicity struck the right note with veterans who had known and respected Johnny Reb and borne the sufferings of war.

At St. Johnsbury the first year a procession offered flowers and evergreens at the new soldiers' monument. Rain interfered at Woodstock in 1869, but on the following Sunday a silent company deposited a miniature flag, with wreath and staff, at each warrior's grave. Burlington honored the unknown soldier in 1870. At Bristol in 1872 they spent the day improving the burial ground. The crowds grew each year; business stopped; the floral arrangements became more elaborate, and bands, choirs, public officials, fraternal orders, fire companies, schoolchildren, veterans of earlier wars, and citizens afoot and in carriages joined the parade. But the bands played softly in the cemetery, barriers between Yankee, French, and Irish tended to lower, and the orators dwelt less on glory than on rededication.

Governor John W. Stewart at Burlington in 1872, when the custom had crystallized, struck the characteristic mood. Preferring quiet meditation to speeches and pomp, he called for remembrance of the devoted dead and for facing the trials and duties of peace. "Smother every remaining . . . spark of animosity between the sections," he concluded. "We cannot afford to perpetuate the hatreds of the war. We should feel today that we can shake hands across the graves with our Southern brethren."[12] Gen. W. W. Grout of Barton, not yet elected to Congress, echoed the same sentiments six years later.

On the other hand, when Jefferson Davis ventured across the Canadian border at Derby in 1867, an indignant woman threw a stone at him, a crowd taunted and booed, and he was refused a

---

[12] *Burlington Weekly Free Press*, 7 June 1872. The whole state press annually gave the holiday full coverage.

visit to a famous herd of cattle. As Vermont carpetbaggers reported Southerners thwarting their Radical program and Vermont came to realize that the Solid South was depriving them of the fruits of victory, they hardened, too.

Freedom was the watchword during Radical Reconstruction, including the constitutional amendments freeing the slaves, making them citizens and giving them the vote. All Vermonters in the U.S. House of Representatives during President Grant's terms supported the Radical program, and Congressman Luke P. Poland headed the committee investigating the Ku Klux Klan. Senators Edmunds and Morrill voted for the impeachment of President Andrew Johnson. Although town and country agreed on the Radical platform, it is noteworthy that all the Vermont congressmen of this period, except for Dudley C. Denison of Royalton and George W. Hendee of Morrisville, came from major centers.

Enforcing the war aims through Radical Reconstruction was one way of continuing the platform on which the Republican Party was organized. Enforcing prohibition was the means of continuing the "temperance" element in that program. Always indifferently enforced until local option took its place in 1902, prohibition was a rallying point for Christian women especially. After a year's whirlwind crusade, the Vermont Women's Christian Temperance Union organized in 1875.[13] The nativism that had erupted into public view with a climax in 1855 still colored the Republican syndrome, as Rowland Robinson expressed it, but it was mainly subterranean. The principles that launched the successful Republican coalition were either realized by the Civil War or still repeated without achievement.

Another way to maintain Republican momentum and deal with new issues in an old context was to promote the men who had fought for freedom and union. The Grand Army of the Republic was a nationwide pressure group for pensions and jobs, but in Vermont its encampments from 1868 on were primarily for old comrades to swap war stories. The G.A.R. paraded on national holidays, decorated graves on Memorial Day, and campaigned for candidates rather than chose them. More likely the Reunion Society of Vermont Officers, organized by Redfield Proctor, Wheelock G. Veazey and others in 1864, influenced the choice of veteran candidates. With few exceptions, only colonels or higher ranks advanced politically to the top Vermont political offices.

Veterans held less than a third of Vermont's highest offices in the fifteen years after the war. Unless they intended to be politicians like C. H. Joyce and Redfield Proctor, they gave priority to

---

[13]See Deborah P. Clifford, "The Women's War Against Rum," *Vermont History* 52 (Summer 1984), 141-160.

fixing up their farms, rebuilding or starting their businesses. Although the danger of Democratic resurgence was slight in Vermont, Republicans here as elsewhere nominated or appointed former Democrats like Paul Dillingham, Luke P. Poland, Asahel Peck, and Bradley Barlow, to insure their not returning to the opposition. It helped that these candidates came from places with many votes. Many good Republicans like Peter T. Washburn and Julius Converse had long been waiting in line for the governorship and asserted their seniority. The following list of war heroes rewarded with elective or appointive office is remarkably short: thirteen out of forty-one individuals first serving between 1866 and 1880 in twelve federal or statewide offices.[14]

> Gen. George J. Stannard (1820-86), St. Albans, 2d Vt. Brigade, Collector of Customs, 1866-72
> Col. Stephen Thomas (1827-1903), West Fairlee, 8th Regt., Lt. Gov., 1867-69; pension agent
> Lt. Col. Peter T. Washburn (1814-70), Woodstock, 1st Regt., Vt. Adjutant General, 1861-66, Gov. 1869-70
> Col. George P. Foster (1836-79), Burlington, 4th Regt., U.S. Marshal, 1870-79
> Gen. William Wells (1837-92), Burlington, 6th Cavalry Corps, Collector of Customs, 1872-85
> Lt. Col. Charles H. Joyce (1830-1916), Rutland, 2d Regt., U.S. House of Representatives, 1875-83
> Col. Redfield Proctor (1831-1908), Rutland, 15th Regt., Lt. Gov. 1876-78, Gov. 1878-80
> Capt. Walter C. Dunton (1830-90), Rutland, 14th Regt., Vt. Sup. Ct., 1877-79
> Col. William W. Henry (1831-1915), Burlington, 10th Regt., U.S. Marshal, 1879-85
> Col. Wheelock G. Veazey (1835-98), Rutland, 16th Regt., Vt. Sup. Ct., 1879-89
> 1st Lt. Kittredge Haskins (1836-1916), Brattleboro, 16th Regt., U.S. Dist. Attorney, 1880-87
> Lt. Col. Roswell Farnham (1827-1903), Bradford, 12th Regt., Gov. 1880-82
> Maj. John L. Barstow (1832-1913), Shelburne, 8th Regt., Lt. Gov. 1880-82

Beside the hero of Ticonderoga, Vermont chose a civilian to represent the state in National Statuary Hall, answering a congressional joint resolution of 1865. Tourists in Washington ask, "Who is that man beside Ethan Allen?" The choice of Jacob Collamer (1791-1865) of Woodstock as Ethan's "standing mate" balanced a frontier radical from the west side with an east side conservative

---

[14]Compiled from *A List of the Principal Civil Officers of Vermont from 1777 to 1918*, ed. John M. Comstock (St. Albans: St. Albans Messenger, 1918), and *Revised Roster of Vermont Volunteers . . . 1861-66*, comp. Theodore S. Peck (Montpelier: Watchman Publishing, 1892). Highest rank cited, omitting brevets. All served in Vermont regiments, and one reached regimental rank in a midwestern unit. Except for Stannard, Wells, Henry, Thomas, and Foster, their military service was brief. Except for Thomas, Farnham, and Barstow, they lived in Burlington, Rutland, or the large villages. Except for Foster and Wells, they were all forty-four or older when they took office. Thomas moved to Montpelier when he became pension agent, or before.

whose useful life spanned the period since Vermont's admission to the Union. It was not just an out-of-perspective act honoring a recently departed senator. Chosen spokesman of his town of Royalton to welcome Lafayette in 1825, foreshadowing Ralph Waldo Emerson when he called for a national literature in 1828, influential in the 1835-36 debate to substitute the state senate for the governor's council, three-term congressman, postmaster general during Taylor's year as president, antislavery moderate and economic conservative like his constituents, Collamer was indeed a representative Vermonter.

Some of the best jobs in Washington, abroad, or in the conquered South went to earlier faithful who were not replaced when rivals challenged them. DeWitt Clinton Clarke, former *Burlington Free Press* editor, was executive clerk of the U.S. Senate for nine years until his death in 1870. Former Congressman George Perkins Marsh of Burlington also served (1861-82) until his death as Minister to Italy, one of the top ten diplomatic posts in pay and perquisites. John Sullivan Adams of Burlington, eleven years Secretary of the State Board of Education, resigned in 1867 to become postmaster, commissioner of immigration, and collector of customs at Jacksonville, Florida.

The principle of rotation survived for the governor and the legislature, but opportunities were cut in half by the institution of biennial sessions. The tradition of two terms ended for the legislature and governor, although state senators from ten large towns won re-election in the seventies.

What appeared to be a new tradition of three terms for the federal House failed because of fierce competition, which cut Dudley C. Denison, Bradley Barlow, and James M. Tyler short, and brought longer tenure to L. P. Poland, C. H. Joyce, and nearly all incumbents elected after 1880. Infirmity, death, or elevation to the U.S. Senate ended the tenure of most twentieth century federal Representatives. Senators Morrill and Edmunds had already set the pattern. This left fewer congressional openings for eager veterans.

Vermont veterans did not swarm to enlist with the Fenians, the zaniest movement to invade Vermont on the heels of the Civil War. In the restless spring days of 1866 and 1870 masterminds in New York conspired to collect arms and forward a thousand Irish into the Eastern Townships of Quebec as a blow in support of Irish republicanism. Crossing the border at Franklin and Highgate, the Fenians were checked with a few casualties and retired. Other Civil War veterans and sympathizers in Burlington and St. Albans areas helped them while Yankees watched and their officials seized their arms, arrested their leaders, and gave the boys tickets back home after the outing.

Vermonters, remembering the St. Albans raid of October 1864, and feeling that the Canadian court let the raiders go, were willing to see the British attacked. They were glad that the reciprocal trade inaugurated with Canada in 1854 ended in 1867, and expected to see Canada annexed to the United States. Most agreed with Warren Robinson, historian of Highgate, to whom it seemed "a round-about way to give freedom to Ireland."[15]

It was one thing to forestall the danger of factionalism with Civil War symbols, and another to ignore voters noisily pressing their needs. Before the war, villages got much of what they wanted in spite of rural predominance through a large majority of small town representatives in the General Assembly. Would this still be true in postwar conditions? By 1870 a majority of the towns had only a quarter of Vermont's population. For most nominating conventions the Republican Party strengthened the small-town vote by giving each town one delegate plus extras depending on the size of the Republican vote in the previous election for governor. The Council of Censors had for twenty years and more itched to amend the constitution to represent population rather than towns, that is, to enhance the power of villages.

The bipartisan Censors of 1869, however, ignored the issue (as unwinnable?) and proposed six amendments that they themselves could not agree on. The 1870 constitutional convention accepted two. It rejected a general corporation law (passed as an 1872 statute, however), gubernatorial appointment of supreme court judges, filling House vacancies in joint assembly (adopted in 1924), and woman suffrage, forced upon the state by the nineteenth amendment in 1920. They abolished the Council of Censors, adopting a method of amendment even more weighted against change, and moved to biennial sessions. In a postwar atmosphere of frenzied lobbying for corporate advantages, especially among railroads until the Central Vermont consolidation of 1870, the smell of corruption around the Grant administration, and the danger of factionalism, the amendments were aimed to sort out differences in a clean way, without giving the Democrats a crack to leak through.

Villages maintained their predominance because the rural majority of poor towns called on the state to assume more and more of its tax burdens, and the villages had the personnel to staff the new state offices. In agriculture, transportation, education, and all the areas where towns felt too poor to carry the tax burden, state functions expanded. This urbanized state government in spite

---

[15]In A. M. Hemenway, *Gazetteer*, 2:268.

of the continued rhetoric of town autonomy.[16] Centralization of the public school system seemed to be on the march. Every session to 1894 enacted some school law, showing that the most urbanized parts of Vermont, with the professional approval of still more urbanized areas outside of Vermont, could win paper victories. In 1864 the legislature chartered one state agricultural college and the next year attached it to the University of Vermont. Without much patronage from the state's farmers or money from the legislature, the Agricultural College did what it could to serve the Dairymen's Association, organized in 1869, test fertilizers, send its Professor George H. Perkins to lecture at farmers' institutes, and, after the Hatch Act of 1887 provided funds for experiment stations, expand its research on farm problems. In 1865 the state also established a reform school in Waterbury (moved to Vergennes after the building burned in 1874), and in 1866, normal schools in each congressional district. It mandated use of texts from an approved list. In 1867 children between eight and fourteen had to attend school three months a year. Under ten they could not work in industry, under fifteen no more than ten hours a day.[17]

In practice, however, the extreme localism of the school districts continued. The town system was not mandatory until 1892. Until then, only twenty-five towns, mostly the largest, adopted it and kept it. Three struggling academies lobbied to divide teacher training funds; Johnson and Castleton normal schools continued feeble past 1880. Towns recaptured choice of texts; compulsory attendance was a dead letter and child labor continued in the mills, evading the restrictions. The founding of a reform school and a state agricultural college were milestones, the latter as much a victory for Burlington as the 1857 statehouse fight and later normal school contests were defeats. But real progress in agricultural and mechanical arts awaited the establishment of an experiment station in 1888 and the strengthening of "the applied sciences" at the University of Vermont toward the end of the century.

With town debts high from Civil War bounties, rural poverty, and bonding for railroads, towns spent too little money for buildings, equipment, and teachers, and the better teachers moved

---

[16]Samuel B. Hand and D. Gregory Sanford's forthcoming book on the Vermont Republican Party (see above p. 103), Edwin C. Rozwenc, *Agricultural Policies in Vermont, 1860-1945* (Montpelier: Vermont Historical Society, 1981), and Robert O. Sinclair, "Agricultural Education and Extension in Vermont," *The University of Vermont: The First Two Hundred Years* (Burlington: University of Vermont, distributed by University Press of New England, Hanover, 1991), 179-186, deal with these issues.

[17]On the postwar educational system see John C. Huden, *Development of State School Administration in Vermont* (Montpelier: Vermont Historical Society, 1943), 70, 80-83, 162-167, 231, 242-244; *The Revised Laws of Vermont, 1880* (Rutland: Tuttle, 1881), Title 10, 152-191; and the annual and biennial school reports.

to larger towns with graded systems or left the state. Once more school reform allowed a few centers to meet new needs. The new needs they felt were secular: for business schools to teach commercial correspondence, bookkeeping and shorthand; for select schools to teach manners and "accomplishments"; for military training. The Vermont Episcopal Institute in Burlington featured drill and tactics for a mainly out-of-state clientele. Burnside Military School survived at least the first five years of peace and prosperity in Brattleboro. Norwich University, after its building burned in 1866, finally escaped from the shadow of Dartmouth to Northfield, but struggled past 1880 with inadequate finances, enrollment, and staff. After 1874 the University of Vermont always had a professor of military science and tactics as called for in the Morrill Act. Burlington's business school was the most nearly continuous of several in Rutland, Brattleboro, and a few other villages.

Education was an avenue to freedom from a restricted past for most students. It meant dollars, recognition, and all the other blessings of this life. Genteel culture as a means of enjoying these blessings was not important to the vast majority. Either they could not afford it, or were too tired from working dawn to dark to enjoy it. On their time off they went to baseball games, circuses, minstrel shows, billiard halls and bowling alleys, panoramas, prizefights, *sub rosa* cockfights, horse races on ice or land with purses, betting, and liquor. Restrictions were looser for all of these plebeian amusements, although Rutland did prohibit ballplaying in the business section.

The popular myth of Vermont's eternal fight for freedom easily pieced the Civil War onto Vermont's revolutionary tradition. New features of Fourth of July parades were merchants' floats, while uniformed veterans filled the lines. Towns honored visiting generals. Bennington Battle Day, 16 August, began to get statewide attention as Philadelphia centennial fever revived the movement to erect a memorial tower, accomplished in 1891. The literary counterpart of the Bennington monument was Abby Maria Hemenway's *Vermont Historical Gazetteer*, five huge volumes of local information on every conceivable subject, cajoled out of hundreds of citizens from 1860 until her death in 1890.

Vermont had private, social libraries in the eighteenth century, but by the mid-1870s public libraries, with a small measure of free access and circulation, were growing in the larger villages. Of the thirty librarians, ten were paid, and presided over collections ranging from the State Library and that of the University of Vermont, with about fourteen thousand volumes each, to a few hundred in the smaller places.[18]

For those who could afford it, more and more summer residents from the cities exerted a powerful influence, always for urban ways, upon their service personnel and on resident Vermonters of the same affluence. They patronized new mineral springs at Sheldon and Middletown and revived old ones at Clarendon, Alburg, and Highgate for health and social reasons. They "camped" and fished on lakeshores. They took their guests by carriage, horseback, and afoot to dine at a summit house. A Lake Champlain excursion on the tourist steamboats *Adirondack*, built in 1867, or the *Vermont II* (1871), was limited to the Ticonderoga-Plattsburgh run after the Delaware & Hudson completed the railroad between Albany and Montreal via the west shore in 1876.[19]

Indoors the elite defined their circles by those who received their calls, who were invited to the Vermont Episcopal Institute on New Years' Day for a performance of Sheridan's *The Rivals*, followed by refreshments and music on "Mr. Hopkins' mechanical piano," or who read plays and papers with the Burlington Shakespeare Club or the Rutland Fortnightly. Burlingtonians could attend Italian grand opera and Gilbert and Sullivan, as well as melodramas, concerts, farces, pantomimes, and amateur theatricals after John Purple Howard opened his opera house in 1879. A piano or melodeon in the parlor was both a social advantage for the young miss and an aspiration that professional musicians fostered.[20]

How much did wives choose styles in costume, art, and building, following city fashion? Hoop skirts with murderous tight lacing yielded to bustles in Vermont only after 1870, to the hurt of several local makers of the "beehives," as the press called them. "Teetering," a seesawing gait

---

[18]The median number of volumes for libraries in towns with upwards of twenty-five hundred people was about three thousand and for the smaller places, five hundred. There were also twenty-two small libraries in secondary schools. See *Public Libraries in the United States of America* (Washington: Government Printing Office, 1876), 1172-1173.

[19]T. D. Seymour Bassett, "Documenting Recreation and Tourism in New England," *American Archivist* 59 (Fall 1987): 553-555; Harold A. Meeks, "Nineteenth Century Recreation," in *Time and Change in Vermont: A Human Geography* (Chester, Conn.: Globe Pequot Press, 1986), 140-156.

[20]*Burlington Free Press*, 4 January 1870, 1 January 1880 (V.E.I.); ibid., 20 April 1870 (Shakespeare); *A Meeting Of the Fortnightly In Memory Of Its President* [from 1880], Mrs. Julia Caroline Ripley Dorr (Rutland: Tuttle, 1913); George B. Bryan, "The Howard Opera House in Burlington," *Vermont History* 45 (Fall 1977): 197-220; H. L. Storey, ed. *Vermont Musical Journal* (Burlington, Oct. 1866-?); T. D. Seymour Bassett, "Musicians, Minstrels, and Melodeons," *New England Quarterly* 19:40-42.

affected by village belles, was a fad of these years.[21] Charles A. Cole, an Englishman visiting near Bennington or Brattleboro about 1873, wrote a series of travelogues and summed up the appreciation level of those who bought decoration:[22]

> There is a pretty fair sale of chromos and lithographs of . . . poultry, cattle, flowers, and fruit. . . . Two or three portfolios carried by pedlars of prints from Boston, Albany, and New York, contained very ordinary lithographs of modern pictures, with . . . portraits of Napoleon, Bismarck, and the Emperor of Germany, and female heads.

Burlington's Grasse Mount, the Federal style mansion where Cornelius Van Ness entertained the Marquis de Lafayette, featured stylish black walnut and richer, darker interiors after lumber magnate Lawrence Barnes bought and remodelled it in 1866. Ex-governor John Gregory Smith, writing his wife from Washington, where he was lobbying for his Northern Pacific Railroad, disagreed with her choice of a mansard roof for their new mansion at the top of Congress Street, St. Albans. "Most likely as usual you will conquer at last. You . . . commenced that before we were married & have kept your ground pretty steadily ever since."[23]

One of the arguments against woman suffrage (disregarding single women) was that men were spokesmen for couples who reached agreement privately after the wife had expressed her views freely. Legally women were well on the way to emancipation in Vermont. Divorce was comparatively easy and increasing, although to the conservatives this was degeneration, not progress. Women had a comparatively large measure of control over their property. Yet when the constitutional convention voted on a woman suffrage amendment in 1870 Harvey Howes of West Haven was its sole supporter.

---

[21] *Woodstock Spirit of the Age*, 25 November 1869, 7 April 1870; *Burlington Free Press*, 14 February 1870, quoting *Middlebury Register*.

[22] "Vermont," *Macmillan's Magazine*, 28 (June 1873): 179. The English author signed a third of the series, ibid., 34 (1876): 75. He referred to Jim Fisk, born in Bennington, later of Brattleboro, as coming "from a town hard by where I am writing" (ibid. 28:171).

[23] Herbert W. Congdon, *Old Vermont Houses* (Brattleboro: Stephen Daye Press, 1940), 79-81; David J. Blow, *Historic Guide to Burlington Neighborhoods*, 120; J. G. Smith to Ann Eliza (Brainerd) Smith, 25 April 1866, in the Smith Family Papers, Vermont Historical Society.

"Self-elected, foreign, intermeddling advisers" from Boston and other downcountry cities, including feminists Lucy Stone Blackwell and Julia Ward Howe, invaded Vermont to support the local women's rights movement. The vote against the amendment and the opponents' emphasis on the "foreign" flying squadron distorts the profile of public opinion on this issue. Four newspapers, in Montpelier, Brattleboro, Rutland, and St. Albans, as well as many liberal clergy, gave a measure of support to woman suffrage, and the 1870s saw piecemeal progress in women's rights. In August 1871 the University of Vermont trustees voted to admit women and two graduated Phi Beta Kappa in 1875. By 1880 women had the right to vote in school meetings and to be town clerks and school superintendents.[24]

Does the newspaper press shape or reflect society? It reflected every Vermont interest and institution in this period better than ever before. At the same time the press was more than ever an institution of the two cities, the capital, and a few large villages, although more towns had weeklies. Eleven towns in northern Vermont and the slate region saw their first local journal of any durability in the fifteen years after 1859.[25] The Democratic press suffered a patronage drought. It lost the *Burlington Sentinel* in 1869 after its editor, William H. Hoyt, moved to New York City to become managing editor of the *Catholic World*. The *Rutland Courier* stopped in 1873 with the death of its editor-publisher, John Cain. Hiram Atkins's *Montpelier Argus and Patriot* thrived by becoming more a village than a Democratic paper. The fifty-eight or more weeklies published in 1879 were over twice as many as at the close of the war, with double the circulation.[26]

---

[24] Quotation from *Burlington Free Press*, 2 February 1870; T. D. Seymour Bassett, "The 1870 Campaign For Woman Suffrage in Vermont," *Vermont Quarterly* 14 (April 1946): 47-61, and Deborah P. Clifford, "An Invasion of Strong-Minded Women: The Newspapers and the Woman Suffrage Campaign in Vermont in 1870," *Vermont History* 43 (Winter 1975): 1-19. Eliza M. Clark was Bennington school superintendent in 1872 (*Vermont School Report* (1872), 363.

[25] *Hyde Park Lamoille News Dealer*, 1860-81 (merged with *Morrisville Vermont Citizen* [1879-81] as *Morrisville News and Citizen*, 1881+); *Newport News*, 1863-64, *Republican*, 1864-65, *Express (and Standard)*, 1865+; *Lyndon Vermont Union (-Journal)*, 1865-1941; *Barton Orleans Independent Standard*, 1865-71, *Orleans County Monitor*, 1871-?; *Fair Haven Rutland County Advertiser*, 1866-68, *People's Journal*, 1868-69, *Journal*, 1869-70?, *Era*, 1879-?; *Richford Frontier Sentinel*, 1866-70-?, *Journal (and Gazette)*, 1878+; *Poultney Bulletin*, 1868-75, *Journal*, 1873-1933; *Island Pond Essex County Herald* (also dated at Guildhall), 1873-?; *North Troy Palladium*, 1874-1921 (merged with *Newport News* as *Newport Palladium and News*, 1921-?).

[26] By checking the annual almanacs against S. N. D. North, *American Newspaper Press* (Tenth Census, 1880), 170-171, 182, 186-193, 344-345, I find somewhat smaller totals than North's. He may have counted different editions issued at different times or from different towns separately.

Vermont Periodical Circulation, 1850-80

	1850	1860	1870	1880
Periodicals	35	31	47	82
Average Circulation	46,000	47,000	71,000	130,000
Weeklies	30	28	43	72
Average Circulation	41,000	45,000	56,000	73,000
Dailies	2	2	3	5
Average Circulation	555	750	3,190	4,200
Total Annual Copies	2,568,000	2,579,000	4,055,000	5,681,000

The invention during the Civil War of "boiler plate" or "patent insides" or "outsides" allowed a local editor to buy half his paper ready-to-read. Competition with out-of-state papers required drastic measures like this. The 2,480 people of Hartford, with no paper of its own in 1870, subscribed to 1,066 periodicals, only a third of them from their own county.[27] The Boston weeklies and the *Springfield Republican* invaded the Connecticut Valley in strength, and the New York and Albany press competed on the west side. In the magazine field the *Brattleboro Household*, started in 1868 by G. E. Crowell, rapidly expanded an 1870 circulation of 12,000 to 50,000 in 1872, outranked by only nine American monthlies.

The best defense against out-of-state papers was to emphasize local news. The *Montpelier Argus and Patriot* and the Brattleboro *Vermont Record and Farmer*, the two most widely circulated weeklies, succeeded by this method. Another tactic was to publish weeklies on Saturday for Sunday reading. Only A. N. Merchant's Democratic *Sunday Sentinels*, published in Rutland and Burlington, 1879-80, and never the respectable dailies, published on Sunday.

The major papers enlarged their staffs, spent more for equipment and materials, and earned more income from job printing and advertising. Burlington, Rutland, Brattleboro, and Montpelier publishers earned over half the Vermont printers' bill in 1870; the *Burlington Free Press* and the *Rutland Herald* did over twenty thousand dollars worth of job printing. Most of the well-established publishers had installed power presses by 1870 if they had not already done so before the war. They added more presses and reduced type size to crowd more news and advertising into each column.

---

[27] W. H. Tucker, *History of Hartford, Vermont* (Burlington: Free Press, 1889), 286.

Larger state bureaucracy meant more printing patronage. The *Montpelier Freeman* had the most state printing jobs for the dozen years after 1862, followed by G. A. Tuttle & Co. of Rutland. This made up for the discontinuance of most federal printing patronage after 1872.

Bigger journalism meant differentiation of function. No longer could journeymen expect to become editors. Editors, paid a salary by publishers, usually came from the professions or the publishers' families. The Vermont Editors and Publishers Association organized in 1868, perhaps because the typographers' unions were excluding them but more likely for business reasons, e.g., to abolish subscriptions on credit. In spite of a Civil War strike on the *Rutland Herald*, printers were not well organized until the twentieth century. At best an ambitious printer could start a weekly in a small village, or become foreman of the chapel (the printing office) in a large one, or leave the state for better pay on a metropolitan daily or for greater independence in the West. Almost a quarter of newspaper employees were women in 1870, compared to a twentieth in 1850. They probably checked the upward spiral of wages and perhaps sobered and steadied the traditionally intemperate printers. Even reporters had become a separate group.

Reporters were most needed on dailies, whose presence in a town was a sure indicator of urbanism. In December 1865 the *Rutland Herald* installed telegraph wires and instruments in its editorial rooms. Now they could print news faster and receive state news directly. With about 1,450 subscribers in 1870 the daily *Herald* was well ahead of its Burlington and St. Albans rivals. Half a dozen other Vermont papers tried dailies but found they did not pay. Their villages were too small to provide enough subscribers who needed local and telegraphic information they could not get from their neighbors. A population of seven thousand proved to be the minimum necessary to support a daily where capital and communications were adequate.[28]

By 1880, the two budding cities of Rutland and Burlington and several urbanized villages were making adjustments to their new conditions of congestion and looking forward to renewed prosperity. The French Canadians had come and gone or stayed and settled into their new homes. The veterans had "gone to their reward" or scattered or returned and were claiming their rewards at home. A younger generation rose to control in business and politics and chose to ignore many of the social standards set for a period upon which the second war for freedom—freedom for urban

---

[28] T. D. Seymour Bassett, "The First Vermont Dailies: A Chapter in Newspaper History," *Vermont Quarterly* 14 (October 1946): 155-162. The 1870 census circulation figures for the *Rutland Herald* daily show 1,540 on the schedule of social statistics and on the manufacturing schedule, 424,704 newspapers printed, or an average of 1,357 per issue.

industry as well as for the slave—shut the gate. These new people had experienced the worst effects of a centralizing society, the creeping paralysis of a depression, yet they weighed loss with profit and did not hesitate to proceed. They had confidence that the evils of urbanism could be conquered for they had already taken first steps to cope with urban problems.

11. Burlington: A Vermont City

Within a few years after the Civil War, Burlington and Rutland crossed the urban threshold. Over a dozen Vermont towns had met the old census definition of urban, having 2,500 or more people, since Windsor, Woodstock, Springfield, and Bennington achieved that level in 1810. Thirty years later, Burlington was only a little more populous than a dozen other "urban" towns that met this minimum. But after another thirty years, Burlington was more than just larger in 1870. Whereas Rutland's population was scattered over the whole town, "the principal village being comparatively small,"[1] Burlington's central gridiron of streets was densely packed with people, both those who lived there and those who came periodically for business and pleasure. The visitors were numerous and diverse in styles and aims. Many people moved in and out while the Queen City flourished. Burlingtonians were heterogeneous in occupations and origins. Although the jack-of-all-trades could still be found, and some wanting to work at their trade had to accept common labor, most workmen chose to exploit special skills. Burlington's social strata were more complex. Its contacts were more often impersonal and indirect than in good old rural days. It boasted institutions that villages could not afford: a daily newspaper, a university of three colleges and a dozen resident faculty, and by 1879, a public library, a hospital, and an opera house. In particular departments another town might lead, as did Rutland's real estate developers and building trades and St. Johnsbury's Athenaeum, but as a constellation of institutions, Burlington outshone the rest by virtue of numbers and resources.

Burlingtonians were boosters, shooting with no goal in their sights. Their idea of the good life tended toward paternalist or communitarian extremes. Some assumed that if troubles arose, the bosses would take care of them. Others had the vague feeling that their community could work things out democratically. Many who had seen the big cities and did not like them were sure that urban evils could not happen here. Here, in spite of diversity, each element expected to share somehow in a higher standard of living and of civilization.

---

[1] U.S. Department of the Interior, Bureau of the Census, *Tenth Census* (Washington: Government Printing Office, 1883-?; 18?v.), 10:351.

How did Burlington deal with the little urban evils that rapid growth and depression brought the city before 1880? Because basic needs are invariable, what this largest urban nucleus in Vermont did about them was representative of places crossing the urban frontier everywhere. On the other hand, its peculiar Champlain Valley landscape, the balance and direction of its commercial and industrial interests, and its blend of New England and New York background produced a social organism like no other.

Like any small city a century old, Burlington had its mix of a few families with inherited wealth, refined by experience abroad, and raw new men from the hills or abroad who had recently made their fortunes. The distinctive flavor came from the Green Mountains, not the Blue Ridge; travel on business to Boston, New York, or Montreal, not to Baltimore or Philadelphia; or to the edge of the northern wilderness. The first class had selective foreign experiences. The Wheelers, Hickoks, Hungerfords, Torreys, and Marshes had connections with British universities and thinkers and had seen continental art galleries and Mediterranean ruins. The Heman ("Chili") Allens and Marvins of Grassmount had traversed Latin America or California and the seas between. On the other hand, Lawrence Barnes, the lumberman, Judge David A. Smalley, originally from Jericho, and many lesser, rough-cut men, when they traveled, stuck to business. They were more likely to spend and risk when they saw possible gain than to pinch pennies and avoid taxes. Burlington has steadily accepted new money into its leadership. If not Ira Allen, then Thaddeus Tuttle, then the new bank cashier or dry goods tycoon from Troy, then the lumbermen from Canada.

Burlington's unique lake-and-mountain scenery was powerful enough to eclipse the urban blight near the wharves, "savagely raw and shabby" as Henry James found it.[2] Perhaps the mechanic, clerk, or common laborer, walking past the Battery to and from the shops in the sunrise or sunset, was too tired to notice the sparkle, the shadows, and the changing hues of Lake Champlain and the Adirondacks. Can natural beauty, if it soaks in long enough, subtly temper the harsh winds of poverty and nourish creativity in those lucky enough to have leisure? The college alma mater, a hymn to Lake Champlain, written about this time, instinctively touched Burlington sentiment.

The traveler of 1840, returning at the end of the Civil War, would have found the setting familiar in spite of changes. From the breakwater, intermittently extended to some three thousand feet since its construction in 1837, he could still see the presiding dome of the college. St. Joseph's

---

[2]*Outsiders Inside Vermont; Three Centuries of Visitors' Viewpoints on the Green Mountain State* ed. T. D. Seymour Bassett (1967; Canaan, N.H.: Phoenix Publishing, 1976), 88, quoting James's 12 August 1870 letter to *The Nation*.

spire to the north (1850) and to the south, "Overlake," the French chateau of LeGrand B. Cannon (1859), now flanked it on the hill. There were twice as many houses, especially workmen's cottages northeast of the Battery to St. Joseph's, and tenements were thicker near the docks. Near Church Street were new steeples and many three- and four-story blocks. Smoke arose from the rebuilt Pioneer Shops at the foot of Cherry, containing a new foundry and machine shop started by Dr. B. S. Nichols, formerly of Davey & Nichols's ironworks at Fair Haven and East Middlebury, and from the planing mills. Thousands of feet of lumber covered land filled since the forties, and the industrial district, once ending near King, reached two or three blocks farther south. A larger, faster, more luxurious steamer brought a few travelers, but most of them came via the Union depot at the foot of College Street. A carriage ride the next morning might have passed the abandoned Maple Street station, soon to be used briefly by the Burlington & Lamoille Railroad. The hackman would explain that an impassable bridge over the old railroad track blocked the North Bend drive along the bluff overlooking the intervale and the ridge toward the lake through which the Central now tunneled.

The streets were unpaved, except for a quarter-mile of stone blocks and almost as much in cobbles. Church Street might be jammed with haywagons and wood carts. Curbing and sidewalks had not kept pace with city growth, but the property owners' habit of planting elms promised shade and beauty within a generation.

Such was Burlington to the casual visitor. To Dr. Samuel W. Thayer, city health officer, "no terms in the English language" could convey the enormity of existing nuisances.[3] Thayer, using these words as a parting shot in his 1866 report, was a man of medical prestige whom taxpayers would listen to. Reared in a small-town doctor's household, graduated from the Vermont Medical College at Woodstock in 1838, after fifteen years in Vermont medicine he had been since 1853 dean and professor of the University of Vermont Medical Department. His familiarity with urban public health conditions came freshest from experience as state Surgeon General organizing care of Vermont casualties in Washington and other city hospitals after the battle of Gettysburg, and after that in charge of the Burlington army hospital until the end of the war.

In the memory of a good many citizens cholera had visited Burlington in 1849 with immigrant Irish, and with the renewal of immigration in 1866 they expected it again. Thayer began and ended

---

[3] In Burlington *City Report* (1866, imprint varies), 100. Given the most prominent place, after the mayor's message, among the annual statements of officials, Thayer's twenty-one-page indictment is the source of my description.

his report with a warning to expect this dread disease as a judgment upon the city's social and moral condition unless it took immediate action. (Cholera did come to North America that year, but Burlington escaped a serious epidemic.) Filth was somehow the source of disease, contemporaries unaware of the germ theory assumed. Thayer's three house-to-house inspectors had carefully gathered a mountain of horrendous evidence to scare the most reluctant taxpayer into prompt action.

They found that the Aqueduct Company was supplying water to five hotels, five livery stables, the two railroads, fifty-nine stores, saloons and the like, and a thousand other persons in this city of seven thousand. The maximum capacity of its pumps working all the time, and of the springs of its reservoir above Williams near Pearl, was about twelve hundred hogsheads a day, half of what the city needed. Eighteen hundred persons depended on inadequate cisterns; another twelve hundred had wells or springs; eight hundred relied on their neighbors or on casks hauled from the lake.

Thayer prescribed a "water cure," a new waterworks immediately. He persuasively pointed out the many advantages: lower fire risk and fire insurance costs, better drinking water, better health, cleaner streets, more tourists to a city whose lifeblood, water, would flow freely through faucet and fountain.

But adequate supply without adequate disposal would be futile, Thayer continued. Sanitary inspection found nearly six hundred houses without drains, and almost as many whose clogged "sewers" merely shifted the noisome burden to neighbors. Less than fifty houses used the main city sewer, that is, the partly covered rivulet in the ravine from Maiden Lane (now Union, north of the present YMCA) to the lake below Howard Street. Only a complete sewer plan that included the dredging of South Cove and the removal of stagnant waters could cleanse these Augean stables.

The worst congestion occurred around Court House Square, a whited sepulchre of a park-crossroads, its back alleys and yards littered with "heaps of straw and ashes, . . . scraps of leather and cloth saturated with filthy water and . . . swill, decayed vegetables, meat, fish and even human excrement."[4] The dirt of poverty enveloped the tenement district. Often two or more families slept in one sometimes windowless room, blackened with smoke, the wooden sink spouts rotten. Cellars reeked a damp stench; contents of slop basins and chamber pots coated exteriors; yards, if any, had hogs at large or in rarely cleaned pens. As health officer without defined powers, Thayer presented a seventeen-point list of recommendations for disposal of solid wastes, cleaning procedures, control

---

[4] Ibid., 85.

of swine, establishing a city dispensary and a new cemetery, doctors' reporting deaths, infectious diseases, and smallpox vaccinations, and police enforcement of health officer's orders.

Reports of superintendents of schools reinforced Thayer's indictment. The Rev. Eldridge Mix, pastor of the First Congregational Church, in 1866, and Prof. Matthew H. Buckham the following year, found the school buildings and grounds dirty, crowded, and badly ventilated. The Union High School was a disgrace to its prominent position on the corner of College and Willard. "Two-thirds of all the children . . . are from non-American families," wrote Buckham, because the Yankees patronize select schools. Rich taxpayers, he claimed, packed district school meetings and defeated all proposals for improvement. A successor called district meetings "those little hiding places of moneyed terrorism."[5]

Other city officers had their bits to add to the horror story. The overseer of the poor listed among his expenses the funeral charges and family aid for three killed by a Pioneer Shops explosion and one killed while working on the Cathedral of the Immaculate Conception. Mayor Albert L. Catlin noted the temporary need for a "much larger" police force until after demobilization, and the chief of police listed prostitution as the fourth most common cause of arrests. After the discharge of the soldiers and the closing of the army hospital this offense subsided.

The total impact of the reformers' blast jolted the city fathers into action. Samuel Thayer had seen to it that the "main" question should come first. In 1866 the voters authorized issuing $150,000 in water bonds. In 1867 the city bought out the Aqueduct Company and appointed Daniel C. Linsley, an experienced railroad engineer who had built the railroad tunnel under North Avenue, to construct the works. From a Worthington pump on a pier below the Battery the conduit ran near the north lumber yards and Pioneer Shops to the old storage basin and across the campus to the new reservoir on upper Main Street. Pumping started on Christmas Day, 1867.

One of the worst fires in Burlington history to 1880 underlined the urgency of the job. On 11 June 1867 it destroyed the twenty-thousand-dollar Howard House, three tenements, shops and barns near St. Paul and Main streets. The following March a Skinner's Lane fire, northeast of Church and Main, threatened to wipe out the most valuable part of the business section when someone remembered the new hydrant a block away, and water hosed from there finished the blaze. That night the hitherto skeptical admitted that the waterworks had saved its initial cost.[6] Fire losses

---

[5]*City Report* (1866), 101-106, (1867), 7, 15-19, (1868), 11, (1877), 81.

[6]*City Report* (1868), 31-46, 54, including history of waterworks construction, (1869), 71, 99.

were comparatively light in the next decade. Over three hundred volunteer firemen, mostly in hose companies without enough good hose, stood ready to respond to alarms announced from one of the fifteen boxes of the new telegraphic system. This innovation, which only half a dozen cities under twenty thousand northeast of Pittsburgh had installed, was tested and gave railroad time at 9:15 every morning.

Water mains improved fire protection and benefited property owners who could afford plumbing, but not the tenement district. Smallpox, brought from Montreal in July 1873, pushed the city into adopting the sewer plan of 1874. The epidemic spread through a tenement population that flouted quarantine in spite of patrolmen, dodged vaccination, and could not be dragged to the existing pesthouse. Again fear opened pocketbooks at the rate of six to ten thousand dollars a year of city money until 1877. The ravine, from whose stream stock were said to drink in 1863, a decade later was a miasmal "black and putrid mass of filth."[7] It was gradually put underground, despite an owner who tried to block work on his property. When the work lagged, Dr. Thayer stepped in again. In 1878 he won over $750 in damages because the city let sewage flow through his property in an open ditch, but settled for immediate completion. Over six miles of sewers by 1880 looked creditable, but aside from the ravine they were only three or four downhill outlets or laterals from Pine to Prospect. Not a foot of pipe served the disease-breeding areas for which the health officer demanded priority. Professor Peter Collier in 1874 found pollution by the intake sixty feet from the dock, in the drift from the sewage outlet, but the city disregarded the health officer's recommendation to extend the intake beyond the breakwater.

By 1880 the health officer controlled garbage disposal in some areas, and the city had provided for regular street cleaning and the removal of dead animals. It had banished hogs from a circle within three-quarters of a mile of the Howard Opera House, that is, nearly all the thickly settled part of the city, and evicted the soap factory from Mechanics Lane. The privy problem was under control and few depended on wells that might become contaminated. The city required doctors to report contagious diseases and quarantined infected schoolchildren. It paid for smallpox vaccination but did not require it. Burlington had the only private general hospital in Vermont, except for sanitaria conducted in part for profit, and a pesthouse at its poor farm two miles from city hall in South Burlington.

---

[7]*City Report* (1874), 42.

In 1865 only three or four lots were left for sale in each of the "Protestant grounds," requiring a new cemetery. Located between St. Joseph's orphanage on North Avenue and the Vermont Episcopal Institute, the new Lake View Cemetery had by the 1870s become self-supporting, landscaped and beautified by the donations of John Purple Howard and his sister Louisa.[8]

The city's three burial grounds, with the Elmwood Cemetery landscaped and ornamented in 1879, became virtually part of the park system because of their leisure-time use. Few small American cities had as much green space. Battery Park fitted between a slum and a better working-class district, at the very center of business was Court House Square, and the college campus was also surrounded by settlement. The city market by the ravine between Main and College streets, somebody's brainchild of the late 1860s, was not green space, but served as a weigh-station and parking lot for hay, wood, and coal wagons that would otherwise have snarled business traffic. The building later stored churns and "bureau creameries" (refrigerators patented in 1876 by James F. Ferguson) made in the Pioneer Shops, and provided office space for an expanded local bureaucracy.

Schools received attention next because, like the cemeteries, they were stuffed to bursting. Beyond the mere need, it took the sting of the superintendents' revelations to wheedle the minimum from grudging taxpayers cushioned by prosperity. All the gains requiring voter approval through the elected Board of School Commissioners passed during the five years before the depression beginning in 1873. The 1867 legislature amended the city charter to provide, among other changes, a city school system, abolishing the districts. The first board included three spokesmen for the college interest in a vigorous public school feeder, a Roman Catholic voice in William H. Hoyt, editor of the Democratic *Burlington Sentinel*, and businessmen, a continuing balance.

With control taken from the districts, the superintendent pointed out that a graded, city-wide system could not operate in a collection of broken-down district schoolhouses. Number four on Maiden Lane (on the present Memorial Auditorium site) was a "tumble down pile of bricks." At Winooski Falls, "water fills the cellar in the spring" and mold lasts through the year, and so on through the eleven disgraceful buildings.[9]

In a perpetual tug-of-war between the professionals with a vested interest in expansion and the pay-as-you-go businessmen, the board gradually added school space by pennywise makeshifts and

---

[8] *City Report* (1866), 76, 93 and references annually thereafter; David J. Blow, *Historic Guide to Burlington Neighborhoods*, ed. Lilian Baker Carlisle (Burlington: Chittenden County Historical Society, [1990]), 14-15.

[9] *City Report* (1870), 79, 80; see also 83-85.

piecemeal additions. It remodeled the vacant Pine Street Methodist building, later replaced by the Converse school, for twelve thousand dollars. It chose an outsider, the lowest bidder, for the new high school at College and Willard, whose work proved defective. It funded the model Adams and Pomeroy schools, one in the growing south end and the other near upper North Street, by collecting from the U.S. Deposit Fund, selling four schoolhouses, winning a special appropriation vote, and then blithely exceeding its budget.

Temporarily checked city growth brought institutional progress. Public school property had trebled in value in the dozen years after 1868. Attendance had increased a third although enrollment advanced less than eight percent. The staff, including five college graduates, a dozen more with normal school training, and eleven apprentice teachers, was half again as large. That meant smaller classes in more space. Except for the high school principal, paid fifteen hundred dollars a year, and two part-time men assigned to night schools in the "tough" sections where pupils tended to drop out early, all the teachers were women, as they had been since the war, their median salary about $530.00 a year.[10]

Postwar city politics, especially as the immigrant element swelled, grew partisan as there were more plums to pick. The Democrats in 1870 elected Daniel C. Linsley, the former engineer of the railroad tunnel and the reservoir, as the new mayor, as well as four aldermen and a school commissioner. The 1870 council, with a six to four Republican majority, nevertheless appointed Democrats as constable, overseer of the poor, and chief of police. These officials had the most contact with poor voters. The constable collected delinquent taxes; the poormaster had hiring patronage as foreman of street gangs and goodwill from dispensing wood and other supplies to the needy; the police kept order in the tenement district. Noble B. Flanagan, former laundryman, alderman, and overseer of the poor, became the city's first full-time chief of police when Mayor Linsley appointed him in 1870 and donated his own two-hundred-dollar salary to swell Flanagan's. In 1872 the three wards became five, submerging the Democrats in four of them. Democrats

---

[10]G. E. Waring, Jr., Special Agent, *Report on the Social Statistics of Cities. Part I. The New England and the Middle States* (Washington: Government Printing Office, 1886) (Tenth Census) 17:84; reports of superintendents of schools in *City Reports*, passim; *Gazetteer and Business Directory of Chittenden County, Vermont, for 1882-83*, comp. Hamilton Child (Syracuse, N.Y.: Hamilton Child, 1882), 117-118.

contested elections through the 1870s with the same minor successes, but without electing another mayor until 1898.[11]

The police and the overseer of the poor had steady business during flush times, first regulating demobilized soldiers, then the multiplying immigrants, and always the victims of liquor. Their main job, especially during the depression, was to discipline the poor and the unemployed. Relief and police costs, number aided, arrested, or housed overnight, areas patrolled by police, all point to the same conclusion. The city tended the poor according to their severest needs. This kept them needy, or moving on. The poormaster's story is short and bitter, like the state's painful experience in the 1850s.[12] A. B. Lowry, first appointed overseer of the poor in 1870, lost his patience after five years and proposed whipping or stone breaking and peat digging to cure loafers or send them packing.[13] The four thousand dollar cost of poor relief in 1867 had nearly doubled by 1880.

This sentiment or lack of it enacted the tramp and railroad police laws of 1876 and established the workhouse in Rutland.[14] One law authorized sentencing unemployed vagrants, if threatening to injure persons or property, to serve up to six months' hard labor, if not provided for by the county sheriff or at the town farm, by assignment to a private employer. Another law authorized commission of railroad employees to clear the cars of free riders and depots of idlers, just as lumberyard watchmen were already wearing the badge to prevent theft and arson. Burlington officials tried assignment to the street commissioner for road repairs or threatened the poorhouse for "undeserving" paupers and their relatives who drifted in from the hills to spend the winter. What lessened the relief burden was the return of better times. Meanwhile, the Ladies' Aid Society attempted to channel private charities to the poor and find them jobs.

The most vexing welfare problem was the growing load of relief to people in their homes. Soon after the war, the poormaster began to distribute fuel free instead of selling it at cost. In 1874

---

[11]Linsley left Burlington in June 1870 to survey for the Northern Pacific Railroad, and resigned the mayoralty in October. *Burlington Free Press*, 25, 29 February, 2, 5 March, 6, 7, 12 April, 30 June 1870.

[12]See above p. 80.

[13]*City Report* (1876), 97-99; see also (1877), 22, (1878), 139-140.

[14]*Vermont Laws* (1876), 47-55 (Rutland workhouse), 91-94 (railroad police), 187-189 (suppression of vagrancy); *House Journal* (1878), Appendix D, 470-479 (Governor Proctor's announcement of 8 December 1878 that the House of Correction is ready to receive prisoners). See also *City Report* (1876), 110, (1878), 47, (1879), 162.

the mills stopped using shavings for landfill or making it available to the poor and used it for their own fuel.

The poor farm harbored an odd lot of humanity: the senile, the feeble-minded, the mildly insane, the epileptic, syphilitic or consumptive, the temporarily ill, the unmarried girls who ran away to have their babies, alcoholics, "grasshoppers" stranded after tallying lumber during the summer, transients; a little of everything. The city fitted the police station with berths and sent tramps there after 1 July 1870; thereafter arrests for vagrancy declined.

A strengthened police force and many unemployed after 1873 combined to increase arrests involving transients back to the peak of 1870-71. The peak of Canadian arrivals was also the peak of arrests for vagrancy, liquor violations (mostly for intoxication, otherwise for violations of prohibition), and blue-law enforcement (playing cards on Sunday, gambling, disturbing schools and religious meetings). Some of the arrests reflect periodic brothel raids or the first enforcement of a poorly understood ordinance of 1872 to let off first offenders, mostly juveniles, with a warning. Burlington, which voted heavily for prohibition in 1853, demonstrated its failure to prohibit the sale and use of alcoholic drinks. In 1868 the police counted thirty-four "diving bells" or "blind pigs," saloons operating behind a facade of groceries.[15] Police chief L. A. Drew pointed with pride in 1879 to a "successful raid . . . on the houses of ill-fame," which sent one madame to state prison and swept the city of the rest, except for one who forfeited a large bail.[16] The next year police arrested one prostitute and four brothel-keepers.

The street department had charge of sewers as well as surfaces, because mains must be laid at an established grade before finishing surfaces. The department provided the principal work relief of the depression years, along with school construction. In 1872 a city council committee rejected Chief Flanagan's proposal to put petty offenders and paupers to work breaking stone and installed a Blake crusher at Willard's Ledge south of Ledge Road. Repairing gullies and potholes was imperative lest the city be sued for damages to teams and carriages.

The Queen City of Vermont, as Burlington had begun to call itself before it was a city, contained in 1880 twelve thousand people inside a triangle with concave sides, its points the road to Shelburne beyond Howard, North Avenue and North Street, and Upper Main Street, Winooski.

---

[15]*City Report* (1869), 87; cf. Jane M. Dewey, "Biography of John Dewey," in Paul Arthur Schilpp, ed., *The Philosophy of John Dewey* (Evanston and Chicago: Northwestern University, 1939), 8, on the speakeasy problem when the philosopher's father was town liquor agent before the war.

[16]*City Report* (1880), 59.

Burlington Arrests, 1865-80
(Compiled from annual reports of the chief of police[*])

Year	Total	Liquor	Violence	Property	Sex	Other	#Lodgers
1865	248	160	34	16	33	5	e25
1868	339	159	93	16	10	30	-
1869	423	242	104	36	7	34	-
1870	610	404	98	58	10	50	58
1871	618	449	87	43	10	29	-
1872	412	280	79	20	10	23	78
1873	433	299	67	34	7	26	87
1874	520	322	84	41	8	+65	180
1875	540	320	127	76	2	15	884
1876	615	426	94	48	23	24	653
1877	463	292	56	56	43	16	493
1878	430	257	77	68	12	16	362
1879	387	232	73	48	22	12	414
1880	490	296	90	65	8	31	41
Total:	6,528	4,138	1,163	656	205	376	3,675

[*]In *City Reports* (none for 1866-67). A change in the fiscal year left 1873 representing eleven months.
[#]In the police station; e=estimated. [+]Abnormal from 49 arrests for violation of some new ordinance.

As Henry Clark, editor of the *Rutland Herald* prophesied in 1868, Burlington and Winooski were beginning to be one place,[17] with people commuting in both directions to their work. Half of the twelve thousand were crowded into less than a quarter of that triangle, close to the Winooski mills and near the lake.

While Burlington had a smaller census count than in 1870, more people were permanently attached as trade and industry prospered. Through the Burlington and Lamoille Railroad, Burlington added a connection with St. Johnsbury and Portland, although as soon as the new road was completed, the Central arranged to let the B. & L. rolling stock use its own spur from Burlington to Essex Junction. Since the hinterland was agricultural, "the retail trade of the city extends some 20 to 30 miles inland, while the wholesale trade reaches through much of northern Vermont. During the summer season a good trade is carried on with the lake towns, steamers making two trips a day."[18] Burlington also became a major coal distribution point for towns along the railroad.

---

[17]*Rutland Herald*, 7 November 1868.

[18]G. E. Waring, Jr., *Social Statistics*, 17:79.

Social Statistics of Four Northeastern Cities in 1880*

	Burlington	Rutland	ConcordNH	RomeNY
Population, 1870	14,387	9,834	12,241	11,000
Population, 1880	11,364	12,149	13,843	12,194
Miles of streets	50	17	30	30
Ann. street dept. cost	$13,500	$5,000	$20,000	$4,000
No. street lamps	147	80	120	75
Cost of waterworks	$450,000	$10,000	$350,000	$181,000
Gal. used per capita	58	66	72	66
Income from water rates	$22.00	$11.50	$25.00	$9.00
Water meters	35	0	few	0
Sewerage plan	1874	none	1876	none
Fire alarm boxes	15	0	21	-
Capacity of largest hall	1,200	1,000	1,100	1,500
Acres in public parks	14	10	4	2
Ann. approp. for parks	$500	nominal	0	$50
Regular police	10	7	5	6
Real estate value per cap.	$257	$271	$726	$445
Tax per $100 valuation	4.01	2.18	1.70	1.70

*Compiled from G. E. Waring, Jr., *Social Statistics* (1886), v. 17, passim. I have chosen the figures in *City Report* (1881), 31, 33, 67, instead of Waring's, for water use, water meters, and street lamps.

The social geography of Burlington in 1880, the interaction of humans, other animals and plants with the terrain near the lake and the Winooski River, was affected by its internal transportation system, the location of its institutional buildings, the distribution of its public utilities, its views, and its history. Embryo districts with different functions could be discerned in 1840, but by 1880 they were clearly marked. Industry and wholesale trade preempted the lakeside and retail trade the Church Street neighborhood. Tenements were near the mills, working people filled the North End with the thickest concentration of French Canadians, while smaller groups of laborers lived at the South End, in boardinghouses near Church Street, and near Chase Street by the Falls. Employers and professionals monopolized the thoroughfares and the rim of one or two blocks from the Church Street stores. The cream of the well-to-do had begun the accelerated removal to hill sites that were, with general expansion north and south, the major real estate development of the next twenty years.

The junction of depot and wharf at the foot of College Street was the focus of heavy carting, the center of the industrial-commercial web. Several hundred men came to work at the waterfront daily, mainly from within two blocks of Battery Street. At least five steamboats as well as coal and lumber barges used the port of Burlington, with shops and yards as far north as the waterworks under the Battery bluff, and south even beyond Howard Street near the Rutland tracks.

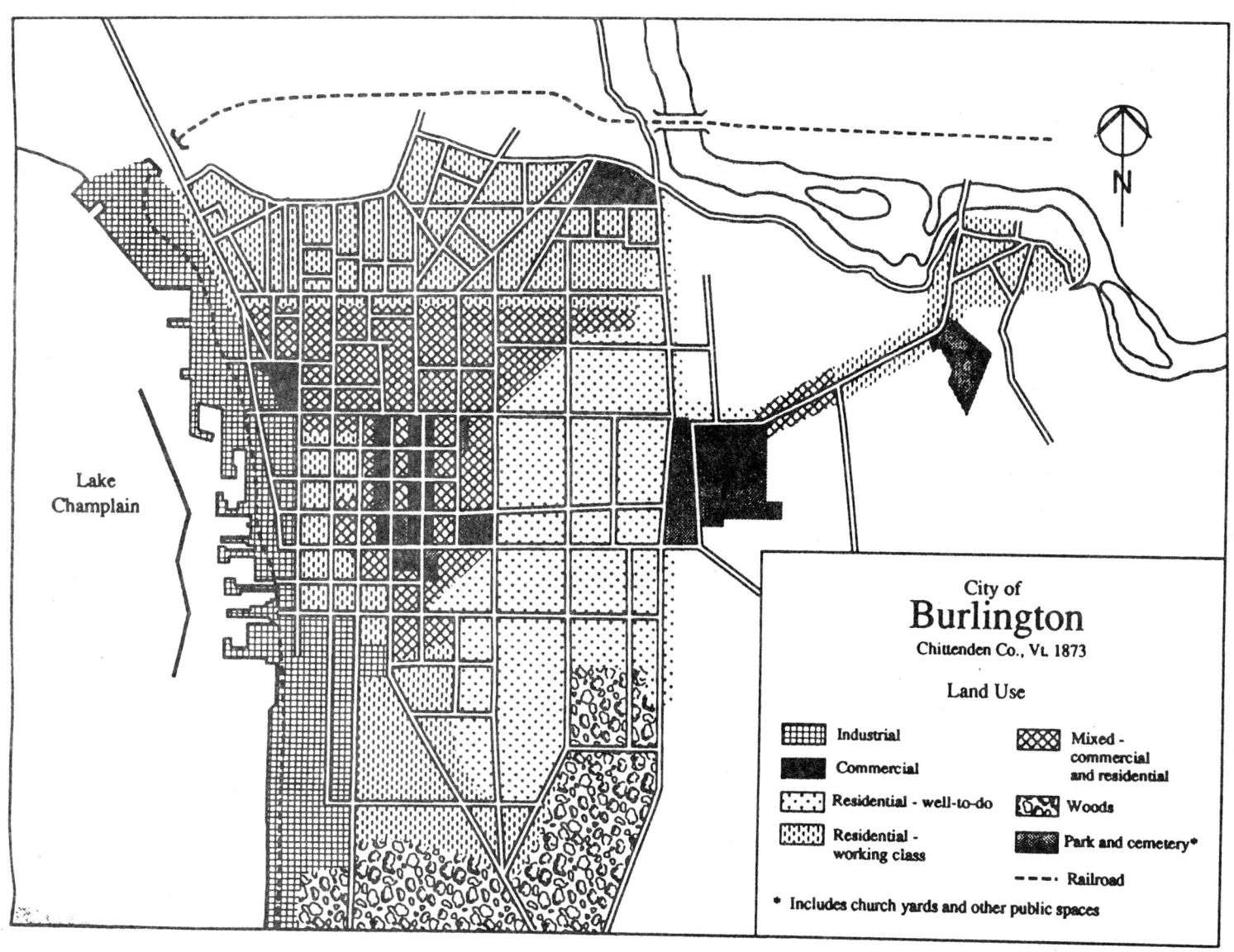

City of Burlington, Vt., 1873. Land Use. By Susan Kennedy, Assistant Professor, Department of Geography, University of Vermont, and graduate students Stephen P. Hanna (Geography) and Eric Hanson (Historic Preservation).

The lumberyard of Shepard & Morse, a big company with headquarters in Boston and other yards in East Saginaw, Michigan, Tonawanda, New York, and Canada, occupied a key position near the foot of College Street. Only a fifth of its reported three hundred workmen identified their employer to the canvassers for the city directories,[19] an omission that suggests the seasonal nature of the work and the transitory character of the help, many of whom worked for another lumber or woodworking firm three years earlier, or were not in town. As with Burlington industry in general, French Canadians and Irish were on the payroll in about equal proportions, while Yankees dominated both clerical and managerial staff. The tiny Tampico Dressing Company of E. B. & A. C. Whiting had moved recently from St. Albans and was to grow steadily throughout the next century as a brush factory. Nearly all the turners working for Wing & Smith were French living in the North End. The firm had come from Niagara Falls thirty years before and made lasts, boot trees, and crimps. Hardly a Frenchmen worked in Brink's foundry or Nichols's machine shop nearby, which made most of Burlington's hydrants and street lamp posts. The gasworks, converted in 1879 from coal to petroleum, stood at the foot of Bank.

Almost as central were the wharves at Main, King, and Maple, used by wholesalers and steamboats. In the loft of the old depot, the Wakefields demonstrated the decline of sail navigation by their move from the old stone store in 1879 and their shift in emphasis from sailmaking and rigging to awnings, tents, wagon covers, flags, and cordage. Steam powered all the mills using the level land to the south: the two marble mills, the weaving department of the cotton mill at the Falls occupying a former furniture plant, spool and bobbin and box factories and planing mills. Add such light industry as the Queen City Laundry, near lower Main, handy to the hotels, Arbuckle's cigar and candy makers on lower Maple, a brewery at the south end of Champlain, and the largest of half a dozen wheelwrights' shops. With the livery stables and blacksmith shops behind the hotels the carriage makers comprised the 1880 equivalent of modern auto sales and service.

The larger of the lakeside firms maintained their own fire companies and police-watchmen and were early served by public utilities. To reach the level of the routes leading out of town, the city had built a plank road up the side of the Battery bluff. When wear had made the ramp dangerous, the city put in its heaviest materials to repair the road: stone mill waste and stone broken

---

[19]The description of Burlington districts is based on an analysis of the city directories for 1879-81, and Hamilton Child, *Chittenden County Gazetteer*, 423-521, which is the first directory to give street numbers; also with reference to F. W. Beers, *Atlas of Chittenden Co. Vermont* (New York: F. W. Beers, A. D. Ellis, & G. G. Soule, 1869), 23, and *Bird's Eye View of Burlington and Winooski Vt.* (Madison, Wisconsin: J. J. Stoner [drawn by E. Meilbek, lith. by Shober & Carqueville, Chicago], 1877).

from "unsightly and dangerous boulders" found about the city. Pine Street received over a thousand tons of marble chips, broken brick, and cinders from the water works in 1878.[20]

Smaller industries whose products did not weigh enough to require their location near rail or boat were scattered about downtown. On College Street, for example, the thoroughly improved connector between shoreline and store line, were two shoe factories and a leather shop, two large wholesale druggists and patent-medicine mixers, four in the book and printing trades, a steam stone mill at a corner of the park, shirt and glove factories and the largest merchant tailors. College had city blocks for a quarter mile both sides of Church Street, yet mixed in were a few fine mansions of managers, showing a process of differentiation still in transition.

Wells, Richardson & Company rocketed out of the depression on Lydia Pinkham's advertising technique. The Wellses had worked into a Waterbury firm that moved to Burlington in 1867 and divided a few years later into a drug wholesale house including the founding Henry family, and a proprietary medicine business. Henry, Johnson & Lord majored in N. H. Downs' Elixir, Baxter's Mandrake Bitters, Henry & Johnson's Arnica and Oil Liniment, and toilet articles. Wells, Richardson produced butter color, Kidney-Wort, and aniline dyes. They put a new "Diamond Dye" trademark on their dime packages of the dyes (was a pun intended?) and sold over a million and a half in 1881. Their $150,000 spent on advertising that year reaped two-fold rewards. In the 1880s they acquired the patented Paine's Celery Compound, invented by E. E. Phelps, M. D., long a lecturer at Dartmouth Medical College. They sold this concoction of "celery, coca [containing cocaine]. . . cascara sagrada, . . . hops, dandelion, buchu, mandrake, sarsaparilla, and chamomile," with an ever-increasing budget for suitably deceptive, brazen, and illustrated advertising. Their late Victorian palaces on the upper Hill testified to the value of God's gift for modern nervous disorders.[21]

Federal, county, and city and lawyers' offices had multiplied since 1840 near Court House Square. Church and Main was the governmental crossroads. Fifty employees from postman to customs inspector at the docks reported to the federal building diagonally opposite city hall. The

---

[20] *City Report* (1879), 92, (1878), 221. The city's payment of $150 to the Burlington Manufacturers' Union in 1875, considered with the police report (1876), 109-111, 176, suggests payment for extra protection during labor disturbance.

[21] Hamilton Child, *Chittenden County Gazetteer*, 465; Wells, Richardson & Co., *Aniline Dyes: What They Are and How To Use Them* (Burlington: Wells, Richardson, 1873), their *Vermont Album* (no imprint, ca. 1895), containing the formula for Paine's Celery Compound, and *A History* (no imprint, ca. 1890).

new, 1873 Mansard gothic county courthouse south of the post office housed half a dozen Burlington officials. The city filled the pond behind it in 1875, and the lot east of the federal and county buildings in 1878, but citizens still pitched garbage and trash into the hollow next to Main. Local officials with a hundred-odd regular and seasonal employees managed and maintained the city's $600,000 worth of property, $400,000 indebtedness, and the expenditure of $100,000 in taxes and other receipts. They spilled over from city hall into the city market and the old courthouse, which also housed fire equipment and upstairs, the Fletcher Free Library.

Hotel, printing, insurance, and banking services crowded the rest of the park's periphery. At its southwest corner three landlords managed most of the city's three hundred hotel rooms. The Van Ness, located where the Howard House burned in 1867, advertised its elevator and bathrooms. Around the hotel corner clustered the better restaurants, the Western Union office, express companies, barbershops, and hostelries.

More business blocks lined Church Street, even into the last block near Pearl. With scarce a gap from the post office to the Unitarian church, some seventy specialized retail outlets occupied the frontage, with druggists on corners, jewelers bunched near Bank or Cherry, the largest dry goods establishments renting the ground floor of the new Howard Opera House and next to it. The quickest way to rise socially was the trade route, traveled by many grocers, tailors, and druggists. Andrew Boutin had risen to run a department store, hiring a traveling salesman, three milliners, and a paperhanger, and enjoying an extensive wholesale trade. Future merchants were clerking in stores they would eventually run: J. O. Middlebrook in A. G. Peirce's feed store, F. B. Boynton and John Gould in shoe stores, Hobart Shanley in Samuel Huntington's bookstore, and F. D. Abernethy with Lyman & Allen's dry goods. West around the corner on Pearl, Woodworth's pottery was a fading reminder of the days when homes, stores, and shops were mixed together. The Burlington Telephone Company and the U.S. Weather Bureau in the opera house were harbingers of the new era. Burlington's telephone exchange, with thirty-five miles of wire and 170 subscribers in 1880, was the largest of five Vermont telephone companies.

Surrounding the trading center for two or three blocks in every direction was a zone of mixed functions and spotty real estate values, but primarily residential. The men of authority and substance still living here seemed to provide the social cement that smoothed labor relations in the shops, divided the labor vote, and made up in personal attentions the inadequacies of public charity. Yet their presence may not have made the wage earners' hearts grow fonder, as they were nearby landlords, their homes were standing reminders of their neighbors' restricted circumstances, and their paths more often crossed than joined the workmen's. On the whole a democracy of manner and an acceptance of leadership survived from the period of unsegregated dwelling.

The rim of Battery Park bore the same relation to the northern industrial district as northern Pine Street did to the central waterfront, with several homes of managers and merchants. Professionals serving clientele in the North End included the Rev. John D. Rossier, pastor of the French Baptist mission at Archibald and Spring, Swedish doctor W. B. Lund and Franco-American physicians Alphonse Method and J. E. Montmarquet. No other professionals lived north of North except the Sisters of Providence teaching at the Nazareth (French) school on Allen Street, where the new St. Joseph's would soon be built (1883-87), and Father Jerome M. Cloarec on Archibald near the old French church. The North End had city water but no sewers. The porous soil absorbed the drainage except when frozen and then water stood in the streets, yards, and cellars.

At the opposite social pole from Battery and the North End was the Hill, southeast of the old ravine. The corresponding upper residential section north of the Pearl artery had laterals pushing northward in active subdivisions during 1873-75. At the far end of North Prospect, Fern Hill, the estate of the public-spirited John N. Pomeroy, looked across the street at the French Catholic center and the homestead of the benevolent Fletchers, who had within the decade endowed the hospital and the library.

South of Pearl, hill residents maintained carriages, coachmen, and other servants, and did not need to stay within a short walk to their work. Exceptions were the dozen professors who had entrée on the hill and could walk to their lectures. Students not living in the "Old Mill" or with their families boarded as far downtown as George Street, Grant Street, and Elmwood Avenue. College, Main and South Willard probably had the most wealth per dwelling. The trunk routes, Union south of Main and Pearl above Winooski Avenue, were the most fully occupied by the upper class. The most expensive street construction of the 1870s was the macadamizing of Union Street as far south as Spruce, and lining it with Kingston, New York, flagstone sidewalks and Isle La Mott curbing. The total cost the city and private citizens over six thousand dollars.

The city's growing edges were outside the rectangle bounded by Maple to Pearl and Willard to the lake, defined as thickly settled by the 1874 ordinance requiring licenses for wooden construction within that area. Symbolic of South End growth was the gradual extension of the name St. Paul Street to cover the settled part of Shelburne Street. In 1840 St. Paul stopped at the hotel corner, in 1873 at Adams, and in 1880 the old name applied only to the highway south of Ledge Road. The next step in completing the street pattern would be to extend Elm to the former White

Street at Main, now that the sewer was in and the pond behind the courthouse drained, and south to St. Paul, calling the whole South Winooski Avenue. Laterals from these streets entering the city from the south were scenes of active subdivision, as thrifty mechanics and small shopkeepers or clerks, with the revival of business, left tenement and boardinghouse to set up housekeeping at the South End. Similar growth peopled the eastern end of Colchester Avenue, mostly below Green Mount Cemetery.

The other gateways to Burlington had handicaps for realtors. College holdings blocked exploitation of the Williston Road frontage. Ledge Road was too remote and precipitous. The Winooski (Lower) Road traversed a steep sandy hill. North Avenue, growing a little at its near end, led nowhere except to Lake View Cemetery, the empty shore, the Episcopal Institute, and Malletts Bay.

Farmland north of town, cut off from South Burlington by the city and from Colchester by the Winooski River, with no bridge between the Falls and the Heineberg bridge near its mouth, was beginning to benefit from the city market for its vegetables, fruit, and dairy products. The area had no public buildings except the North Avenue school.

This sketch shows the crystallization of functional districts, the virtual completion of the inner street network, residential expansion in all directions within the gridiron, and upper class preemption of the areas best served by public utilities. Burlington was again a town of rapidly shifting job opportunities but with less rapid turnover than before 1873. A sixth of the householders of 1879 had disappeared by 1882. Three-eighths of the names in the 1882 directory were not listed in 1879.[22]

The fluctuations of fortune can also be traced in the careers of individuals. Among the overseers of the poor, N. B. Flanagan had eight and G. D. Weller had four occupations, A. B. Lowry five employers, and Henry Greene four addresses during the period 1865-82. From fifty to a hundred traveling salesmen and peddlers, three-quarters employed by local business and the rest out of Boston, added their comings and goings to the busyness of the place. Among these was Alphonse Gravel, who in 1874 became Ward 2 alderman, another example of upward mobility.

Embedded in these mere lists of persons was the humor and pathos of adjustments in a mobile society: husband and wife at different addresses, Mrs. T. C. O'Brien keeping a boardinghouse

---

[22] Checking the names beginning with *S* through *Z* in the 1879 city directory and Hamilton Child, comp., *Gazetteer and Business Directory of Chittenden County, Vermont* (Syracuse, N.Y.: Hamilton Child, 1882), I found 17.6% of the 1879 list missing in 1882, and 37.6% of the 1882 directory not listed three years earlier. About a hundred had moved within the city. Spellings had sometimes changed, e.g. Florent Sturgeon / Florence Turgeon; Tebo/Thibault, Sentamour/St. Amour.

while her man was mining in Idaho, embryo commuters maintaining a residence in a nearby town for want of job or personal security, the pawn shop tragedies observed by the manager of the City Loan Company, immigrants like Joe Smashwood and N. J. Tute (secretary of George D. Sherman's military band) perhaps unaware of the connotations of their anglicized names. We can imagine the shortlived hopes of the Cigarmakers' Union No. 77 (1869-74?) and the Champlain Typographical Union No. 177 (1874-75?), and the ambitions, rivalries, or hurt feelings involved where two or more social organizations (six to thirteen masonic lodges, two of Odd Fellows, two or three Franco-American benevolent societies, five or six brass bands or instrumental groups, four camping or sporting clubs) aimed at the same goals.

Burlington supported specialties beyond Rutland and the principal Vermont villages. It had more purveyors of fancy goods, hats and furs, ladies' furnishings, cleaners and dressmakers, and fewer "clothing" dealers; fewer wheelwrights and more carriage painters, saddlers, livery stables, and horse blanket salesmen. Burlington also led in saloons, eating houses, billiard parlors, tobacco firms, bakers and bottlers; fuel, grain, oil, ice, tea, coffee, and spice wholesalers; plumbing, furnaces, stoves, tinsmithing and gas fitting; jewelry, trunks and leather goods, hairdressers, florists, photographers, and music dealers. Of course, Burlington led in its wealth of professionals, including veterinarians and engineers. Here could be found specialists in apiarists' supplies, sap spouts and buckets, bicycles, junk, steel and rubber stamps, stencils, seals, waxworks, and house moving—all few and far between elsewhere in Vermont.

The village of Rutland offered steadier work for the building trades than Burlington because it grew more gradually and suffered a series of disastrous fires in the late 1860s. Although all townspeople invested in land if they could, Rutland had three who called themselves "real estate speculators" and one "concrete sidewalk maker."[23] Rutland trustees opened fourteen new streets or extensions between 1864 and 1870, when they recommended adopting street signs and numbers. Rutland repeated Burlington's wrangling between civic improvers and tax-sensitive conservatives, with action lagging on a reservoir, street lighting, and sewerage.

Most differences between Burlington and its nearest rivals were in degree and detail, except where some state institution or industrial specialty gave special character to a village. Montpelier, Rutland, and Brattleboro shared preeminence in printing and stationery. Montpelier was high in

---

[23] Evelyn Pierpoint (U.S. MS. *Ninth Census, (1870), Population*, Rutland (household 256-331), James Mace (household 350-441), John Hines (household 480-587); Ben Lampman (sidewalks, household 234-303).

dentists and restaurants (no connection established), Brattleboro in watchmakers, cabinetmakers, and wheelwrights, and Rutland in druggists. Brattleboro vied with Rutland, Bennington, and Burlington in the needle trades.[24] A machine-operated laundry opened in Rutland within a year after the war and eight other towns had one by 1880. Rutland and St. Johnsbury merchants introduced the ten-cent store to Vermont. Bennington had the edge in shoe, hardware, and cigar stores. St. Albans led in little but hair (upholstery?) workers and butter wholesalers—let us hope they kept apart.[25]

Every growing village had its real estate boom, its complaints against too much "fast horse" for public safety, its unrealized horse car project, and its harbingers of spring, the organ grinder, peanut vendor, and gold pen and lightning rod peddlers. Latent prejudice against foreign labor was widespread—witness occasional advertisements specifying only "Americans" need apply.[26] The constabulary was forever inadequate to cope with liquor, brawl, and brothel nuisances. Little Cavendish, in its postwar heyday, had "most everything. . . . French, Dutch, Irish, English, Norwegians, . . . a few 'nymphs of the walk,' and several dealers in poor whiskey," catering especially to the woolen mill operatives.[27]

There was something almost random, certainly unplanned, about the rural reaction to urban invasion, at each turn of the business cycle. From a longer perspective, the encroachment was steady, forking in two paths. One entailed intense competition in cities like Burlington; the other, benevolent paternalism in towns more under the influence of a single corporation, like St. Johnsbury, or Proctor a decade or more later. But even in Burlington the dominant mood was to accept the decisions of business executives.

A reporter for the *New York Evening Express* was struck in 1875 by the healthy, erect, well-dressed, intelligent appearance of the St. Johnsbury scale mechanics. They stayed with Fairbanks their whole lives. Some had money invested. Many owned neat, comfortable, gleaming white homes, stocked with well-bound, well-read classics, a piano—the happy homes of free men who attributed the guiding Fairbanks family's success to the "best material, best machinery, best wages,

---

[24]Thomas Thompson, heirless New Yorker, left $50,000 in trust to the women in the clothing industries of Brattleboro and Rhinebeck, N.Y. See Lucile Eaves and others, *A Legacy to Wage-earning Women: A Survey of Gainfully Employed Women of Brattleboro, Vermont, and of Relief Which They Have Received From the Thomas Thompson Trust* (Boston: Women's Educational and Industrial Union, 1925).

[25]See the town directories and *A Vermont Business Directory for 1880-81* (Boston: Briggs, 1880).

[26]E.g., *Rutland Herald*, 13 May 1868.

[27]Correspondent in *Woodstock Spirit of the Age*, 16 November 1868.

best management, best credit and best markets." A historian of manufacturing noted another characteristic:[28]

> The theory of individual responsibility is so fully carried out, that the name or initials of the sealer is stamped on the working parts of each scale, large or small, and thus any derangement or inaccuracy subsequently discovered recurs directly to the workmen, who are frequently so anxious to maintain their reputation that they go long journeys at their own expense for the purpose of investigating or correcting alleged imperfections.

Charles Edward Russell, with a populist orientation, reached a different conclusion. St. Johnsbury, as he recalled it around 1880 when he attended its academy, had the restraints of puritanical convention, but beneath their austerity, its people were the kindliest in the country. The Fairbankses ran the town without being responsible to any authority but themselves. People rationalized this rule by the trickle-down theory: the Fairbankses spent their profits, and the working people got some. Also the Fairbankses were Christian businessmen who financed St. Johnsbury Academy, gave the town the unusual Athenaeum, a remarkable library hung with excellent paintings. Horace Fairbanks had been governor; Edward preached at the South Congregational Church; Franklin collected natural history and established a museum; Henry had taught at Dartmouth. Besides, the family owned the factory that employed many men.

Jim Dow, a long-employed Fairbanks machinist in late middle age, self-educated and polished beyond the common school, lived at the academy boardinghouse. Dow believed that everyone works and all are equal, no matter what kind of work they do. He could have been more than a machinist, but stayed on his treadmill job, he said, because he would rather be free after the six o'clock whistle than to have ceaseless responsibilities. Russell twitted him—only once—on the inconsistency of his being a freethinker yet attending church regularly because the Fairbankses preferred pious workmen. After paying his board, Dow had four dollars a week to spend on the refinements that were his real life. Because he did not feel he could ask a woman to live on that pittance, he never married. "I

---

[28]Fairbanks, Morse & Co., *Pioneers in Industry*, 32-33, quoting the *New York Evening Express*, Oct. 1875; John Leander Bishop, *A History of American Manufacturers, from 1608 to 1860* (3rd ed.; Philadelphia: E. Young, 1868; 3v.), 457.

suppose I shall notch beams until I am too old to run the machine," he said. "Then what? Old men's home, I suppose. A man must take what comes to him."[29]

Russell understated popular acquiescence in the unlimited wages of management, the large reward for those business cares that the machinist chose to avoid. Those who looked hard could probably find grumblings, but no overt opposition to Fairbanks control of the village.

Urban penetration of rural Vermont was an antlike advance of a headless army, first persuading villagers, who then seduced the divided and dependent hill regions. Rural Vermonters generally accepted urban industrialism as a liberating force, whose service would be perfect freedom. Farm children, diverted by moral questions of slavery and union, believed the promises of better positions in village or city.

Experience with urban problems of congestion, impersonality, social cleavage and stratification, and the like would revive reform. The managers, seeing the troubles arising from their transformations, called for piecemeal planning of a waterworks, a sewer system, a fire department, because they were in the habit of dealing with difficulties as they arose. They had yet to admit publicly the collectivism of both factory and city, although they assumed that their various operations were interlocked and, therefore, required unified governance—by themselves. Some forces they adjusted to because they could not control them: the price of Argentine wool, depressions born in Europe, migrations, American patent law. To such operators comprehensive planning by government at any level was utopian, although they aimed at it in their own affairs.

Why were the rest of the people silent? In the villages the pinch was less sharp than in the metropolis. The small city of Burlington, where the ills of urbanism were more painful than anywhere else in Vermont, accomplished the most to alleviate them. Personal contact between manager and workman lowered tensions. To Yankees, Irish and Franco-Americans, many matters were more important than sewerage: literacy, church services in French, papal interference in American politics, ambition, fishing, or a sociable glass. Many were lamed before they reached the village by the interminable struggle with the starved soils and hostile conditions of rural New England, Ireland, and Quebec. Their churches, whether Roman or Puritan, were more bulwarks for their traditions than schools of the prophets for change. The move from farm to shanty town, tenement or cottage, however many miles, was one of great social and psychological distance. With

---

[29]Charles Edward Russell, *Bare Hands and Stone Walls: Some Recollections of a Side-Line Reformer* (New York: Charles Scribner's Sons, 1933), quotation, 22; 8-9, 15-22. An excerpt in *Outsiders Inside Vermont*, 95-100, describes the village and academy atmosphere.

scarce a protest, the laborer lapsed into silence and discipline, and most tried to rise in status. The very tempo and turmoil of change made people despair of forethought. The pragmatic answer was the hand-to-mouth solution. Mobile individualism, stamped upon American character by the progressive frontier and the seemingly settled eastern farm, became by the conditions of city growth the watchword of urban America too.

After 1880 Vermont farmers turned toward the metropolitan market, especially for fluid milk, and many not well placed for such production suffered in the transition. Village industry rebounded from the temporary setback of 1873. A new granite industry expanded rapidly. Electricity entered the economy, first in half a dozen village telephone exchanges, as telegraphy had come a generation earlier, then in hydro-electric power plants and in electric cars, lighting, and manufacturing. The twentieth century spread of the internal combustion motor to highway, farm, and mill, and rural electrification, radio, and television, completed the urbanization of the countryside itself. Meanwhile, Vermont democracy moved to widen participation in the solution of social problems. People came to reject the kind of responsibility symbolized by the Fairbanks sealer's initials on his scale parts. More and more they wanted those with power over people's lives to be responsible to them.

Index

Page numbers in italics indicate illustrations; those followed by *n* indicate footnotes.

Abernethy, F. D., 212
Abolition of slavery. *See* Slavery
Abortion, 81
Adams, Charles Baker, 94
Adams, John Sullivan, 92, 187
Adams Mission Home, Burlington, 182
Adirondack (ship), 191
Adolescents, 42
Afro-Americans, 24
Agricultural machinery, 151, 155-56, 164, 165
Agriculture. *See* Farming
Alburg, Vt., 191
Aldis, Asa O., 97
Alexander, Eldad, 78 *n*7
Allen, Alanson, 182
Allen, Ethan, 50, 60, 82, 91, 144, 186
Allen, Heman ("Chili"), 20, 22, 198
Allen, Ira, 33, 50
Allen, Ira H., 65, 72
Allen family, 50
American party, 126
Ancé, François, 39
Antimasonic party, 2
Antislavery. *See* Slavery
Apple. *See* Fruit culture
Aqueduct Co., Burlington, 200, 201
Architecture, 91
Arlington, Vt., 39-40
Art, 192. *See also* Sculpture
Atkins, Hiram, 142, 193
Audet, Jean-Frédéric, 178
Automobiles, 68
L'Avenir National, 181

Bacon, W. A., 77
Bailey, Myron W., 160
Baker, Benjamin Franklin, 90
Balch, Benjamin, 76
Baldwin, C. C. P., 142

Ball, Arnold, 171
Ball, Emeline L., 83
Bands (Music), 90-91
Banks and banking, 74-75, 148, 161
Baptist church, 21-22, 182
Barlow, Bradley, 187
Barlow, Sidney, 23-24
Barnard, Vt., 116, 156
Barnes, Lawrence, 145, 146, 167-68, 182, 192, 198
Barnes, William F., 61, 62, 64, 127
Barney, George, 11
Barre, Vt., 158, 162
Barre & Chelsea Railroad, 158
Barrett, Rockwood, 139
Barron, Hal Seth, 155
Barstow, John L., 146, 186
Barter, 77, 106
Barton, Vt., 52, 65, 106, 151, 163
Batchelder & Sons, Wallingford, 165
Bates, Henry M., 124, 125
Baxter, Carlos, 20, 127
Baxter, H. Henry: in Civil War, 133, 137, 143; industrialist, 62, 147, 171; leaves Rutland, 171-72; residence of, 64
Baxter, Portus, 115, 127
Bellows Falls, Vt., 51, 52; bridge at, 29; churches, 97; fire, 83; hotels, 72; industry, 163, 164; insurance business, 75; publishing, 90; schools, 92
Benedict, George Grenville, 132, 141, 146, 148, 159
Benedict, George Wyllys, 46, 123-24
Bennington, Vt., 26, 153, 197; business, 216; in Civil War, 139; industry, 50, 57, 69, 157, 164-65; police, 83; temperance movement, 79
Bennington & Glastenbury Railroad, 158
Bennington Battle Day, 190
Bennington Battle Monument Association, 82
Bennington Powder Co., 147
Benns, Deacon, 21

221

Billings, Frederick, 125
Bissell, William Henry Augustus, 41, 182-83
Blackall, C. R., 72
Blacks. *See* Afro-Americans
Blackwell, Lucy Stone, 193
"Bolton War," 1846, 35-36, 85
Boutin, Andrew, 212
Bowles, Samuel, 72
Bowman & Mansfield, Rutland, 61
Boynton, F. B., 212
Bradbury, W. B., 90
Brainerd, Ezra, 46
Brainerd, Lawrence, 122-23, 125-26, 129
Brandon, Vt.: churches, 97; industry, 50, 57, 68; militia, 130; organizations, 98
Brandon *Vermont Observer*, 106
Brattleboro, Vt.: banking, 148; census, 99; in Civil War, 141, 144, 145, 146; Civil War hospital, *135*, 145; Civil War induction center, 133, 134, *135*, 140, 145; fires, 83; gasworks, 83; as health spa, 71-72; industry, 57, 69, 164, 215-16; insane asylum, 80-81; insurance business, 75, 76; poor farm, 80; schools, 93; strike, 85
Brattleboro & Whitehall Railroads, 158
Brattleboro Asylum for the Insane, 80-81
Brattleboro *Eagle*, 106
Brattleboro *Household*, 194
Brattleboro Melodeon Co., 164
Brattleboro *Vermont Record and Farmer*, 194
Brattleboro *Windham County Democrat*, 98
Brazil, 68
Bristol, Vt., 50, 184
Bristol Bill, 83
Brothels. *See* Prostitution
Brothers, Oliver, 166
Brothers, William, 166
Brown, C. C., 77
Brown, Henry Kirke, 91-92
Brownson, Orestes A., 40, 41
Buckham, Matthew, H., 183, 201
Bull, Ole, 88
Burden (H.) & Sons, 157
Burdett, Riley, 164
Burlington, Vt., 26, 195, 197-98, 208, 218; banking, 75; "blue laws," 78; brothels, 101, 206; business, 21, 77, 207, 212, 214, 215; cemeteries, 203; census, 16 *n4*, 21, 206-7; charities, 182; churches, Catholic, 20, 38-39, 94-95, 96, 178, 180; churches, Protestant, 20, 21-22, 39, 97, 181-83; in Civil War, 138, 139, 140, 144, 145, 146, 148; description of, 1840, 15-26; description of, 1860s, 198-99; description of, 1880, 208-14;

Burlington, Vt. *(continued)* families, leading, 198; fires and fire prevention, 20, 21, 23, 38, 84, 201-2; gasworks, 83, 210; harbor, *14*, 15-18, 26, 198-99, 208, 210; holiday observation, 184; hospitals, 81, 145, 146, 202; hotels, 16, 21, 72, 212; industry, 21, 24, 174, 210-11; insurance business, 75; land use, *209*; as lumber port, 54, 165, 167-68, 208, 210; map, *19*; organizations, 215; parades, 31-32, 130; police, 83, 204, 205, 206, 207; politics and government, 31-32, 204-5, 212; the poor, 80, 205-6; prohibition, 206; public health, 80, 199-201, 202; sanitation, 82-83, 200-1, 202; schools, 92, 93, 190, 201, 203-4; social life, 191; for state capital, 127-28; statistics, 1880, 208; telephone, 212; water-supply, 200, 201-2
Burlington & Lamoille Railroad, 157, 199, 207
Burlington Cancer Relief Association, 182
Burlington Commercial College, 148
Burlington Cornet Band, 90
Burlington *Free Press*, 104, 148
Burlington Mill Co., 22, 23-24
Burlington *Sentinel*, 18, 193
Burlington Shakespeare Club, 191
Burlington Steam Draining Co., 82-83
Burlington *Sunday Sentinel*, 194
Burlington Telephone Co., 212
Burlington *Times*, 149
Burlington Woolen Co., 166-67, 178
Burnside Military School, Brattleboro, 190

Cabot, Vt., 77
Cain, John, 129-30, 193
Calais, Vt., 25
Calhoun, John C., 117
Camp, Zebina C., 141 *n17*
Camp Holbrook, Brattleboro, *135*, 145
Camp Smith, Montpelier, 144
Canada, 138, 140, 146. *See also* French-Canadians, Patriot War, 1837-1842
Canal boats, 17
Canals, 161. *See also* Champlain Canal
Canfield, Thomas H., 16-17, 62, 127
Cannon, LeGrand B., 139, 199
"Canuck," 175 *n2*
Carpenter, Bisa C., 99
Castleton, Vt., 65, 79, 88-89, 180
Castleton Seminary, 88-89
Castleton *Vermont Statesman*, 106
Catholic church, 20, 44, 79, 94-97; anti-Catholic sentiment, 79, 94-95, 152; convents, 96, 178; converts to, 40-41;

Catholic church *(continued)* French-Canadian parishes, 39, 96, 178-80, 181; Irish parishes, 38-39, 64, 79, 94, 96-97; parochial schools, 180-81
Catlin, Albert L., 76, 201
Catlin, Guy, 23
Catlin, Moses, 23
Cavendish, Vt., 163, 168, 216
Cemeteries, 82
Central Vermont Railroad Co., 159-60, 161, 188. *See also* its previous name Vermont Central Railroad
Chaffee, Frederick, 145
Champlain Canal, 1, 16
Champlain, Lake, 4-5, 15-18, 191
Champlain Transportation Co., 17
Champlain Valley, 3, 4
Chaplin, Moses, 119
Charities, 182
Chase, Dudley, 40
Chelsea, Vt., 75, 155
Chester, Vt., 29, 90
Chester Boot Co., Rutland, 145
Child labor, 42, 189
Children, 42
Chittenden, Lucius E., 74
Churches. *See* names of denominations
Cities and towns, 111
Citizen Soldier, 46-47
Civil rights, 142
Civil War, 1861-1865, 131-32; conscription, 139-41; cost, 131, 132, 138-39, 146; economy, effect on, 146-51; enlistment, 132-33, 137-38; equipment and supplies, 143-45, 146-47; family assistance, 143; hospitals, *135*, 145-46; induction centers, 133-36, 145; officers, appointment of, 136-37; opposition to, 142; recruiting for, 138-39; regiments, 130-31, 132, 133, 134, 137, 145, 155; soldiers, number of, 132, 141; surplus property sales, 146; uniforms, 144-45. *See also* Veterans
Clapp, William, 159
Clarendon, Vt., 53, 72, 151, 191
Clark, Eliza M., 193 *n24*
Clark, Henry, 207
Clarke, Claude H., 89
Clarke, DeWitt Clinton, 82, 127, 187
Clay, Henry, 76, 118, 120
Clement (Charles) & Son, 138
Climate, 4
Cloarec, Jerome M., 213
Clothing and dress, 191-92
Colchester, Vt. *See* Winooski, Vt.

Cole, Charles A., 192
Collamer, Jacob, 123, 186-87
Colleges and universities, 45-47, 94. *See also* names of schools
Collier, Peter, 202
Comings, Elam, 17
Commemoration Day. *See* Memorial Day
Comstock, Peter, 17
Community Church, Island Pond, 44
Congregational church, 20, 79, 97, 183
Connecticut and Passumpsic Rivers Railroad, 65, 67
Converse, Julius, 115, 186
Copper industry, *48*, 61, 147
Corey, Hugh, 140
Corinth, Vt., 140
Corporal punishment, 44
Crain, H. F., 69
Crane, C. R., 142
Crime, 83
Crimean War, 1853-1856, 56
Crowell, G. E., 194
Customs administration, 16, 18, 159
Cuttingsville, Vt., 50

Dairying, 54, 156
Daly, J. B., 96
Danby, Vt., 52, 64
Dancing, 88, 152
Daniels, Reuben, 69
Danville, Vt., 65, 78 *n7*
Dartmouth College, 33, 39, 94
Davenport, Thomas, 68
Davey & Nichols, Fair Haven and East Middlebury, 147, 199
Davidson, Parks & Woolson, Springfield, 69
Davis, George F., 143-44, 145, 146
Davis, Jefferson, 184-85
Davis, Mial, 182
Dearborn, Henry, 27
Decoration Day. *See* Memorial Day
Delaware & Hudson Railroad Corp., 158, 191
Democratic party, 74, 116-17, 119; "bastard tickets," 120; during Civil war, 142; in 1853 election, 122-23; party newspapers, 107-8; and slavery question, 103, 126
Denison, Dudley C., 185, 187
Dentistry, 78 *n7*, 82
Derby, Vt., 162
Dewey (A. G.) Co., Quechee, 69
Dewey, John, 43
Dewey, Julius Y., 76

Dillingham, Paul, 76, 128, 142, 158, 186
Dillon, Catherine Driscoll, 37
Divorce, 101, 192
Dodge, G. B., 110
Dodge, Ossian E., 88
Dorr, Seneca M., 145, 160, 169, 170
Dorr, Proctor & Co., 145
Dorr & Myers, 170
Dorset, Vt., 60, 64
Douglas, Stephen A., 123
Douglass, M. F., 61
Dow, James, 100
Dow, Jim, 217-18
Dow, Mary, 99-100
Dow, Samuel, 99
Drew, L. A., 206
Drugstores, 77-78
Druon, Zephyrin, 96, 152, 181
Dunton, Walter C., 186
Dwight, John Sullivan, 88
Dwight, Timothy, 54

East Montpelier, Vt., 111
Eastman, Charles G., 76, 92, 116, 119, 122
Eaton, Horace, 45, 67, 113
Editors, 104, 113, 195
Edmunds, George F., 128, 172, 183, 185, 187
Education, 41-47, 190. *See also* Colleges and universities, Schools, Teachers
Edwards, Guy, 23
Eldridge, Charles, 29
Elections, 112-14, 117-20; of 1840, 31-32, 112, 113; of 1842, 74; of 1853, 122-23; of 1854, 124-26; of 1864, 142
Emigration. *See* Migration
Enosburgh, Vt., 96
Episcopal church, 20, 39-40, 41, 47, 93, 182-83
Essex, Vt., 52
Essex Junction, Vt., 53-54, 160
Estey, Jacob, 69, 164, 182
Estey & Green, Brattleboro, 145
Ethnic groups. *See* names of individual groups

Fair Haven, Vt., 50, 57, 60, 65, 147, 165, 180
Fairbanks, Charles, 67
Fairbanks (E. & T.) Co., St. Johnsbury, 60, 65-68, 146-47, 162, 216-18, 219
Fairbanks, Edward, 217
Fairbanks, Erastus: businessman, 65, 67, 72; Civil War governor, 131, 132, 136, 143-44; political candidate, 115, 122, 124
Fairbanks, Franklin, 66, 67, 217

Fairbanks, Henry, 217
Fairbanks, Horace, 67, 157, 217
Fairbanks, Joseph P., 67, 129
Fairbanks, Thaddeus, 65, 67
Family, 99-101
Farming: during Civil War, 151; after Civil War, 155-56; clearing of land, 2-4; diversity of, 10-11; marketing of produce, 4-5, 11; seasonal tasks, 5-8. *See also* Agricultural machinery, Dairying
Farnham, Roswell, 146, 186
Farrar and Wait, Burlington, 24
Fast Day, 184
Federal government, 109-10, 141
Felchville, Vt., 144
Fenians, 187-88
Fenwick, Benedict, 39
Ferguson, James F., 203
Ferrisburgh, Vt., 43, 121
Field, Charles K., 127
Field, William M., 144
Fire extinction, 84, 111
Fires, 83
Fisk, Hiram C., 109
Fitzpatrick, John Bernard, 96
Flanagan, Noble B., 204, 206, 214
Fletcher, Ryland, 125, 126, 128, 130, 143
Flint, Martin, 3
Follett, Timothy, 40
Foot, Solomon, 120, 123, 162
Forest products, 11
The Fortnightly Society, Rutland, 191
Foster, George P., 186
Fourth of July, 190
Franklin, Vt., 187
Fraternities, 46
Free Democratic party, 125
Free Soil party, 122-24, 125
Free trade. *See* Reciprocity Act, 1854
Freemasonry. *See* Antimasonic party
French & Kingsley, Rutland, 145
French-Canadians, 79-80, 156, 195; in Burlington-Winooski, 24-25, 39, 96, 178-80, 208, 210, 218; Catholic parishes, 96, 178-80, 181; census, 177-78; described by Rowland Robinson, 175, 177; education, 96, 177, 180-81; emigration to Vt., 2, 175-77; family names, 181; in marble industry, 172, 181; newspapers, 181; as railroad workers, 158
Frontier and pioneer life, 2-4
Fruit culture, 25
Fuller, Levi K., 145, 164, 182
Fullertons & Co., Proctorsville, 144

Gage, Royal, 129
Galusha, Jonas, 74
Games, 42
Gardner, Abram B., 143
Gas manufacture and works, 83, 210
Germania Band, 88
Gilman, James Franklin, 99
Glass manufacture, 21, 50
Gleed, John, 121
Glenwood Seminary, West Brattleboro, 93
Goesbriand, Louis de, 64, 79, 94, 95, 96-97, 140, 180
Gold rush, 76
Goodale, D. C., 108
Goodrich, Chauncey, 25, 107
Gore, John, 68
Goshen Gore, Vt., 159
Gough, John, 153
Gould, Jay, 140
Gould, John, 212
Governors, 114, 115
Grafton, Vt., 51
Grand Army of the Republic (GAR), 185
Grand Isle County, Vt., 4-5
Grand Trunk Railway Co. of Canada, 52
Grandey, George W., 127
Grange in Vermont. See Patrons of Husbandry
Granite industry, *48*, 162
Grant, Miles, 98
"Grasse Mount," Burlington, 22, 192
Gravel, Alphonse, 214
Gray's (A. W.) Sons, Middletown Springs, 165
Greeley, Horace, 118
Green, G. B., 78
Greenbanks, Thomas, 163
Greene, Henry, 214
Gregory, John, 129
Griswold, Alexander Viets, 39
Groton, Vt., 83
Grout, W. W., 146, 184
Guilford, Vt., 51

Hale, Thomas, 123-24
Hall, Hiland, 139
Hamilton, Alexander, 50
Hand, Samuel B., 103
Hanna, Nicholas, 96-97
Harlow, Hiram, 163-64
Harmon, James, 133
Harrington, Giles, 109
Harris, Broughton D., 123-24
Harris, Nathaniel, 78 *n7*

Harrison, Benjamin, 172
Harrison, William Henry, 18, 31, 112
Hartford, Vt., 52, 163, 194
Harvesting, 7
Haskell and Palmer, Woodstock, 107
Haskins, Kittredge, 186
Haswell, John C., 107-8
Hatch, Mr., 144
Haying, 7
Heaton, Homer W., 76
Hedges, Lemuel, 69
Heineberg, Bernhard J., 24
Hemenway, Abby Maria, 40, 190
Hendee, George W., 184, 185
Henry, William W., 186
Henry, Johnson & Lord, Burlington, 211
Hewlett, S. W., 153
Hickok, Henry, 20
Hickok, Samuel, 18
Higgins, Julius E., 130
Highgate, Vt., 71, 96-97, 187, 191
Hills, J. H., 14
Hitchcock, Edward, 72
Hoar, George F., 172-73
Hodges, George, 115
Holbrook, Franklin F., 139
Holbrook, Frederick, 82; Civil War governor, 132, 137, 141, 143, 145; founder of agricultural society, 124
Holidays. See names of holidays
Holmberg, J. B., 88
Home for Aged Women, Burlington, 182
Home for Destitute Children, Burlington, 146, 182
Home for Friendless Women, Burlington, 182
Homeopathy, 82
Hooker, James H., 17
Hope, James, 52
Hopkins, John Henry, 39-40, 41, 46, 93, 191
Hospitals, 80-81, 145-46, 202
Hotels and taverns, 72, 151-52
Houde, Frédéric, 181
Howard, John Purple, 191, 203
Howard, Louisa, 203
Howard Relief Society, Burlington, 182
Howe, Frank, 143
Howe, John, 68, 69
Howe, John, Jr., 143
Howe (John) & Co. See Howe Scale Co., Brandon and Rutland
Howe, Julia Ward, 193

Howe Scale Co., Brandon and Rutland, 68, 147, 165
Howells, William Dean, 68
Howes, Harvey, 192
Hoyt, William H., 40, 193, 203
Hubbard, Asahel, 55
Hubbard, Guy, 55
Hubbardton, Vt., 90
Hubbardton Battle Monument Association, 82
Hubbell, Homer, 75
Huling, M. C., 139
Hungerford, Edward, 181-82
Hunt, Seth B., 165, 180
Hutchinson Family, 88
Hyde, Archibald W., 18, 40, 41
Hyde Park, Vt., 106
Hydrotherapy, 71-72. See also Mineral waters

Immigration. See Migration
Industry. See Manufactures, particular industries
Ingersoll, George G., 20
Insane, 80-81
Insurance, 75-77
Inventors and inventions, 68-69. See also names of products and industries
Irish, 2, 79-80; in "Bolton War," 35-36, 84-85; in Burlington-Winooski, 24-25, 79, 210, 218; and Catholic church, 38-39, 94, 95, 96-97; census, 79-80, 177; in Civil War, 140, 147; as farmers, 156; compared to French-Canadians, 175-76, 177, 181; in marble industry, 64, 140, 172, 181; in politics, 178; as railroad workers, 35-36, 37, 84-85. See also Fenians
Ironside (ship), 151
Iron-works, 50, 147
Island Pond, Vt., 44, 52
Isle La Motte, Vt., 109

James, Henry, 198
Jenison, Silas, 45, 112
Johnson, N. R., 121
Johnson, Richard M., 119
Jones (Ralph) & Co., Port Hope, Ont., 158
Jones, Russell L., 163
Jones & Lamson Machine Co., Windsor, 163-64
Joyce, Charles H., 137, 185, 186, 187
Juniper Island, 16

Kansas-Nebraska bill, 123-26
Keely, Patrick C., 180
Kellogg, Daniel, 123, 139

Kellogg, Loyal C., 116
Kendall, Nicanor, 55
Kidder, Jefferson P., 122
Kimball, Edgar A., 119
Kirkland, Edward C., 157
Kittredge, W. C., 126
Knapp, Chauncey L., 121
Know-Nothing party. See American party
Knowles, John, 68
Kouwenhoven, J. A., 57

Labaree, Benjamin, 46, 94
Labor and laboring classes, 159-60. See also Prices and wages, Strikes and lockouts, Trade-unions
Ladies' Aid Society, 205
Lafayette, Marie Joseph, Marquis de, 22, 187, 192
Lafountain, Charles, 178
Lamson, E. G., 171
Lamson & Goodnow, Windsor, 57
Lamson, Goodnow & Yale, Windsor, 145, 147, 163
Lawrence, Richard Smith, 55, 56, 57
Lawyers, 104, 113, 115
LeClair, Francis, 178
Liberty party, 119, 121
Libraries, 46, 92, 190-91
Lighting, 83
Lime, 54
Lincoln, Abraham, 155
Lincoln Iron Works, 171
Lind, Jenny, 88
Linsley, Daniel C., 201, 204
Liquor laws. See Prohibition, Temperance
Literacy, 8, 44
Literature, 92
Livestock marketing, 54
Local government, 110-11
Loney, Isham, 24
Love, Roger, 171
Loveland, J. C., 69
Lowell, Vt., 96
Lowry, A. B., 205, 214
Lowry, Heman, 21
Lumber industry, 165, 167-68
Lund, W. B., 213
Lyman, Wyllys, 21
Lyndon, Vt., 106
Lyndonville, Vt., 67, 151, 162-63
Lyon, Matthew, 50

McClellan, George B., 142
McCullough, John G., 110
McGaffey, G. W., 77
McGettrick, Patrick, 172
McGowan, Edward, 97
McGregor, John, 178
Machine-tool industry, 57, 58, 163-64, 171
McIndoe, Lyman J., 107
McKeogh, John, 139, 142
Magazines. *See* Periodicals
Manchester, Vt., 83, 106, 110, 151
Manley Brothers, Dorset, 60
Manufactures, 174
Maple sugar, 6
Marble industry, *48*, 50-64, 138, 147, 168-73, 181
Marbleized slate. *See* Slate industry
Marsh, George Perkins, 20, 21, 22-23, 43, 52, 187
Marsh, James, 22
Marston, Jeremiah T., 108
Mason, Lowell, 90
Mattock, John, 120
May Day, 83
Meacham, James, 94, 113, 129, 130
Mead, Larkin G. (1795-1876), 99, 101
Mead, Larkin G. (1835-1910), 60, 91-92, 144
Mead, Nancy, 89
Medicine, 78, 81-82. *See also* Patent medicines
Memorial Day, 184
Memphremagog, Lake, 151
Menard, Mr., Highgate, 97
Mendelssohn Quintette Club, 88, 89
Mentally ill, 80-81
Merchant, A. N., 194
Merriam, E. N., 89
Merrill, Ferrand F., 129
Merrill, Thomas A., 129
Merrill, Prosper, 144
Method, Alphonse, 213
Methodist church, 20, 183
Mexican War, 1845-1848, 47, 55
Michaud, John Stephen, 178
Middlebrook, J. O., 212
Middlebury, Vt., 26, 50, 52, 60, 88, 127
Middlebury *Argus*, 108
Middlebury College, 26, 32, 45, 46, 94
Middletown Springs, Vt., 165, 191
Mietzke, George A., 88-89, 90
Migration, 2, 155-56, 175-77
Militia, 129-31, 146
Miller, William, 31, 40-41
Mills, Ephraim, 18
Mills and mill-work, 49-50, 51

Mineral waters, 191
Missisquoi & Clyde Rivers Railroad, 158
Missisquoi Valley Railroad, 158
Mix, Eldridge, 201
Mott, Theodore F., 24, 88
Montmarquet, J. E., 213
Montpelier, Vt., 26, 81, 215-16; business, 77, 194-95; as capital, 110, 127-28, 162; census, 79-80; churches, 96, 183; in Civil War, 137, 138, 139, 142, 144, 145, 146, 149; division from East Montpelier, 111; gasworks, 83; hotels, 27, 72; insurance business, 75, 76-77; militia, 130; temperance movement, 79; turnpike, 33; on underground railroad, 121
Montpelier and Wells River Railroad Co., 158
Montpelier *Argus and Patriot*, 142, 193, 194
Montpelier *Christian Messenger*, 106
Montpelier *Green Mountain Freeman*, 106, 195
Montpelier Seminary, 183
Montpelier *Vermont Patriot*, 106, 108
Montpelier *Vermont Watchman & State Journal*, 104, 106, 128
Monuments, 82
Moody, Dwight L., 182
Moore, John W., 90
Morrill, Justin Smith, 127, 172, 185; politician, 11, 115, 120, 187; storekeeper, 45, 115
Morton, William Thomas Green, 78 *n7*
Mountain Maid (ship), 151
Mountain rule, 103, 113
Moussette, Antoine, 181
Mowry, F., 77
Music and musicians, 87-91
Myers, John J., 170-71

National Hydraulic, Proctorsville and Windsor, 55
National Life Insurance Co., Montpelier, 76-77, 161
Needham, Horatio, 122
Negroes. *See* Afro-Americans
Nelson, Robert, 17
New York *Tribune*, 118
Newbury, Vt., 52
Newfane, Vt., 110, 134
Newport, Vt., 52, 65, 106, 151, 163
Newspapers, 104-8, 117, 148-49, 181, 193-95. *See also* under towns for specific newspapers
Nichols, B. S., 199, 210
Nichols, Clarina Howard, 98-99, 100
Nichols, George B., 99
Nichols, George W., 98, 122

North Bennington Boot & Shoe Co., 165
Northern Canal. *See* Champlain Canal
Northern Pacific Railroad, 192
Northern Transportation Co., 17
Northfield, Vt., 33-34, 36, 37, 60, 127, 139, 151
Norwich, Vt., 98, 142
Norwich University, 45, 46-47, 82, 94, 190
Noyes, John Humphrey, 100-1

O'Brien, T. C. O., Mrs., 214-15
O'Callaghan, Jeremiah, 38, 94-95
O'Hear, Thomas, 96-97
Old Home Week, 156
Opera, 87-88
Orcutt, Hiram, 93
Organs, 164
Original Metropolitan Opera Troupe, 87
Otis Shepard, Davis & Co., Burlington, 168
Orvis, John, 49, 161

Pacifism, 129-30
Page, John A. (1814-1891), 122
Page, John B. (1826-1885), 132, 157, 158, 169, 171
Paine, Caroline, 33
Paine, Charles (1799-1853), 34-35, 36, 71, 158; gubernatorial election, 32, 115, 120; and Lorinda Stevens, 100; memorial for, 60
Paine, Charles (b. 1830), 35, 36
Paine, Elijah, 32-34
Palmer, Thomas H., 45, 129
Pangborn, Zebina K., 92 *n5*
Pangborn & Brinsmaid, Burlington, 119
Panton, Vt., 71
Paper industry, 164
Park, Trenor W., 125, 139, 157, 169
Parochial schools, 92, 93-94, 96, 180-81
Partridge, Alden, 46
Partridge, Lewis S., 142
Passumpsic Railroad, 54, 72, 153, 158, 162-63
Patent medicines, 211
Patriot War, 1837-1842, 17-18, 109
Patrons of Husbandry, 160-61
Paupers. *See* Poor
Peace movement, 129-30
Peach, Arthur Wallace, 131
Peacham, Vt., 162
Perfectionists, 101
Periodicals, 194
Perkins, George H., 189
Perkins, William S., 39-40
Phelps, E. E., 211

Phelps, Edward John, 53-54, 160, 171
Phelps, Samuel S., 120, 123
Photographers, 77
Picart, François, 64, 180-81
Pierpoint, Robert, 128, 130
Pinkham, Lydia, 211
Pioneer life. *See* Frontier and pioneer life
Pioneer Mechanics Shop Co., Burlington, 167-68, 199, 201, 203
Pitkin, Perley P., 144
Pittsford, Vt., 50
Plattsburgh, N.Y., 16
Plymouth, Vt., 51
Poetry. *See* Literature
Poland, Joseph, 143
Poland, Luke P., 116, 185, 186, 187
Political parties, 11-12. *See also* names of parties
Politics and government. *See* Elections, Federal government, Local government, Mountain rule, State government
Poll-tax. *See* Taxation
Pomeroy, John N., 21, 213
Pond & Morse, Rutland, 145
Poor, 80, 205-6
Portland & Ogdensburg Railroad, 156, 157
Postmasters, 107, 118
Potter, Alonzo, 93
Potvin, John S., 22
Poultney, Vt., 65
Powers, Hiram, 91
Powers, Thomas E., 125, 126, 127
Pownal, Vt., 147, 180
The press. *See* Newspapers
Prices and wages, 148; for factory workers, 67, 178; for farm workers, 7, 11; for quarry workers, 62, 64, 172; for railroad workers, 158; for teachers, 92-93, 204
Prince, William H. N., 68
Printers and printing, 106-7, 149, 194-95
Prisons. *See* Vermont. State Prison
Proctor, Jabez, 55, 168
Proctor, Redfield, 180; marble industrialist, 145, 161, 168-69, 170-71, 172-73; military service, 137, 146, 185, 186; politician, 111, 137, 186
Proctor, Vt., 180, 216
Proctorsville, Vt., 144
Progressive party, 103
Prohibition, 78, 79, 185
Prostitution, 83, 101, 206
Le Protecteur Canadien, 181
Prout, John, 171

Public health, 80, 199-201, 202
Putney, Vt., 101

Quarrymen's Benevolent Association, 64
"Queen City," 206
Queen City Laundry, Burlington, 210
Quévillon, Joseph, 96

Radical Reconstruction, 185
Railroads, 32, 35, 36; accidents, 52-53; freight, 54, 62; map, *48*; passenger traffic, 53-54, 72, 91; and politics, 158, 160-61; post-Civil War boom, 156-58; safety, 160; and Vt. economy, 51-52, 65, 73, 151. *See also* names of railroads
Randolph, Vt., 3, 52, 121
Ransom, Truman, 47, 119
Real estate investment, 73
Reapportionment, 1855-1857, 126
Reciprocity Act, 1854, 51, 146, 167, 188
Reconstruction, 185
Recreation. *See* Social life and customs
Redfield, Isaac F., 116, 168, 171
Redfield, Timothy P., 76
Reed, Charles A., 139
Religious tolerance, 2, 94-95, 152
Republican party: after Civil War, 185, 186, 188; hegemony of, 103; organization of state party, 123-24, 125, 126, 128
Retail stores, 77-78
Reunion Society of Vermont Officers, 169, 185
Revivals, 39-40, 97-98
Reynolds, J. R., 171
Rifles, 51, 55-57
Riggs, Mr., 172
Ripley, William Y., 75, 170
Roads, 27, *28*, 29. *See also* Turnpikes
Robbins, Samuel E., 56-57, 71
Robbins & Lawrence, Windsor, 56
Roberts, Daniel, 75
Robinson, John S., 122
Robinson, Rowland E., 43, 121, 175, 177, 181, 185
Robinson, Rowland T., 121
Robinson, Warren, 188
Rochester, Vt., 162
Rockingham, Vt., 139
Rockwell, William Hayden, 80
Rogan, Mary, 178
Root, George F., 90
Ross, Thomas, 68
Rosier, John D., 213
Royalton, Vt., 52

Royce, G. E., 171
Royce, Homer, 127
Royce, Stephen, 124, 125
Rupert, Vt., 52
Russeguie, Daniel, 98
Russell, Charles Edward, 217-18
Russell, Charles T., 84
Russell, William J., 164
Rutland, Vt., 52, 190, 195, 197; banking, 75; building boom, 73-74, 215; business, 77, 78, 215-16; churches, 96, 97, 98, 180; in Civil War, 133, 137, 138-39, 142, 144, 145, 147, 148; cultural life, 88, 89, 90; fires and fire prevention, 84, 215; gasworks, 83; grand list, 73; hotels, 72; industry, 60, 61, 62, 64, 165, 168-73, 174, 181; militia, 130; organizations, 79, 98, 182, 191; prostitution, 83; sanitation, 82; schools, 92, 190; for state capital, 127, 128; statistics, 208; temperance movement, 79; workhouse, 205
Rutland Academy of Music, 89
Rutland & Bennington Railroad, 157
Rutland and Burlington Railroad, 36, 68, 147, 158, 169; construction, 37; freight, 51, 54; passenger traffic, 53
Rutland & Washington Railroad Co., 52, 53
Rutland *Courier*, 193
Rutland Free Convention, 101
Rutland *Herald*, 104, 148-49, 194, 195
Ruttland Land Co., 72
Rutland Marble Co., 60, 170, 181; under H. H. Baxter, 62, 64, 147, 171-72; under Redfield Proctor, 172-73; *Rutland Marble Company vs. Ripley*, 169
Rutland *Sunday Sentinel*, 194
Ryegate, Vt., 162

Sabin, Alvah, 113
Safford, George B., 183
St. Albans, Vt., 83, 181, 192; business, 77, 216; churches, 97, 180; in Civil War, 133, 136, 140, 148; Fenian sympathizers, 187; railroad junction, 37, 52, 162; schools, 96
St. Albans Foundry Co., 145, 147, 151, 159, 162
St. Albans *Messenger*, 149
St. Albans raid, 1864, 142, 146
St. Clair, Alanson, 121
St. Johnsbury, Vt., *66*, 83, 152, 158, 162, 216-18; business, 216; in Civil War, 134, 137, 146, 149; holiday observation, 184; industry, 60, 65, 67-68, 162; insurance business, 75; organizations, 182; schools, 92, 180
St. Johnsbury Academy, 217

St. Johnsbury Academy of Music, 89
St. Johnsbury & Lake Champlain Railroad, 156
St. Johnsbury Athenaeum, 197, 217
St. Johnsbury *Caledonian*, 104
Salisbury, Vt., 50, 130
Sandbar, 4-5
Sanford, D. Gregory, 103
Sanitation, 82-83, 200-1, 202
Saxe, John Godfrey, 92
Scales (weighing instruments), 60, 65-68, 162, 165
The School Journal and Agriculturist, 92 n5
Schools, 92-94, 189-90; academies, 45, 93; common schools, 42-44; high schools, 93; normal schools, 189; parochial schools, 92, 93-94, 96, 180-81. *See also* Colleges and universities
Scott, Orange, 107
Scottish, 10
Sculpture, 91-92
Searle, Henry, 25
Seed industry and trade, 3
Sewage. *See* Sanitation
Sex instruction, 101
Shafter, Oscar L., 122-23, 124-25
Shanley, Hobart, 212
Shattuck, Ira, 15
Sheep, 9-10
Sheldon, Henry, 37
Sheldon, Vt., 50, 71, 75, 80, 191
Sheldons & Slason, West Rutland, *63*, 170, 171
Shepard & Morse, Burlington, 168, 210
Sherman, George D., 215
Sherman, Richard W., 15, 17
Shoreham, Vt., 50
Slade, William, 113, 120
Slate industry, *48*, 51, 60, 61, 165, 166, 180; marbleized slate, 64-65, 147, 166
Slavery, 120-26, 128, 131
Smalley, Benjamin H., 97
Smalley, David A.: obtains hospital for Burlington, 81, 145; insurance company officer, 76; judge, 170, 198; politician, 20, 111, 117
Smashwood, Joe, 215
Smiley, Robinson, 40
Smilie, Nathan, 116-17
Smith, D. M., 69
Smith, Frederick, 21
Smith, John Gregory, 37, 132, 141, 157, 159, 192
Smith, Joseph, 40
Smith, Oramel H., 76
Smith, William Farrar, 168
Smith, Worthington C., 115, 143, 159
Smith family, 160, 162

Soapstone, 51
Social life and customs, 8-9, 152-53, 190-91
Social welfare, 182
Société de St. Jean Baptiste, 181
Soils, 3-4, 6
Sons of Temperance, 79
Springfield, Vt., 29, 57, 69, 164, 182, 197
Stagecoach lines. *See* Roads
Stannard, George J., 159, 186
Stannard, Vt., 159
State government, 110, 115-16
Steam Stone Cutter Co., Rutland, 171
Stearns (E. A.), Brattleboro, 164
Steele, Benjamin H., 116
Stevens, Lorinda A., 100
Stewart, John W., 184
Still, William, 121
Stockbridge, Vt., 163
Stone, Henry D., 57, 163
Stores, retail, 77-78
Storey, H. L., 88
Stoughton, Edwin H., 136
Stratton Mountain, 9
Strikes and lockouts, 84-85, 148; in marble industry, 62, 64, 85, 147, 172, 181; by railroad workers, 35-36, 85; by typographers, 149; by women workers, 163
Strong, Frank M., 68
Strong, Moses, 72
Students, 46
Styles, A. F., 77
Suffrage. *See* Woman suffrage
Sullivan Machine Co., Claremont, N.H., 171
Summer people, 191
Sutherland Falls, Vt., *See* Proctor, Vt.
Sutherland Falls Marble Co., 147, 169-71
Sutton, Vt., 77
Swanton, Vt., 50, 96

Taft, James, 44
Tampico Dressing Co., Burlington, 210
Taxation, 73, 150-51, 161
Taylor, Nathaniel, 100-1
Taylor, Zachary, 108
Teachers, 43-44, 45, 92-93
The Teacher's Voice and Vermont Monthly Magazine, 92 n5
Telegraph, 53
Telephone, 212
Temperance, 78-79, 122, 125, 153. *See also* Prohibition